P9-BYK-386

Living Beyond Yourself

Beth Moore

LifeWay Press
Nashville, Tennessee

✠

ISBN 0-7673-9275-2
Dewey Decimal Classification Number: 248.843
Subject Heading: WOMEN–RELIGIOUS LIFE \ BIBLE N.T. GALATIANS–STUDY AND
TEACHING \ SPIRITUAL GIFTS

This book is the text for course CG-0477 in the subject area Personal Life
in the Christian Growth Study Plan.

Unless otherwise noted, Scripture quotations are from the Holy Bible,
New International Version, copyright © 1973, 1978, 1984
by International Bible Society.

Scripture quotations marked KJV are from the *King James Version.*

For information on adult discipleship and family resources, training, and events, visit out Web
site at www.lifeway.com/discipleplus or contact Customer Service Center, MSN 113; 127 Ninth
Avenue, North; Nashville, TN 37234-0113; FAX (615) 251-5933;
email customerservice@lifeway.com

Printed in the United States of America

LifeWay Press
127 Ninth Avenue, North
Nashville, Tennessee 37234-0151

*As God works through us, we will help people and churches know Jesus Christ
and seek His kingdom by providing biblical solutions that spiritually transform
individuals and cultures.*

Dale McCleskey, Editor
Pam Shepherd, Assistant Editor
Leslie Irwin, Manuscript Assistant
Edward Crawford, Art Director
Cover Illustration, Alicia Buelow

To Barbara O'Chester

Founder of Great Hills Retreat Ministry

A radiant example of a Spirit-filled woman.

Thank you for your tireless devotion to the Lord's Christ.

You remain one of my most cherished heroes.

I love you.

About the Author

Beth Moore realized at the age of 18 that God was claiming her future for Christian ministry. While she was sponsoring a cabin of sixth graders at a missions camp, God unmistakably acknowledged that she would work for Him. There Beth conceded all rights to the Lord she had loved since childhood. However, she encountered a problem: although she knew she was "wonderfully made," she was "fearfully" without talent. She hid behind closed doors to discover whether a beautiful singing voice had miraculously developed, but the results were tragic. She returned to the piano from which years of fruitless practice had streamed but found the noise to be joyless. Finally accepting that the only remaining alternative was missions work in a foreign country, she struck a martyr's pose and waited. Yet nothing happened.

Still confident of God's calling, Beth finished her degree at Southwest Texas State University, where she fell in love with Keith. After they married in December 1978, God added to their household three priority blessings: Amanda, Melissa, and Michael.

As if putting together puzzle pieces one at a time, God filled Beth's path with supportive persons who saw something in her she could not. God used individuals like Marge Caldwell, John Bisagno, and Jeannette Cliff George to help Beth discover gifts of speaking, teaching, and writing. Twelve years after her first speaking engagement, those gifts have spread all over the nation. Her joy and excitement in Christ are contagious; her deep love for the Savior, obvious; her style of speaking, electric.

Beth's ministry is grounded in and fueled by her service at her home fellowship, First Baptist Church, Houston, Texas, where she serves on the pastor's council and teaches a Sunday School class attended by more than two hundred women. Beth believes that her calling is Bible literacy: guiding believers to love and live God's Word. *Living Beyond Yourself: Exploring the Fruit of the Spirit* grew from her fervent desire that women know greater intimacy with God.

Foreword

I met Beth Moore by phone while I was serving on staff at Green Acres Baptist in Tyler, Texas. We met personally at the taping of the first women's discipleship study LifeWay published in 1995, *A Woman's Heart, God's Dwelling Place*. Little did we know then what would happen with these God-inspired studies, how women's lives would be changed, how some would come to know Him as personal Savior, how the studies would be a catalyst for beginning or revitalizing women's ministries in churches across the country. Beth has become a sweet friend and co-laborer in Kingdom ministry. Her heart for teaching God's Word to women is so evident, with all glory going to Him. God continues to use Beth's obedience to write and teach as you will see through this study.

Biblical discipleship studies are a part of a larger picture of women's enrichment ministries in churches today. What is happening in your church? Are women being reached and discipled for Christ? What a privilege we have as women to be used by God to touch the lives of other women. As you study, I pray His fruit will become more and more evident in your life.

Chris Adams
Women's Enrichment Ministry Specialist
Discipleship and Family Adult Department
LifeWay Christian Resources

CONTENTS

Introduction

Welcome to *Living Beyond Yourself: Exploring the Fruit of the Spirit.* In the next few weeks I pray that you will learn about, but much more importantly, grow in and experience the work of the Holy Spirit. We will be studying the wonderful Book of Galatians and concentrating on Galatians 5:22-23.

Perhaps you are familiar with *A Woman's Heart: God's Dwelling Place, A Heart Like His: Seeking the Heart of God Through a Study of David,* or *To Live Is Christ: The Life and Ministry of Paul.* You will find *Living Beyond Yourself* to be similar in format but quite different in content to these previous studies.

All four Bible studies are 10-week interactive courses inviting your personal involvement. Each week contains five lessons which will each require 30-45 minutes for completion. If you spend this kind of time in the Word of God, I assure you, He will change your life. I urge you not to miss a single lesson. Ask God daily what He wants to say to you personally.

Living Beyond Yourself differs from the previous studies in a significant way. This study does not involve video. Thus *Living Beyond* groups are planned for one-hour rather than two-hour meetings. Ideally, these courses are targeted for group participation once a week.

Each week's introduction includes five Principal Questions. Each Principal Question is derived from one of the five lessons for the week and is marked with a leaf symbol in black (✿). Discussing the answers to these questions weekly in small group will help ensure each person's basic understanding of the material.

In addition to these five content-oriented questions, you will find Personal Discussion Questions in each lesson. These questions appear in green marked with a green leaf (✿). These learning activities help group members personally apply the material to their own lives. These are also formatted for discussion each week; therefore, the weekly small-group discussion will ordinarily consist of five Principal Questions and five Personal Discussion Questions designed to further enrich each person's experience.

No one will ever be expected to share personal experiences with the group. Sharing is strictly voluntary, and I hope no one will share anything causing herself or others discomfort. Please answer the questions in each lesson whether or not you choose to share them in small group. Any questions you skip will reduce the effectiveness of the study in your personal life. I want you to get the very most out of this journey! God will do amazing things among us if we grant Him full access to our minds, wills, and emotions!

Each daily lesson is introduced by a Scripture called Today's Treasure. Your daily treasure is the Scripture best representing the theme of the lesson.

Each lesson will invite your full participation through Bible reading and various kinds of questions and activities. You may find multiple choice exercises, yes/no activities, fill-in-the-blank statements, creative thinking exercises, hypothetical situations, or straightforward questions which you will answer in your own words. These interactive exercises are designed for your sake. I don't want you to simply read my journey through Scripture. I want this book to become your journey. Your full participation will guarantee God's freedom to accomplish a fresh and wonderful work in your life.

I primarily use the *New International Version* of the Bible in *Living Beyond Yourself.* If you do not own one, you will still be able to answer virtually every question without significant confusion. If you're able to get your hands on an inexpensive paperback NIV, however, I think you would be blessed by an easy-to-read version which, in my opinion, does not compromise the text.

Allow God to do a fresh work in your life for the next 10 weeks. Let every journey through His Word be a new experience, a new opportunity. Resist comparisons to other studies. Welcome changes. Invite Him to have His perfect way for the next 10 weeks.

I conclude each lesson with a margin question asking you to consider how God wants you to respond to what He showed you today. I encourage you to expand your learning beyond the pages of *Living Beyond Yourself.* Keep your own personal journal. Record what God does and teaches you as you pursue this journey.

Week 1

Free at Last!

Freedom! What a glorious word. A song lyric from the '60s said: "People everywhere just want to be free." Christians want to be free, but I fear that so few are. Galatians makes an astonishing statement about Christian freedom: *It is for freedom that Christ has set us free. Stand firm, then, and do not let yourselves be burdened again by a yoke of slavery.* This week we begin our journey together. The goal of our trip is genuine freedom—the freedom that comes only through a life filled with the Holy Spirit. Such a life displays the character traits the Bible calls the fruit of the Spirit.

We'll begin our study with an overview of the wonderful Book of Galatians. The apostle Paul wrote Galatians to young Christians in danger of losing their freedom in Christ. In it the apostle tells us how to be filled with the Spirit and free from the bondage of sin.

Principal Questions

Day 1: How did Paul respond to persecution in the city of Lystra?

Day 2: What are four major reasons Christ died for us?

Day 3: What reasons might Paul have cited to avoid confronting Peter?

Day 4: On what basis is righteousness credited to us?

Day 5: After careful deliberation, when did God decide to adopt you?

Day 1
Many Hardships

"Strengthening the disciples and encouraging them to remain true to the faith. 'We must go through many hardships to enter the kingdom of God,' they said" (Acts 14:22).

I am thrilled beyond measure to begin this journey with you! What could be more important than learning to be a Spirit-filled believer? Over the next 10 weeks, we are going to have the opportunity for Christ to alter our personalities from the inside out. We are going to discover that the character of Jesus can be a genuine reality in the life of an everyday believer.

To let Christ have access to everything needing alteration, we must give Him permission to get very personal with us. The enemy will do everything he can to discourage you from allowing God into the deepest places of your heart. If Satan succeeds, you lose. On the other hand, if you grant God full access to every part of you over the next 10 weeks, you will never be the same. You win.

Write a prayer of dedication to God as you begin this course. Allow nothing to prevent you from completing the journey.

Heavenly Father I am asking that you allow me to complete this course and in so doing change me from the inside out.

Staying true to context is a crucial part of Bible study; therefore, we begin our study by overviewing all six chapters of Galatians. We will then proceed to a more in-depth study of the fruit of the Spirit and the issue of living in the Spirit.

The Book of Galatians is vital to the New Testament. Without it you would be living a far different kind of spiritual life as a believer in Christ. I pray that very soon you will begin to develop a great love and appreciation for Paul's letter to the people of Galatia.

Keeping in mind the importance of a proper foundation, we will begin tomorrow with chapter 1. Today let's get acquainted with the region of Galatia and the types of people to whom Paul wrote. On their first missionary journey, Paul and Barnabas established four churches in the Roman province of Galatia (modern-day Turkey). The four cities where these churches were settled are named and described in Acts 13 and 14.

Read Acts 13:14-47. Below draw and label a time line representing the sequence of important historical events in the nation of Israel.

Egypt |desert 40yrs |destroyed 7 nations in Canaan 450yrs |Saul (King) 40yrs |David

Read Acts 13:48–14:23. What were the names of the four Galatian cities on this missionary journey? (Check one or more.)

☐ Ceasarea   ☑ Lystra   ☑ Derbe
☑ Antioch   ☐ Cholesterol   ☑ Iconium

What is the good news and the bad news of Acts 13:49-50?

Good News	Bad News
Spread the Word	Persecution of Paul & Barnabas
traveled on to Iconium	threw them out of region
Antioch believers full of Spirit	leading Stirred men of city & Gentile women

Before we proceed to the next question, let's take a closer look at Acts 13:50. I believe the verse contains a very important message to us.

Who did the Jews purposefully incite first? _Leading men_

How did Paul describe these women? _Gentile_

What did these women stir up? _wives have power over_
(influence) husbands

For reasons we may never know, God entrusted to womankind a most wonderful and terrible gift: the power of influence. This is the foremost quality highlighted in our earliest heritage.

To whom did the serpent go when he sought the ruin of Adam and

Eve? (see Gen. 3:1). _Eve._

Do you suppose the serpent believed Eve could talk Adam into anything? Consider the power of feminine influence. God selected us as the bearers of children and, in our society, women assume the greatest role in childrearing. Our day-cares, Mothers Day Outs, schools, and Sunday Schools are overwhelmingly staffed with women. With the divorce rate escalating and millions of children growing up without a father in the home, mothers possess incredible influence. For better or worse, your self-esteem has probably been influenced most at the hands—and mouth—of your mother.

How do you use the fearful gift of influence? At its best, it teaches, nurtures, encourages, exhorts, evangelizes and disciples. At worst, it cripples and kills. The line between influence and manipulation is extremely fine. Influence is so easy to use, it's frightening. Maybe it's the reason God exhorts us to "gentle and quiet" spirits. We need to think before we speak and act. The warnings in

Scripture are not provided because we are so lowly, but because we possess such an awesome gift.

Today let's risk some honest answers to the question of influence. How do I use the gift of influence in my home? in my church? in my workplace? When you consider your capabilities, both positive and negative, do you see the extreme necessity of learning to live in the Spirit?

"Father, please make us teachable through this study, that we might learn to wield our influence only under the authority of the Holy Spirit who dwells within us!"

How do you respond to Acts 13:50, remembering that these were "devout and honourable" women who were so easily incited to become persecutors (KJV)? (Check one or more.)
❑ If they could so easily become persecutors, so can I.
☑ Yes, I recognize how I have used my influence in destructive ways.
❑ No, I am above falling into any trap like those women did.
❑ Other ___Be alter___

In verse 52, how did the disciples respond to the persecution?

___full of the Spirit___

Do you think you would have responded the way Paul and Barnabas did in Acts 14:2-3? Why or why not?

Probably not - strong faith

Read 14:19-20. How did Paul respond to the persecution in Lystra?

Returned to town!

Read verse 22, today's focal passage, and fill in the following blanks.

"___Strengthen the souls of___ the disciples and encouraging them to

___continue to remain true___ to the faith."

"We must go through many ___troubles___ to enter the kingdom of God," they said.

What does this verse teach you concerning the popular "prosperity gospel" of health and wealth based on the depth of a person's faith?

influence - to assist person
manipulate - self motivated

Our nation today knows very little about true persecution. We too rarely hear accounts of people like John and Betty Stam, young missionaries to China, who were beheaded just one month after their arrival in Tsingteh, leaving behind a three-month-old infant. Or, what about Peter and Lydia Vins, missionaries to the former Soviet Union? Peter was imprisoned and never seen again. Lydia's imprisonment followed later. Such a heritage might be enough to dissuade a child from faith in the gospel. Not so. Their son, Georgi, surrendered his life to the same pursuit, on the same field, and was ultimately imprisoned as well. Enough is enough, right? Nope, his son, Peter, Jr., grew up, dedicated his life to Christ, and followed the same path to prison.

In 1979, under Jimmy Carter's leadership, the surviving Vins family members were released from prison, and they continue to serve faithfully in the United States and abroad. Consider this excerpt from *The Hidden Price of Greatness*, written by Ray Beeson and Ranelda Mack Hunsicker:

> It seems a paradox that the death of Christians could be the key to church growth. Yet as surely as the cross of Christ was essential to our salvation, the sacrifice of believers is crucial to world evangelism. That is as true today as ever.
>
> In fact, the rate of Christian martyrdom has risen dramatically in recent years. The World Evangelization Research Center estimates that there were approximately 35,600 Christian martyrs in 1900 compared to an estimated 325,000 in 1989. Martyrdom is a fact of life in at least fifty countries. The Center concludes from its research that out of the two thousand or so plans for global evangelization by A.D. 2000, "martyrdom is probably the most potent and significant factor of all."[1]

When we read such accounts, we wonder if people like the Stams had any idea what their commitment might cost them. Would they have dared surrender to such a sentence? Consider this excerpt from a speech delivered to the Moody Bible Institute graduating class of 1932:

> Let us remind ourselves that the Great Commission was never qualified by clauses calling for advance only if funds were plentiful and no hardship or self-denial involved. On the contrary, we are told to expect tribulation and even persecution, but with it victory in Christ....It is ours to show, in the salvation of our Lord Jesus Christ, and in personal communion with Him, a joy unspeakable and full of glory that cannot be affected by outside circumstances.[2]

The speaker? John Stams, just before his departure to China.

No, we are not acquainted with this sort of persecution, but Beloved, we must pray for those who are! Yet, we indeed experience a constant persecution of sorts, waged by the most vicious of all persecutors. Just like the Stams experienced, his allied forces are closing in and his captives are many. But so subtle is this battle that all around us people are being spiritually beheaded while we often remain unmoved. Heads are rolling. This is war.

It's a matter of influence. And that just happens to be our specialty.

How does God want you to respond to what he showed you today?

_____

_____

_____

_____

_____

_____

_____

Pleasing God

This week we establish a foundation for our study of the fruit of the Spirit. We began on day 1, researching Paul's experiences in the region of Galatia, particularly in the cities of Antioch, Iconium, Lystra, and Derbe.

From the following list, check the events reported in Acts 13:14–14:23.
❑ **Paul used Hebrew history to preach Jesus to synagogue members.**
☑ **Unbelieving Jews stirred up God-fearing women to persecute Paul and Barnabas.**
❑ **John Mark turned back because of persecution.**
☑ **The crowd in Lystra tried to worship the disciples as Greek gods.**
☑ **Paul and Barnabas organized the churches and appointed leaders.**

I am awed by Paul's spiritual tenacity. After being stoned and left for dead, his heart still ached for the lost people of Galatia and for the spiritual protection of the new believers. These new churches were Paul's babies; he cared for them, admonished them, and nurtured them. Soon you will see that he had some strong words to say to the churches. Take a moment now to slowly and thoughtfully read aloud Galatians, chapter 1. Reading aloud allows both your heart and ears to absorb God's Word. After you have read the entire chapter, reread the salutation in verses 1 through 5. Do you ever wonder why on earth God went to the trouble to save you? I certainly sometimes wonder why He saved me! The older I get and the more I know myself and HIM, the more I wonder! Scripture clearly offers at least four major reasons Christ died for us.

FOUR MAJOR REASONS WHY CHRIST DIED FOR US

↪ **Fill in the blanks from the following Scriptures.**

1. "Who gave himself for our sins to _deliver us out of this_ _present evil_ age, according to the _will of Our God's Father._" (Gal. 1:4).

2. "For Christ died for sins once for all, the righteous for the unrighteous, to _bring us to God_. He was put to death in the body but made alive by the Spirit" (1 Pet. 3:18).

3. "For God so _loved_ the world that he gave his one and only Son" (John 3:16).

---

4. "But God <u>demonstrates His own love</u>
for us in this: While we were still sinners, Christ died for us"
(Rom. 5:8).

Take another look at the four reasons. Christ died for us: (1) because He wanted to rescue us from evil; (2) because it was His Father's will; (3) because He wanted to bring us to His Father; and (4) because He loves us. Why did He choose to save us?

Psalm 115:3 sums it up nicely for us: "Our God is in heaven; he does whatever pleases him." God chose to save us simply because it pleased Him. Stop for a moment and thank Him that your salvation pleased Him!

Now look back at Galatians 1 and answer the following questions.

Why was Paul astonished or amazed? (v. 6).

<u>Because God called you by the grace of Christ</u>

On what basis does Paul claim his gospel is true? (vv. 11-12).

<u>Rec'd by a revelation of J.C.</u>

One of the clearest proofs of God's power is the evidence of a transformed life. Paul shared his testimony with the Galatians in verses 11 through 24. Isn't it noteworthy that God did not save Paul from poverty but from prosperity! He had been a man of both position and purpose.

How did Paul describe his position? (v. 14). <u>Zealous.</u>

What did Paul see as his purpose? (v. 13). <u>distruction</u>

When did God set Paul apart? (v. 15).
- ☑ at birth
- ☐ on the Damascus Road
- ☐ at his bar mitzvah
- ☐ at the Jerusalem conference

Read Romans 8:29 and fill in the blanks: "For those God
<u>knows (foreknew)</u> —chosen— **he also** <u>sets apart to be like His Son</u> ."

Perhaps you continually struggle with the fear that if God had known some of the mistakes you were going to make and the sins you were going to commit, He never would have chosen you. Scripture is clear—God foreknew you from birth to death, yet He predestined you for His very own. It's called grace. I don't understand it either, but I praise the name of the One who offers it!

As you can see, the tone of the Galatian letter is very emotional. Paul surely wished to remain and disciple every young church he helped to build, but that was not his assignment. Clearly, what he feared most in those baby churches nourished on truth was the infiltration of lies and the poison of false doctrine. Are only young Christians susceptible to false teaching? No, indeed Matthew 24:24 says, "false Christs and false prophets will appear…to deceive, even the elect–if that were possible."

What does Peter identify as the motivation of false teachers?

(2 Pet. 2:3). _____ Greed _____

One major motivation propels false teachers. They are greedy for power, position, and popularity. How can you spot them? They draw attention to themselves and away from the Word, so that the follower can no longer discern Truth from lies.

MAJOR CHARACTERISTICS THAT MAKE US EASY TARGETS

The Scriptures suggest three major characteristics that make us easy targets for false teaching.

1. Read 2 Peter 2:1-2. How can we guard against false prophets of the sort Peter mentions? distruction _____

We cannot possibly recognize a lie if we don't know the Truth. Ignorance of God's Word makes us easy targets for false teaching!

2. Read 2 Corinthians 11:3-4. What difficult-to-admit reason for being led astray do these verses suggest? Eve's scene _____

As much as it hurts me to say it and while few would ever admit it, I believe another reason some are weak to false teaching is boredom. The "simplicity" (KJV) and the constant devotion to One and only One can translate to boredom for those who seek thrills and sensationalism.

Have you ever felt, or do you now, feel bored with the Christian life? On the following scale, place an "X" to mark the period of your life when you felt most disinterested in growing as a disciple. Then place a "✓" to indicate where you see yourself today.

○━━○

Bored Stiff   **Excited**

If you are easily diverted from the Christian life, something is wrong and you are at terrible risk. I pray that this study will help "fan the flame"! (2 Tim 1:6).

3. **Galatians 1:10 reveals another major characteristic that makes us targets. Fill in the blanks below using Galatians 1:10.**

"Am I now trying to win the ___favor___ of ___men___, or of

God? Or am I trying to please ___men___? If I were still trying to

please ___men___, I would not be a ___servant___ of Christ."

Look carefully at what you've written. Few things on earth cause as much unhappiness as trying to win the approval and affirmation of people. Note the phrase, "Or am I trying to please men?" The Greek word for *please* is *aresko* and it means "to fit, to gratify, to accommodate oneself to, or to be acceptable."[3] Under the leadership of the Holy Spirit, I took a few moments to reflect on the worst mistakes I've ever made and the most abominable sins I've ever committed. The overwhelming majority of those poor choices were a result of seeking someone's approval and acceptance...a desire to fit in.

Can you think of a time when seeking someone's approval ultimately proved to be a very negative influence in your life? ❑ Yes ❑ No

Recently in Houston, several teenage boys tortured, terrorized, and murdered two teenage girls walking home from a party. Their motive? To win the approval of gang members. Who can forget the endless video replays of Ronald Reagan's attempted assassination? The motive? Not for war, mutiny, or money, but to win the attentions of a movie star with whom the gunman was obsessed.

The apostle Paul knew all too well that seeking people's approval can lead to sin. Did you notice that the verse says, "If I were still trying to please man." In other words, this text strongly implies that at one time Paul was seeking to please man. Was he referring to Paul's zealous persecution of Christians as an attempt to gain the approval and popularity of his superiors?

Remember this important fact about God. He never asks anything of us to make Himself look better. The demands He makes on our lives are NEVER for His personal gain. We cannot make Him any more God than He already is. He would be no less Lord of lords if no one believed. Every urging and exhortation of God to us is for one major reason. He desires that we have the pleasure of knowing, serving, and sharing Him. God reserves the sovereign right to be sole authority over our lives for our good, for our completion, for the conforming of our lives to that of His Son.

Why, then, is seeking the approval of man so harmful to us? Look again at Galatians 1:10. Notice Paul begins by talking about approval and ends by talking about servanthood. "If I were still trying to please men, I would not be a servant of Christ." What does one issue have to do with the other? Approval and servanthood are connected because we become immediate slaves to the person(s) from whom we seek approval. You can trust only One to constantly be on the lookout for your best interest. Only One holds the future in His hands and knows your part in that future. Only One cares for you with a perfect and unconditional love. Only One can make "all things work together for good" (Rom. 8:28, KJV). Only One can safely, yes, gloriously enslave you!

**How does God want you
to respond to what He showed
you today?**

_____

_____

_____

_____

_____

_____

_____

Attaining the approval of others does not mean seeking the approval of others. Praise God if, in seeking to please Him, you accidentally end up pleasing others. God certainly does not bless us according to how many others curse us, and we'd be wise never to expect or encourage rejection.

Read each of the following passages and answer the questions.

To what were we enslaved before we met Christ? (Rom. 6:19-23).

Impurity, wickedness, death - Sin

To what are we enslaved in Christ? _Eternal Life._

What does Isaiah say would have been the result if Israel had been obedient? (48:17-19). _Blessing to flow..._

In what way do we need to seek God? (Jer. 29:11-13).

He knows the Plan!

What will be the basis for rewards from Christ? (Rev. 22:12).

What he has done

✍ **For you, what would it mean to seek only God's approval?**

Blessings & Reward

☙Today's Treasure:

"I have been crucified with Christ and I no longer live, but Christ lives in me. The life I live in the body, I live by faith in the Son of God, who loved me and gave himself for me" (Gal. 2:20).

Day 3

Crucified

Begin today's study by thoroughly reading Galatians, chapter 2; then answer the following questions:

Describe what you see as the major theme of this chapter.

Paul's authority as an apostle

Why did Paul oppose Peter? _for being a hipocrate_

1st livengw/ Gentile & then the Jews.

What a wonderful and timely message for those growing in Christ! Did you ever get the feeling that once the disciples were baptized with the Holy Spirit, they suddenly became flawless? It's obvious that such an assumption is false! Every single day, they fought the same battle with the flesh that we do, and sometimes they lost. Notice another important point. No matter how high their spiritual stature, the disciples were not beyond confrontation or accountability.

∾ What reasons might Paul have cited to avoid confronting Peter?

_____

Have you ever been questioned or confronted by someone you might have considered spiritually "beneath you"? Think about it a moment. Isn't it interesting the folks God will sometimes use to chasten or redirect us? Can you welcome such admonishment? Paul was younger than Peter, not one of the original twelve, and not part of the church's Jerusalem leadership.

We are going to spend the remainder of today studying our focal passage, Galatians 2:20. Reread Today's Treasure aloud. Perhaps, like me, you have read and heard this verse countless times and even memorized it, but what does it really mean to be "crucified with Christ"? The term means identifying with Him in His death in such a way as to allow Him to live through you.

Christ chose to walk a certain path to His death so that, at the end, He could proclaim, "It is finished!" Permit me to draw a parallel. We must also agree to walk the path of the cross to allow the Spirit of Christ to live through us.

Although every believer has been "crucified with Christ" in the ultimate sense of victory over sin and the grave, we must make certain choices to be crucified with Christ for victory in our daily battle with sin. Today let's walk the road to Calvary and see what it truly means to "identify" with Christ in His death to self. To choose this same road is to allow the finished work of Calvary to have its immediate way! Read these Scripture passages describing the final events of Jesus' journey to the cross. We will then make parallel connections to the crucified life.

TEN CHARACTERISTICS OF THE CRUCIFIED LIFE

Read John 16:5-18. On the following scale place an "X" on the spot to indicate how well you think the apostles understood Jesus' mission and coming death.

Understood   **Clueless**

1. Few will understand.
If you seriously decide to live a life crucified to self and alive in Christ, you will discover that few will understand. More importantly, those who misunderstand will most likely be the ones you have to relate to the most. Galatians 2:20 describes a radical change that many find confrontational.

Read Matthew 26:36-46. How did Jesus resolve His struggle? (v. 39).

Face down & prayed

2. You must abandon your own will and your own agenda.
As long as you cleave to a personal agenda and continue to nurse your own will, the personalized daily will of God will be thwarted in you.

How was Christ able to overcome His negative feelings toward His death? (Heb. 12:2).

Fixed eyes on Christ

How can we find solace in the death to our own will and desires? (1 Cor. 2:9-10).

Spirit

Read Matthew 26:56. How did the disciples respond when Jesus was arrested? (Check one.)
☐ **They stayed with Him.**
☐ **They followed to see what would happen.**
☑ **They fled in fear.**

3. Your intimate spiritual companions will be few.
I am not suggesting or encouraging spiritual elitism; nothing could be further from God's will. I am, however, suggesting that there may be few who choose to walk this same road with you. Those with whom you can pray deeply and agonize spiritually are unique, indeed! Be thankful for them!

Check Jesus' response during a time of great stress (Matt. 26:36-39).
☑ **He prayed alone.** ☐ **He prayed with others.**

4. Intense times of aloneness with God are required.
Not even your intimate spiritual companions are invited to attend some meetings with God! He reserves the right to meet with you One-on-one. The best preparation you will ever receive for your most agonizing trials will be when you are the only student attending class. In the midst of your deepest difficulties, have you ever looked around and thought, *Where is everybody?* Sometimes God reserves the right to withhold others and to pull you aside with Him so that you can experience what David did in 1 Samuel 30:6, "David found strength in the Lord his God."

Read Matthew 26:57-67 and 1 Peter 3:15-16. What do these two passages have in common?

Good conscience

5. You will be constantly on the witness stand.

Matthew describes Jesus' trial. Peter challenges us to be prepared to give an answer. There will never be a time when we are not subject to the observation of others. We will be held under the strictest scrutiny of non-believers and believers alike, continually called to the witness stand.

> **Read Hebrews 13:12-14. Which of the following statements best reflects the meaning of the passage?**
> ☑ Jesus bore shame and disgrace; we must be willing to face the same.
> ☑ Jesus suffered outside of Jerusalem; we must be willing to leave the comforts of home.
> ☑ Jesus was unashamed of us; we should be unashamed of Him.

We must decide what we value most. Do we most want to be conformed (to the image of Christ), or do we want to be comforted? Each of the three statements above are true. The first best reflects the meaning of Hebrews 13:12-14.

6. You must go "outside the camp."

The second response to the activity above also expresses a practical truth. Do not be surprised when God continually forces you outside your comfort zone. When was the last time you were required by God to leave your comfort zone?

> **Read Matthew 27:27-31. Stop to reflect on the shame and indignity Jesus endured for us. Write a brief prayer thanking Him for enduring what you and I deserve.**

_Heavenly Father, I want to thank you for suffering
The shame & indignity for me, my family and all the world_

7. There will be times when your dignity is forfeited.

The words of Whitney Houston's hit song, "The Greatest Love of All," still ring in my ears from time to time: "I decided long ago never to walk in anyone's shadow. If I fail, if I succeed, at least I did what I believed. No matter what they take from me, they can't take away my dignity...." Wrong, Whitney. They can take away your dignity. And we'd better learn to walk in Someone's shadow, because in those moments when we are vulnerable and exposed, the shadow of the Almighty may be the only covering we have! (see Ps. 91:1).

> ✍ Read Matthew 27:32-44. Put yourself in Jesus' place. How difficult would it be to surrender your rights and not "come down from the cross and save yourself"?

◯───────────────────────◯

Very Difficult   **Easy As Pie**

8. You must forego your rights.

Christ was the Son of God, the "fullness of the Godhead bodily!" As the song says, "He could have called ten thousand angels." He could have spoken in His own defense! He could have opened up the earth to swallow His every foe. But He did not. You have many rights of your own. You may have the right to be angry, the right to be bitter, the right to leave your husband or give up on that wayward teenager. But to be crucified with Christ means that you volunteer to forego all your personal rights except one: your right as a believer to be filled and led by the Spirit of Christ who dwells within you. Don't make the mistake of trying to simply ignore your rights when they are so difficult to lay down. Surrender them to Christ and ask Him to replace them with a supernatural work of the Spirit: with healing, with power, with wisdom!

> **Read Matthew 27:34,48. The drink offered to condemned men was an anesthetic to dull the pain. In your opinion, why did Jesus refuse the drug? (consider Heb. 2:9).**

To remain alert - keep the devil away

9. You must accept that death is painful.

When I was troubled over the painful death of a friend's child, a nurse said words I'll never forget: "If there is an awareness at the time of death, there is pain. Simply said, death hurts." Does it ever. At times, to choose the will of God over our own is excruciating. We love our flesh and it hurts to have its desires crucified! Never misunderstand pain as permission to forego the will of God.

So, what in the world makes all this worth it? Read John 20:1-18.

What makes it worthwhile is that, as Christ's life is resurrected in us, others might exclaim in the words of Mary Magdelene, "I have seen the Lord!" This is the highest calling of all humanity.

Our experience totally differs from that of Christ's in only one place. Conclude by comparing Matthew 27:45-46 to Romans 8:38-39 and Hebrews 13:5. Because our Savior agreed to have the sins of the world heaped upon Him and experience separation from the Father, we will never be forsaken.

10. Because He was forsaken, you never will be.

In many ways we identify with Christ. In many ways He shares our lives and experience. Here, however, the parallel ends. Jesus bore the full force of rejection by humanity and separation from the Father. Because He was forsaken, you never will be.

> **Which one of the characteristics of the crucified life spoke most personally to you and why?**

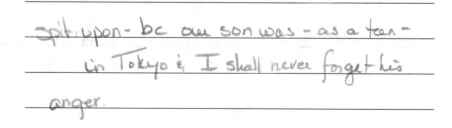

spit upon - bc our son was - as a teen - in Tokyo & I shall never forget his anger.

How does God want you to respond to what He showed you today?

_____

_____

_____

_____

_____

_____

_____

Day 4

Credited Righteousness

"Consider Abraham: 'He believed God and it was credited to him as righteousness'" (Gal. 3:6).

Today as we continue building a foundation for our study of the fruit of the Spirit, let's turn our attention to Galatians 3. Please read those 29 verses now.

No doubt you noticed the temperature of Paul's letter rising quickly. He admonished them so strongly because of their attempts to add works to faith to equal salvation. Jewish believers in Christ were heartily trying to convince Gentile converts that, in addition to accepting Christ as Savior, they had to be circumcised and keep the law. Once again, the simplicity of the gospel became a stumbling block. They could not believe effort had no bearing on acceptance.

What is the only qualification necessary for salvation? (Eph. 2:8-9).

grace

The greatest risk we'll ever run is growing casual with the basic precepts of "so great a Salvation." May God grant us a fresh approach as we attempt to understand these two crucial building blocks of our salvation: grace and faith. The Greek word for *grace* is *charis* which means:

That which causes joy, pleasure, gratification, favor, acceptance, for a kindness granted or desired, a benefit, thanks, gratitude. A favor done without expectation of return; the absolutely free expression of the loving kindness of God to men finding its only motive in the bounty and benevolence of the Giver; unearned and unmerited favor. *Charis* stands in direct antithesis to *erga,* works, the two being mutually exclusive. God's grace affects man's sinfulness and not only forgives the repentant sinner, but brings joy and thankfulness to him. It changes the individual to a new creature without destroying his individuality.[4]

Reread the above definition of grace. In the definition, underline words that speak to your heart. Why did you choose those words?

Now let's consider the actual definition of faith. The Greek word for *faith* is *pistis,* and it means "firm persuasion, conviction, belief in the truth, veracity, reality....Objectively meaning that which is believed."[5]

Look carefully at Today's Treasure. On what basis did God credit Abraham with righteousness?

Believing

ʟ **On what basis is righteousness credited to us? (Rom. 3:22-24).**

Faith.

Verse 22 provides the perfect definition of faith: "through faith in Jesus Christ to all who believe." Very simply, faith is believing God. The Galatians were not the only ones who needed a lesson on the continuing theme of faith through all the ages. Compare Paul's words in Romans 4.

Read carefully all 25 verses; then answer the following questions.

Many Jews believed that circumcision was the mark of God's appropriated righteousness to man. Was Abraham credited by God as righteous (circle one) before or after circumcision?

To whom is Abraham a father? (vv. 16-17).

Abraham's descendents

What promise of God did Abraham believe? (Gen. 12:1-3).

desc./nation/blessings

What odds were stacked against Abraham's belief? (v. 19).

Had to leave - Sarah taken to Palace.

Why did Abraham believe God? (vv. 20-21).

King gave orders

Do you believe God? Has He ever promised you anything more outrageous than numberless offspring when you were childless and one hundred years old? My precious friend, God's specialty is making impossibilities possible.

Observe the wonderful words of Romans 4:17: "the God who gives life to the dead and calls things that are not as though they were." In my life God took the broken pieces and made me something I was not—and still am not—except by grace. Basically Romans 4:17 means God can add 2 and 2 and make 10.

ʟ **Can you describe an instance in which you were challenged to "believe" God and He showed Himself faithful?**

_____

_____

_____

God reveals His majesty most clearly against the backdrop of apparent hopelessness. The moment you sincerely believe you have received a promise from God, pray to flourish in your belief through the tests that will follow. For the remainder of today, let's concentrate on the last half of Galatians 3. In verse 15, Paul began to express the relationship between the promise and the Law.

Did the Law do away with the promise? ❏ Yes ☑ No

WHO was the "Seed" who received the promises with Abraham?

Christ

Why was the Law put in charge? (v. 24).

until Christ arrive

How does the Law contribute to bringing us to Christ? (Rom. 3:20).

awareness to sin.

Paul attempted to teach the Galatians about God's unfolding revelation. First Peter 1:10-12 beautifully demonstrates how God revealed His great salvation step by step.

Did God allow any of the prophets to receive the completed revelation? ❏ Yes ☑ No

Do the angels know every plan of God? ❏ Yes ☑ No

The "Progressive Revelation" revealed in Galatians 3 is this:
- God exclaimed the PROMISE: I will bless a people for My name's sake! (see Gen. 12:1-3).
- God exposed the PROBLEM: "All have sinned and fall short" of My glory! (Rom. 3:23).
- God extended the PRESCRIPTION: "God made him who had no sin to be sin for us, so that in him we might become the righteousness of God" (2 Cor. 5:21).

READ!

I will never forget the sarcastic words spoken to me by one woman early in my ministry. Before I had even spoken to her group, she stated: "I love how you people do things. You're really great about telling us what is wrong with us, but you really stink when it comes to telling us what to do about it!" Those words are a continuing standard for me every time I teach: "Have I pinpointed problems? Have I extended a biblical solution?"

God never points out sin for the purpose of instilling hopelessness, guilt, and poor self-esteem. God convicts of sin for two major reasons:
- to convict the lost of sin and offer the gift of salvation
- to convict the saved of sin and offer the gift of restoration

God's whole point in expending His endless energies on humans is to have a people for His name. All that He does is to that end.

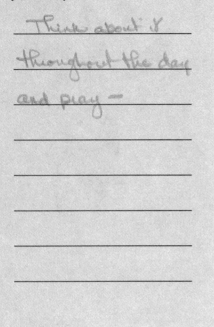

How does God want you to respond to what He showed you today?

Think about it throughout the day and pray —

🐟Today's Treasure:

"Because you are sons, God sent the Spirit of his Son into our hearts, the Spirit who calls out, 'Abba, Father'" (Gal. 4:6).

Does God seem to continue to "pick on" you about an area of personal sin? Do you ever wonder why He's so hard on you? so persistent? so insistent? God paid a very high price not only to save you but also to fellowship with you.

What, today, is hindering that free flow of fellowship?

Let's conclude by comparing Galatians 3:26-29 and Judges 6:34. Gideon was facing similar odds to those Abraham confronted in the battle God called him to fight: "Then the Spirit of the Lord came upon Gideon." The Hebrew word for *came upon* is *labesh* which means "wrap around, to put on a garment or clothe."[6] *The Interlinear Bible* reads, "and the Spirit of Jehovah clothed Gideon with Himself." In that moment, God Himself became both the covering for Gideon's guilt and the armor for Gideon's victory. Can you imagine? You should because you, my fellow warrior, have likewise been clothed with Christ.

D a y   5

Abba, Father

We will conclude week 1 by considering Galatians 4. Take your time and read the Scriptures aloud. Look for one prevailing theme.

Below, write what you identify as the theme of chapter 4.

Son — grace

I hope you discovered one of the key themes of Galatians 4 to be sonship (and daughtership). The focus is described beautifully in Today's Treasure, Galatians 4:6. Today our entire study will be devoted to an increased understanding of the parent-child relationship we've been invited to share with God.

Look carefully at verse 6. Because we are His children, where did God send the Spirit of His Son?

into our hearts.

Have you ever wondered where we get the doctrinal basis for "inviting Jesus" specifically "into our hearts"? As you can see, it's not just a warm and tender concept, it's scriptural.

Now take a look at Romans 10:8-10. What vital role did the heart play in salvation? *believe in your heart Jesus is Lord*

Belief overflows from the heart to God and, in turn, the Spirit overflows from God to the heart. Another "member" of your body also plays a vital role in salvation according to these two verses.

What is that body part and what must it do?

mouth must confess Jesus is Lord

The Greek word for *confess* is *homologeo* and it means "to assent, consent, admit; to promise; to concede...confess. Hence, to confess publicly, acknowledge openly, profess."[7]

Before whom was our confession made? (1 Tim. 6:12).

Many witnesses

Take a look at 1 Timothy 6:13. Even Christ confessed with His mouth before men! This passage is referring to the "confessions" of Christ in John 18:33-37.

What specific confessions did Christ make in John 18:36-37?

Care of body - no bones broken / look upon whom they pierced.

At what point in your own life did you publicly confess Christ as Lord? _7 yrs - 12 yrs._

Turn to Matthew 1. What do you see recorded in verses 1-17?

Genealogy of Jesus.

Beloved, the moment you believed with your heart and confessed with your mouth that Jesus Christ is Lord, that genealogy became your own. Your heritage became a holy one. You're lineage became royalty. Your spiritual bloodline stems all the way back to Abraham...you are a child of promise. By what means have we been born into such great wealth? The answer can be found in Romans 8:14-16. We are added to the family of God by way of blessed adoption!

Oh, how God increased my understanding of this glorious truth through our time with Michael, our adopted son for seven years. I can't begin to recount the serious deliberation that transpired between my husband and myself while we considered adopting Michael. We agonized far more over his adoption than the natural births of our two daughters. We considered the risk over and over again.

We knew, that in many ways, the adoption would cost us far more than a natural birth. Because Michael was old enough to have developed his own will and ways, we knew he might never respond to us as "real" parents. We knew that there was only so much we could do for him if he did not have the will to overcome the obstacles and habits of his "formative" years. Michael's natural father was against the adoption but unwilling to care for him. We knew it was possible he could fight us throughout Michael's young life and even attempt to steal

him from us for his own personal gain. We had to be sure that we wanted him regardless of the price.

Turn to Ephesians 1:3-6 and read the proceedings of your own adoption.

◓ After careful deliberation, when did God decide to adopt you?

bef. the foundation of the world.

Through what "agency" did He acquire your adoption?

Why did God go to all the trouble to adopt?

Love

Along the way, many people have asked Keith and me what motivated us to adopt an older child with special emotional needs. We wholeheartedly agree that we had two reasons: the will of God and our own ignorance. We are both so thankful we had no idea what lie ahead. Fear and dread may have hindered us from receiving one of God's most precious gifts to us.

Because of what we've experienced, it is more than I can fathom to consider that God adopted each of us knowing exactly what was ahead. He knew every time we would: fail Him, deny Him, desert Him, choose someone over Him, or make choices that would break His heart.

Jesus knew how difficult it would be to convince us to break old habits and to overcome our previous heritage. He also knew how endless the battle would be with our previous "parent," the devil, who was so unwilling to give us up. And having this full knowledge, He did it anyway–because it pleased Him.

Not only did we receive a new Father, but we also were invited to partake in a very distinct relationship with that Father. Both Romans 8 and Galatians 4 say that the Spirit of Christ given to believers enables them to cry out, "Abba, Father!" *Abba* is a term of extreme endearment expressed by a young child to his beloved father, his hero, the one who kisses his scraped knee and dries his fresh tears. *Abba* would be the word used only for a parent who was familiar, available, trustworthy, and comforting. Literally, it is "Daddy, my Daddy."

When Michael first met us, he observed, "Those girls call you 'Mommy.'" I replied reluctantly, "Yes, they do." He then said, "I don't have me a Mommy." That precious child was able to say so much with so few words. "I've had a mother, but she was not a Mommy. And you're a Mommy, but you're not mine." *Abba* literally means "you're a Daddy, MY DADDY!"

I thought these were the only two places in Scripture this term was used, but I was mistaken. Tucked right in the middle of chapter 14 of Mark's Gospel is one more occasion when the word *Abba* appears. Read Mark 14:32-36. How my heart breaks. How, then, must the Father's heart have broken.

Conclude your study today by noting what kind of Father your adoption has afforded you according to the following Scriptures.

How carefully does your Father watch to know what you need? (Matt. 6:8).

Knowledge bef. you know.

 **In what way did the Father show His great love for you, and what does His demonstration suggest about His willingness to meet your needs? (Rom. 8:32).**

Crucified His Son for us! Will give us all things.

How does 2 Corinthians 1:3 suggest that the Father can share your hurts?

Father of mercies & God of all comfort.

Read Ephesians 2:18. Circle the word that best describes the Father.

distant   (approachable)

How would you describe the Father's attitude about gift-giving? (Jas. 1:17-18).

Every good thing bestowed upon us & every perfect gift

How does God want you to respond to what He showed you today?

_____

_____

_____

_____

_____

_____

_____

How does the Father regard you? (Deut. 7:6).

his possession of all on the earth!

Now, that's a Father! Accept Him fully as your own today.

[1]Ray Beeson and Ranelda Mack Hunsicker, *The Hidden Price of Greatness* (Wheaton, IL: Tyndale House Publishers, Inc., 1991), 212.
[2]Ibid., 213.
[3]Spiros Zodhiates et al., eds., *The Complete Word Study Dictionary: New Testament* (Chattanooga, TN: AMG Publishers, 1992), 251.
[4]Ibid., 1469.
[5]Ibid., 1162.
[6]James Strong, from the *Hebrew and Chaldee Dictionary* of *The Exhaustive Concordance of the Bible*, (Nashville: Holman Bible Publishers, n.d.), 58.
[7]Spiros Zodhiates et al., eds., *The Complete Word Study Dictionary: New Testament* (Chattanooga, TN: AMG Publishers, 1992), 1045-1046.

Week 2

To Live by the Spirit

The Holy Spirit. The Spirit of the Living God. How are we to understand and relate to God the Spirit? This week we will examine what the Bible says about the Holy Spirit. We will consider the Spirit's many roles in our lives. He works to bring us to salvation. He seals us as members of God's family. He leads us as we seek to know and grow in God. The Spirit empowers us to fight life's inevitable battles with the world, the flesh, and the devil. In every way and at every turn we are utterly dependent on the Holy Spirit of God.

This week we will study much of what the Bible says about the Holy Spirit. We will consider the divinity of the Spirit, the ministries of the Spirit, and how we can walk in constant companionship with the Holy Spirit. Come along as together we examine the following issues.

Principal Questions

Day 1: What part did the Holy Spirit perform in creation?

Day 2: What is the mystery God has chosen to make known?

Day 3: What does the Spirit do with the words of Jesus?

Day 4: What do you believe it means to "live by the Spirit"?

Day 5: Why is one without the Spirit incapable of understanding the things of the Spirit?

Day 1

Three in One

This week we continue building a foundation for our study. We seek to broaden our understanding of the Holy Spirit and consider His importance in our daily lives. We will study what Galatians 5 and 6 have to say about the third member of the Trinity.

Today we examine passages throughout Scripture in the form of a "character study" of the Spirit. Many of these points may be assumptions you already possess concerning the Holy Spirit, but remember, assumptions are not facts until you find them in God's Word. You may be very familiar with these Scriptures, but I trust that the exercise of organizing them into categories will be of help. In today's study, we will seek to answer several important questions:

1. Does Scripture prove the Holy Spirit to be God—just as divine as the Father and the Son?
2. If so, what characteristics or attributes do the Father, Son, and Spirit have in common?
3. How is the Holy Spirit unique?

Let's discover the facts by searching the following Scripture passages and answering the accompanying questions.

Compare Isaiah 40:13 and 1 Corinthians 2:12. What does the fact that the Spirit knows the thoughts of God suggest to you?

He is God - 3-in one

Read Psalm 139:7-10. What characteristic of God does the Spirit display in these verses? (Check one.)
❑ all powerful   ☑ present everywhere   ❑ all knowing

↻ Read Genesis 1:1-2 and Psalm 104:30. What is the Spirit's role in creation? _Power of God moving over the waters (Creator)_

Job 33:4 tells us that the Spirit not only acted in the world's creation, but also the Spirit created us as individuals. _Made me & gave me life_

What evidence do you find in Luke 1:35 that the Spirit is God?

The Spirit rested upon the Virgin Mother

The Today's Treasure:

"So I say, live by the Spirit, and you will not gratify the desires of the sinful nature" (Gal. 5:16).

Did you note the parallel statements? The angel said, "the Holy Spirit will come upon you, and the power of the Most High will overshadow you." The Spirit does what only God can do. Since Jesus was begotten of the Holy Spirit and since Jesus is the Son of God, the Spirit is God.

Luke 1:35 makes plain that the Spirit accomplished Christ's birth. What past action does Hebrews 9:14 say the Spirit also accomplished?

Christ's death

 **How did Jesus fulfill His ministry? (Acts 10:38).**

Yes (?) Anointed

Read Romans 8:11. Where does the Spirit dwell? (Check one.)
❏ with God in heaven   ❏ everywhere   ☑ in you

And what will He ultimately do with our mortal bodies?

Take us to heaven.

In what names did Jesus command that believers should be baptized? (Matt. 28:19).

Father , _Son_ , and the _H.S._ .

Don't you love the security that comes from searching Scripture, our one and only standard of truth? Surely you are convinced that the Holy Spirit is indeed the third member of the Trinity and divine in every respect.

As we search, we will discover divine attributes that the three members of the Trinity have in common. We will also determine how their roles differ. Consider the act of creation as an illustration which proves how the Father, Son, and Holy Spirit are one and yet distinct in many functions.

Locate Genesis 1:1 in your Bible. Our first hint of each member of the Trinity's intimate involvement in creation is the Hebrew term used for *God* in the fourth word of Holy Writ: "In the beginning *Elohim* created." The word *Elohim* is a plural form of the Hebrew word for *God*. The singular form is *El*. The plural word suggests more than one yet less than many.[1]

New Testament believers understand the meaning of *Elohim* more clearly: God is three in one—the Father, the Son, and the Holy Spirit. There are several imperfect analogies which help to explain the triune nature of God. For example, water is made up of three parts (two parts hydrogen, one part oxygen), yet remains one in substance. Water can take on the form of ice, liquid or vapor, yet it's still water. You may be a daughter, a wife, and a mother, yet you're still you. Each of these analogies help us to glimpse God's triune nature in some tiny way, still each of these examples is pitifully limited. The best we can do is recognize that our one God is Father, Son, and Spirit.

The plural form of the word *Elohim* speaks of the Trinity's involvement in creation, but does Scripture delineate responsibilities? Let's find out.

Take a look at John 6:38 and 8:28. What does Christ cite as His key responsibility?

To do the Will & Everything of the Father. (Authority)

Now look at Colossians 1:13-17. The passage demonstrates Christ's intricate involvement in creation, yet as we have seen in John 6:38 and 8:28, the Son never does anything on His own. He does only what pleases the Father.

Now look at John 1:1-3. By what name is Christ called?

God.

In this passage, the Greek term for *Word* is *Logos,* which means "the power of speech, delivery, oratory, eloquence. The Word of God, meaning His omnipotent voice, decree."[2] Christ came as the Word made flesh, dwelling among us (see John 1:14) and by the *Logos,* all things were created.

What part did the Holy Spirit perform in creation? (Gen 1:1-2).

moved over the waters.

The word "hovering" or "moved" (KJV) means to "flutter, move, shake."[3] What you are seeing in Genesis 1:2 is the Holy Spirit acting in His role as Energizer, applying the power and energy of the Godhead to the act of creation.

Now let's compile what we've discovered about each member of the Godhead and determine how creation demonstrates the Triune God at work–one God, in three distinct personalities. "Hear, O Israel: The Lord our God, the Lord is one" (Deut. 6:4). That one Lord accomplished all of creation through the Father's **will,** the Son's **Word,** and the Spirit's **way.** The Father willed it, the Son spoke it, and the Holy Spirit energized it into being.

The same God who willed, spoke, and energized the universe into being directs all His care and distinctive direction to your precious life. He continues to direct you through these same methods: the Father first wills, the Son speaks the Father's will to you through His Word, and the Holy Spirit supplies the power for you to obey.

Have you been feeling a little insignificant lately? unimportant? How's this for a change in perspective? The entire Godhead is intimately involved in your daily life using the same power and glory with which He commanded creation into being. He must find you rather significant!

Let's conclude with a wrap-up of these thoughts. The Father has a perfect plan for your life. Jeremiah 29:11 says that plan is "to prosper you and not to harm you, plans to give you hope and a future." In advance, the Father has **willed** and tailor-made a plan for your unique life to bring you to one "expected end." That perfect plan has been afforded you by the precious blood of His Son, Jesus, who has extended His **Word** to direct you in your path. The Holy Spirit, then, teaches you His Word and empowers you to obey and follow it, thereby providing a **way** for simple humans to perform godly tasks. Without the Holy Spirit, you would live in the constant frustration of qualifying for a race, having the finish line in sight, but having no energy to finish the race.

How does God want you to respond to what He showed you today?

[handwritten] Make this message loud & again send it to His Children. Be more consciense of His presents - every moment of every day & night

🕊Today's Treasure:

"Now it is God who makes both us and you stand firm in Christ. He anointed us, set His seal of ownership on us, and put His Spirit in our hearts as a deposit guaranteeing what is to come" (2 Cor. 1:21-22).

Read Philippians 2:13. How does this verse reaffirm today's study?

[handwritten] at work in me. Awareness of his purpose

Can you recall a time or circumstance in your life that illustrates all three members of the Trinity at work? Describe that event.

[handwritten] Vision!

Day 2

An Eternal Guarantee

In our previous study, we explored the truth that the Holy Spirit is both divine and distinctive. Today we will continue by studying seven ministries of the Holy Spirit.

Before I offer a brief explanation about each ministry, please search the following Scriptures and note the obvious activity of the Holy Spirit.

John 16:7-11 tells us that the Spirit acts as our Counselor. Of what things does the Spirit convict us?

[handwritten] Concerning sin, righteousness & judgement

What does Titus 3:5 tell us the Spirit does for us?

[handwritten] saves us by mercy

First Corinthians 12:13 says that "we were all *[handwritten]* made one **by one Spirit."**

What does 1 Corinthians 6:19-20 call the "temple of the Holy Spirit"?

[handwritten] Who is in you! You are not your own, but bought w/a price. Glorify God in your body

? Ephesians 4:30 tells us that our behaviors can *[handwritten]* lift **the Spirit.**

What command does Ephesians 5:18 contain? *[handwritten]* Be filled

THE MINISTRIES OF THE HOLY SPIRIT

Notice that the first ministry of the Holy Spirit is to convict or reprove.
Conviction is the ultimate good news/bad news. Before we come to Christ, the Spirit provokes us to an awareness of our sinful state—the bad news. Then the Spirit points us to the Savior—good news indeed! The Holy Spirit convicts His children for a different reason—to restore fellowship and spiritual productivity.

As we study the ministries and manifestations of the Spirit, we might come to the sobering realization that we've thought these were our responsibilities.

• Have you ever tried to convict a lost person of his sin of unbelief?
• Have you ever tried to convict a saved person of her sinful ways?

Praise God, conviction is not our job. Such responsibility is reserved for God. It doesn't matter how powerfully we present our testimonies or arguments. If the Holy Spirit has not drawn a person to Christ, our efforts are futile. Certainly we may be used as vessels through which the Spirit extends the invitation, but we are powerless to bring results. We have only one true source of results and that is intercessory prayer. We can pray diligently for the Holy Spirit to intervene in the life of an individual and for that person to respond favorably.

The second ministry of the Holy Spirit is regeneration.
The Greek word for *regeneration* is *paliggenesia*, which is a compound word formed from *palin* meaning "again" and "genesis" or "beginning." Regeneration "refers to the spiritual rebirth of the individual soul."[4] This term is defined perfectly by Christ Himself in John 3:1-8.

What is Christ's command in John 3:7?

Must all be born again

✎ Oh, Beloved, are you thankful you've had the opportunity to "begin again"? What is the clearest difference you remember experiencing as a person reborn in Christ?

Glorying in Nature = God

The third ministry of the Holy Spirit is baptism.
The Greek word for *baptizing* is *baptizo*, which means "to dip, immerse, submerge, to overwhelm, saturate.... First Corinthians 12:13 refers to this Spirit baptism as "an act performed by God in joining all true believers to the body of the Lord Jesus."[5]

The word *baptizo* was often used to describe the procedure in which a piece of cloth was dipped into dye, resulting in an entirely new color. Surely we have been dipped into the precious blood of our Savior, emerging as white as snow.

Confusion over the exact moment of the believer's baptism by the Holy Spirit divides denominations and individuals. Many of our fellow believers who are charismatic in their practices of the gifts of the Spirit have been taught that the baptism of the Holy Spirit is the onset of the gift of tongues.

Please look carefully at 1 Corinthians 12:13,30. Verse 13 says that we are all baptized by one Spirit. Verse 30 assumes we do not all speak in tongues. No matter how you feel about the gifts of the Spirit, the baptism of the Holy Spirit and speaking in tongues are not the same thing. If you have been born again, you have been baptized by the Holy Spirit.

The fourth ministry of the Holy Spirit is His glorious indwelling!

> ✎ **Read Colossians 1:25-27. What is the mystery God has chosen to**

make known? _He is within us._

Prior to the Day of Pentecost in Acts 2, the Holy Spirit did not indwell the hearts of all children of God. Less than one hundred people recorded in all the Old Testament had been filled with or empowered by the Holy Spirit. Furthermore, the Holy Spirit came and went as He willed. Scripture records that the Holy Spirit not only anointed Saul, but also departed from him as well. Read in Psalm 51:10-12 the repentant, pleading words of David after his sin with Bathsheba.

> **What specific petition does David make concerning the Spirit of God?**
>
> _joy which comes from salvation_

David knew God's Spirit was indeed a gift. He knew from the experience of Saul that he could lose the Spirit's powerful presence. Now look at John 14:16 and Romans 8:38-39.

> **How is the presence of the Spirit different in present-day believers?**
>
> _remain forever w/in us!_

→ That's exactly why the Day of Pentecost was such a unique celebration! The moment we are born again, we have the wonderful guarantee of the Holy Spirit's residence in us with the abiding promise that He will remain forever!

The fifth ministry of the Holy Spirit is the sealing.
He gives to all believers. The Greek word for *seal* is *sphragizo,* which has a twofold meaning in Ephesians 4:30. First, to seal is to "close up and make fast with a seal signet such as letters or books so that they may not be read." Secondly, it means "to set a seal or mark upon a thing as a token of its authenticity or approvedness."[6] The seal of the Holy Spirit is for protection and identification. We are identified as joint heirs with Christ, and we are protected from the entrance of any other entity.

Please understand this crucial biblical precept. Because you have been sealed by the Holy Spirit, you cannot be inhabited by any other spiritual force. Some years ago I met a woman who was positive she was born again, yet she was experiencing such difficulties that a man was attempting to exorcise demons from her to no avail. I firmly believe that a born-again believer cannot be possessed by a demon. We are sealed. Demons have no way in. We may be oppressed, and the Bible contains prescriptives for such occasions, but we cannot be possessed.

The sixth ministry of the Holy Spirit is to fill the yielded believer.
A marked difference separates the filling of the Holy Spirit and the other ministries He performs. Regeneration, baptism, indwelling, and sealing all take ← place the moment we accept Christ as Savior and Lord. On the other hand, the burden of the filling of the Holy Spirit rests on us. The Holy Spirit is always ready and able to fill the believer, but He will not agree to perform this ministry unless He is in present control of the one He inhabits.

Ephesians 5:18 says, "be filled with the Spirit." We are as filled with the Holy Spirit as we are yielded to Him and controlled by Him. The ramifications of being Spirit-controlled are amazing. We have much to learn about the supernatural outcome of the Spirit's filling during the remainder of our study.

The seventh ministry of the Holy Spirit may be difficult to understand. Scholars are divided over the force at work in 2 Thessalonians 2:6-12.
Some believe Paul spoke of human government restraining evil. I am convinced, however, that the passage speaks directly about the Holy Spirit. It describes the Holy Spirit's ministry of restraining. The Spirit will not permit ← Satan to spread his evil without limit in this present age. The fact that you can look around you and see any good at all is evidence of the Restrainer's work. The fact that Satan cannot stop the growth of the church or the spread of the Word is evidence of the Restrainer. Open Bibles in the hands of people where Christianity is banned is testimony that the Restrainer functions in this age.

Certainly we live in a dark and sin-damaged world, but stop and think what the planet would be like if evil were unleashed completely. Write a paragraph describing what life on earth would be like.

Discribed prior to the great Flood.

_____

_____

_____

_____

Write a prayer thanking God for the restraining power of the Spirit.

_____

_____

_____

_____

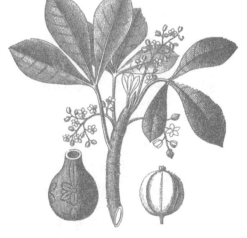

As we conclude today's study, let's summarize what we've learned about the seven ministries of the Holy Spirit.

How does God want you to respond to what He showed you today?

_____

_____

_____

_____

_____

_____

_____

List as many of His ministries as you can from memory. After you have written what you readily retained, go back and review your notes. Then complete your list.

1. _Regeneration_____
2. _Baptism_____
3. _Indwelling_____
4. _Sealing_____
5. _Counselor_____
6. _Filling -_____
7. _Restraining_____

Circle the number of ministries that occur the second we receive Christ as Savior.

1   2   3   ④   5   6   7

Which one of the seven ministries is dependent upon our ongoing relinquishment of control?

_restraining_____

❧Today's Treasure:

"Since we live by the Spirit, let us keep in step with the Spirit. Let us not become conceited, provoking and envying each other" (Gal. 5:25-26).

Day 3

Led by the Spirit

The previous session was devoted to a basic study of seven ministries of the Holy Spirit, most of which took place the moment we were born again. Today we are going to uncover six different ways the Holy Spirit reveals Himself to us in an ongoing fashion.

Read the following Scriptures and determine each distinctive manifestation of the Holy Spirit.

❧ **What does the Spirit do with the words of Jesus? (John 16:12-15).**

_Give to us._____

? We are _Sons_ by the Spirit (Gal. 5:18; Rom. 8:14).

Which of your needs does the Spirit meet? (Rom. 8:16).
☐ security   ☑ blessing
☐ assurance of salvation   ☑ abilities/talents

Romans 8:26 says the Spirit helps us to _pray_ . *love this verse!*

✎ **Describe a time when you had to depend on the Spirit in this way.**

"Parents' death.

List ways 1 Corinthians 12:1-11 describes the Spirit meeting the needs of the church and individual believers.

Gifts, messages, power, interpretation, communication, serving.

The Spirit gives gifts, but Galatians 5:22-23 states that He develops

love, joy, peace, patience, **in the lives of believers.**
kindness, goodness, faithfulness, humility, self-control.

I pray that you are beginning to grasp just how active the Holy Spirit of God is in your personal life! Review the list you completed above. Remember, these activities are ways the Holy Spirit manifests Himself to you—reminders of the Spirit's presence. Every time you understand the Word of God, the Holy Spirit has manifested Himself to you as Teacher. Every time you realize God has "somehow" pricked your heart to discern direction, the Holy Spirit has manifested Himself through leadership. Every time you edify the body of believers through service, the Holy Spirit is evidenced as the Giver of gifts. Every time you express love for someone you never could have imagined even tolerating, you've witnessed the fruit of His Spirit. He continually "bears witness" with your tendered spirit; He prays for you when you don't have a clue how to pray.

Describe the last time your spirit was willing, but you had no idea how to pray in a given matter.

Val.

How did God eventually respond to meet your personal needs in that matter?

still waiting

Who do you think prayed for God to respond to specific needs you had at that time? **The Holy Spirit,** who is ever anxious to intercede for God's children. The intercession of the Holy Spirit is not license to avoid prayer. I have actually heard people say: "I haven't had time to pray in a week! Oh, well, the Holy Spirit's interceding for me." This type attitude is not what Paul described in Romans 8:26-27. Look back at these verses for a moment.

The Holy Spirit "helps us in our _weakness_**" (v. 26).**

The Spirit intervenes in our weakness, but not in our avoidance. First Thessalonians 5:17 tells us to "pray continually," but when the weakness of our human state results in a loss of words and direction, how comforting it is to know that the Holy Spirit intercedes with groanings on our behalf.

Through our brief study of the Holy Spirit's ministries and manifestations, you can learn volumes about His personality, His creativity, His awareness, His consistency, His "protectiveness," His tenderness, and His loyalty. Let's spend some time now increasing our awareness of two ways we can affect the Spirit.

First Thessalonians 5:19 tells us not to restrain the H.S.

We can quench the Holy Spirit. The NIV says "put out the Spirit's fire." The Greek word for *quench* is *sbennumi*, which in this context means "to dampen, hinder, repress, as in preventing the Holy Spirit from exerting His full influence."[7] Very simply, to quench the Spirit is to say "no" to God.

As we have already noted, the Holy Spirit never withdraws His presence. We have also noted that God has an "expected end" toward which He continually moves us. He desires for us to acknowledge Him as completely sovereign over every decision and direction of our lives. His insistence is not based on His ego. Remember, His commands for us are exactly that: for us. His insistence is based on our success, on our victory.

Jeremiah 10:23 says God owns the rights to: (Check one or more.)
☑ **our lives**　　　　❑ **our families**　　　　❑ **the church**

When we resist the authority of God and say "no" to His leadership, we are quenching or shrinking the Holy Spirit. In the life of a believer, the opposite of Spirit-filled is not Spirit-"emptied" but Spirit-quenched.

Let's consider a second way we can affect the Holy Spirit. On day 2, we looked at Ephesians 4:30 concerning the "sealing" of the Holy Spirit.

Fill in the blanks from Ephesians 4:30:

"Do not _____make_____ **the Holy Spirit of God, with whom you**

were _____marked_____ **for the day of redemption."**

The Holy Spirit can be grieved. The Greek word for *grieve* is *lupeo* and it means "to afflict with sorrow, to cause grief, offend."[8] In everyday language, to grieve someone would be to "break his heart." The word implies that the third member of the Holy Trinity is able to feel pain. The Word of God cites only one causal agent of His pain: those He inhabits—the very ones who also are a source of His joy. How can we grieve the Holy Spirit? Take a look at the verse following Ephesians 4:30.

What behaviors or attitudes does Ephesians 4:31 demand that we

"get rid" of? bitterness, passion, anger — no more insults, shouting, hateful feelings

Sin in the life of the believer causes the Holy Spirit to grieve. Consequently, the Holy Spirit's pain will not cease until we "get rid" of the sin. How do we get rid of the sin? Through true confession and repentance. These are such familiar words to us, yet so often we misunderstand their literal intent.

Many of us learned to pray repeating the words, "and forgive me for all my sins." Since the word *repentance* means to turn and walk in the other direction, we can't possibly repent of something vague and unspecified. For the Spirit to be released from grief and to fulfillment, every known sin must be the object of repentance. Blanket prayers of forgiveness with no thought to the object of God's disfavor are a waste of time. We cannot confess what we will not face. We must be specific. ✗

Second Corinthians 7:10 contains another crucial component of repentance. What leads to true repentance?

w/out regret → leading to salvation.

As long as we experience no sorrow for a sin, we have not fully turned from that sin. We cherish some sins; we treasure them. We do not want to let go of them; therefore, we admit to God we have committed them, but we lack the sorrow that would give us the strength to turn away.

Have you ever held on to and nurtured the memory of a past sin?
❑ Yes ❑ No If so, what was the effect on your closeness to Christ?

_____

What can we do when we discover we lack sorrow in the area of a known sin? Ask God to quicken us in a sorrow which leads to repentance. Oh, Beloved, we are so often enslaved by memories—even those we cherish. All the while we have no idea how those cherished sins are holding us enslaved and vulnerable to our enemy. God longs to pour out His blessings upon every believer, but we withhold His hand when we hold on to past sins with our hand. Quench not the Holy Spirit: say yes to God. Grieve not the Holy Spirit: say no to sin.

Day 4
Flesh vs. Spirit

We are now beginning to pour the last bit of concrete for the foundation of our fruit of the Spirit study. Throughout this week, we have been broadening our understanding of the Holy Spirit—the One who makes it possible for us to live beyond ourselves. Today we will turn our attention to Galatians 5 and 6. Read both of these chapters with a view toward Paul's theme of contrast between the flesh (the sin nature) and the Spirit.

How does God want you to respond to what He showed you today?

_____

_____

_____

_____

_____

_____

_____

❧Today's Treasure:

"For the sinful nature desires what is contrary to the Spirit, and the Spirit what is contrary to the sinful nature. They are in conflict with each other, so that you do not do what you want" (Gal. 5:17).

In the two columns below, organize every detail these two chapters provide concerning the flesh and the Spirit.

THE FLESH	THE SPIRIT
immorality envy	joy self-control
impurity drunkenness	peace
sensuality carousing	love
idolatry	patience
sorcery	kindness
jealousy	goodness
outburst of anger	faithfulness
disputes	gentleness

Take a good look at the details listed in the preceding columns. What you are confronting is summed up perfectly in Galatians 5:17: "For the sinful nature desires what is contrary to the Spirit, and the Spirit what is contrary to the sinful nature. They are in conflict with each other." Beloved, one of our biggest reasons for failure in daily struggles is our vain attempt to balance the Spirit and the flesh—to make them function as coworkers. It is absolutely impossible. It has nothing to do with strength versus weakness. It's just not possible. They can't work together because they are polar opposites.

From what you have learned thus far, what do you believe it means to "live by the flesh"?

trouble / distruction

What do you believe it means to "live by the Spirit"?

Eternal life & peace while on Earth

In his letter to the Romans, Paul became even more descriptive in his struggle with his old nature. Please read Romans 7:7-25 aloud, with great concentration, even more than once if necessary. Feel the emotion in Paul's voice; sense his frustration. Read it as words from your own mouth because you have been there and so have I. Thank goodness, most of us do not live every single moment in the kind of agony Paul described, but there are times when the desires of the flesh are almost overwhelming.

Notice two key phrases in Romans 7:8 and 7:11: "sin, seizing the opportuni- ✱
ty." Oh, my friend, how sin does seize the opportunity. No sooner have we
made a vow or a spiritual resolution than it seems our flesh begins to find every
opportunity to trip us. Even if we didn't struggle with evil principalities, our
own flesh is enough to sabotage us. We cannot always say, "The devil made me
do it." Scripture reveals that redeemed humankind possesses three enemies.

Make note of the enemy identified in each Scripture passage:

1 John 2:15-17 _The World._

1 Peter 5:8 _Sobriolity_

Galatians 5:19 _immorality, impurity, sensuality_

The world system is our enemy. You need only take a spin down the freeway
and read the billboards to know that the world is speeding head-on into spiritual destruction. Satan is our enemy and he heads an army of enormous proportions. Finally, our sin nature, or what we refer to as our "flesh," is our enemy.

👁 In a society that, at its best, preaches "follow your heart," what
does Jeremiah 17:9 have to say?

The heart is more deceitful than all else is
desperately sick.

We can't even trust our own hearts! The world, the devil, and the flesh—pretty strong foes, wouldn't you say? Are you feeling a little defeated?

Write your own paraphrase of 1 John 4:4: _Christ is greater_
than self.

Now look again, closely, at what you've written. Beloved, you are staring at
the reason for this study. Greater is He that is in you than he that is in the
world! You see, this verse tells us that God has given us victory over all three of ← _? again?_
our enemies if we will follow Him in "triumphant procession" (2 Cor. 2:14)!
The Holy Spirit of Christ, who inhabits this flesh and exercises dominion over
it at our mere invitation, is greater than "he" who is the prince of this world (see
John 12:31) and dictates the personality of this world. He that is in us is the key
to overcoming "he that is in the world," all that is "of the world," and all that
is of the flesh.

What has the Spirit given to us? (2 Pet. 1:3-4).

His precious & magnificent promises

How does God want you to respond to what He showed you today?

_____

_____

_____

_____

_____

_____

Today's Treasure:

"We have not received the spirit of the world but the Spirit who is from God, that we may understand what God has freely given us" (1 Cor. 2:12).

Why has He given us all we need? (v. 4).

you may become partakers of the divine nature

Fill in the blanks below using 2 Corinthians 9:8:

"God is able to make all _____grace_____ abound to you, so that in all

_____ at all _____, having all that you _require_,

you will abound in every good _cause_."

My precious sister, if you are born again, you possess everything you need to be victorious. You are "thoroughly furnished unto all good works." You are dressed for success. Through the next eight weeks, may the One "who is able to keep you from falling and present you before His glorious presence without fault and with great joy" teach us to a victorious degree what we already possess in Jesus (see Jude 24). Make His Praise Glorious!

Day 5

Spiritually Mature

Today we will conclude our overview of the Book of Galatians and complete our foundation for the fruit of the Spirit study. Stop now and read Galatians 6.

Now look back at Galatians 6:1. To the praise and glory of our merciful God, restoration of a fallen brother or sister is a vital function of the body of Christ.

What kind of person does the apostle Paul pinpoint as the instrument of God's restoration?

_____

What does the phrase "you who are spiritual" mean? Thankfully, Paul included a lesson in his letter to the church at Corinth concerning the spiritual man.

Please read 1 Corinthians 2:6–3:3. Answer the following:

For whom is the "message of wisdom" (2:6)? mature Christians

How long has God destined this secret wisdom to be ours (2:7)?
❏ since Christ died on the cross
☑ since before time began
❏ since we trusted Christ for salvation

What does the Holy Spirit have to do with God's perfect plan for your life? (2:9-10).

The secret – which no man thought would occur.

Why have we received the Spirit of God rather than the spirit of the world (2:12)? (Check one or more.)
- ❏ because we're really good people
- ☑ so we may understand what God has freely given us
- ❏ so we may be empowered to live Christlike lives

✎ How does the Holy Spirit "speak"? (2:13).

Words taught by H.S. – spiritual thoughts w/ sp. words.

✎ Why is one without the Spirit incapable of understanding the things of the Spirit (2:14)?

not spirit filled / foolish to him

What is the wonderful paradox presented to us in 2:15?

?

How do you feel about the statement in 2:16, that we have the mind of Christ?

Frightening – is that when we are all tog. / certainly not alone

How did Paul have to address the Christians of Corinth (3:1)? (Check one.)
- ❏ as mature saints
- ☑ as spiritual babes
- ❏ as faithful co-laborers
- ❏ as fellow sufferers

What was the outward manifestation of inward immaturity (3:3)?

Walking like mere man.

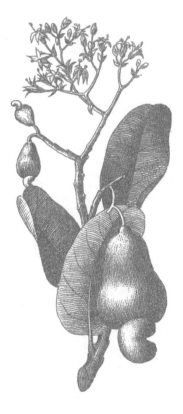

The apostle Paul addressed three distinct groups and every person alive can be placed in one of these groups. First Corinthians 2:14 introduces the first "type" of person—"the man without the Spirit." For the sake of clarity, let's refer to him as King James does: he is the natural man. The natural man is the unredeemed person.

1. The Natural Man

Romans 8:9 says, "If anyone does not have the Spirit of Christ, he does not belong to Christ." The unsaved man or woman cannot discern the spiritual things of God. Those without Christ are spiritually dead (see Eph. 2:1), alienated from the Spirit of God.

Believers struggle with this truth. We cannot understand why our lost friends cannot understand. We say: "But it says it right there! Can't you see it?" No, they cannot; it is foolishness to them. In a very real sense, it does not compute.

Let me explain this in rather simple, mechanical terms. If I have a fax machine, it doesn't matter how pertinent and life-saving the information I need to send may be if the person who needs the information has no fax machine. I can fax the information all day, but my message will never reach him. He does not possess the equipment needed to receive the fax. As basic as this week's study has been, you could not have comprehended it without the Spirit of God in you to receive and process the information.

Natural persons have no means by which to be truly victorious over sin. They are driven solely by their own natures. We should not be surprised at the depravity that surrounds us. I am somewhat puzzled by a common attitude in today's church. We believe that abortion clinics, godless school districts, pornographers and the like are the hindrances to revival in our land.

Who does the burden of revival and the healing of a nation fall upon? (2 Chron 7:14).

Titus 7 good S. Filled man.

God expects unredeemed people to sin. Revival has nothing to do with unsaved people. If God's people would humble themselves, pray, and seek His face, then this nation would be healed in spite of every bar, every gambling hall, every gang, and every crack house. Now let's look at the second "kind" of person: the man of deadly spiritual complacency.

2. The Carnal Man

Check out 1 Corinthians 3:1-3. Note everything you can glean from these three verses that describe the worldly or carnal person.

milk vs. solid food

fleshy - mere man

The final question in these three verses delivers a precise summation of the worldly or carnal man: "Are you not acting like mere men"?

What does Paul mean by "mere men"?

unsaved

The worldly or carnal men Paul addressed in these verses are positively saved. Paul defines the worldly man in 3:1: they are "mere infants in Christ." They act very much like someone who does not have the Spirit of Christ, who is not born again…they act like "mere men."

This sobering truth should caution our tendencies to judge the state of someone else's salvation. I once attended a very prestigious lunch at a Houston country club. All the women were God-honoring, church-serving Christians. A lady asked me: "So, Beth, how do you feel about our president? Don't you think he's lost?" I am horrified when I consider how in former years I might have dogmatically answered that question. Thankfully, I have learned a few things since then and have had a few too many peeks at my own sinful nature. I could only respond, "After the mercy it took for God to save my own sinful soul, I would be far too afraid to guess." Beloved, we are not the judges.

3. The Spiritual Man

Finally, let's look at the third type of person. The apostle Paul calls this person the spiritual man. Second Corinthians 2:15 tells us that, the spiritual man "makes judgments about all things." The Greek word is *anakrino*, and it means "to discern, judge, to examine accurately or carefully."[9] What are the things we are to discern or judge? Look back at 2:14: "the things that come from the Spirit." The spiritual man does not judge people. He or she judges "things." Very specifically, those "things that come from the Spirit."

No wonder Galatians 6:1 says only those "who are spiritual" should restore one who has fallen. Only a spiritual person could judge the situation without judging the sinner. Go back and review the passage. God even warns that the spiritual individual must restore very carefully and soberly, "or you also may be tempted"! The spiritual man is constantly aware of the fine line which separates him from the carnal man—a split second's hesitation.

The spiritual man is the person in which the mind of Christ is activated! He or she is a person who delights in the meat of God and not just the milk. Her mind is open to those things which "no eye has seen, nor ear has heard, no mind has conceived." She lives and thinks in a capacity far beyond that of "mere man." Why? Because she "lives in the Spirit"!

Do you see it all coming together now? This is who we want to learn to be as we walk through this study. The spiritual woman! The woman who "lives in the Spirit," who is "led by the Spirit." The one who keeps "in step with the Spirit" and is "filled with the Spirit."

If you are a young Christian, would you like to hear some really good news? These terms do not refer to the time you've spent, but to the today you've surrendered. You may be a new Christian who has just surrendered your heart, but if you're surrendered, you are just as "spiritual" as one who has known Him for 30 years.

Certainly God wills us to "grow in the knowledge" of the Lord Jesus Christ, that we may be thoroughly furnished; but the issue of spirituality rests upon "yieldedness" to the Holy Spirit's control. Please, please understand the most important ingredient of yieldedness. Yieldedness is always the result of a deliberate choice to yield…to consciously surrender. The spiritual life will never come "naturally."

Have you noticed that you never have to make the conscious choice to sin? Left to what comes naturally, regrettably, we all will sin. That's what the carnal man is all about. He just does what comes naturally from his old nature. If we are going to live as a spiritual man, it will result from a deliberate, conscious surrender to the Holy Spirit of God.

Surrender must be a daily choice. We can be spiritual one day and not the next. We can be spiritual one morning and not that night. (Have you noticed, oddly enough, that spirituality seems to be taxed by husbands and children?) We are spiritual when we are out of control and the Holy Spirit is in control. "So, Beth," you ask, "how will we ever know if we are 'in the Spirit?'" The answer is simple: by the fruit of the Spirit. I can't wait to get started, can you? Until then:

> Let us not become weary in doing good, for at the proper time we will reap a harvest if we do not give up. Therefore, as we have opportunity, let us do good to all people, especially to those who belong to the family of believers (Gal. 6:9-10).

Just a word of conclusion. Today some of you who are trying so diligently to complete this study, to stay focused, to be victorious in the face of ever-increasing odds, are completely exhausted. My heart aches for you. I have been there. You keep working and trusting and still you don't see any change in your husband, in your teenager, or your circumstances. The striving is exhausting. Please hang in there and remember two things:

1. God brings results from your obedience; you do not. Let Him do His job in His "proper" time. He'll do it, all right. His name depends on it and He cannot lie. Keep waiting because:

> They that wait upon the Lord shall renew their strength; they shall mount up with wings as eagles; they shall run and, not be weary; and they shall walk, and not faint (Isa. 40:31, KJV).

2. You have everything you need by virtue of the Holy Spirit within you to bear your load. If He had energy enough to speak the worlds into being according to the Father's will and the Son's Word, He has the energy to carry you through your burden. You've got the Father's will and the Son's Word on it. Keep in mind, when we power walk in the Spirit, it is He who carries the weights.

Let me close with a little fun reading. Some years ago I wrote this poem after hearing the groans of exhausted women. It occurred to me that much of the reason we felt so weary was because we had bought the lie of television's successful, worldly woman. Over the next eight weeks, let's grasp and hold on tight to the truth which has already been bought for us. Hope it brings a smile today.

SUPERWOMAN'S FREEDOM PLEA

Oh, Lord, who said there's just One Life to Live?
I'm sure I'm livin' a thousand!
The few times I do awake to pray
All My Children start arousin'!

Uh, oh! No time for quiet now
Think quick! The day's beginnin'!
I'll try to recall all Oprah's advice…
Then my head starts spinnin'.

Make those younguns religious, cautious but not suspicious
And watch their self-esteem!
Yet you be professional, look sensational
And keep that house squeaky clean!

And perish the thought you'd forget the needs
Of that marvelous man you married
Why, throw yourself before him when he raises his eyebrows
And quit thinking, "I'd rather be buried!"

Oops, now I'm late for work, the kids hate their clothes
And the baby's got a cough
As the World Turns so quickly, I'm severely tempted
To take the next jump off.

Surely they're kiddin', Is there anyone left
Who's honestly Young and Restless
As for me, I feel centuries old, completely worn out
And cellulite infested!

It's gonna take more than Ryan's Hope for this woman to survive.
I cannot abide another deep breath of these Days of our Lives!
Superwoman? She's a curse. To fake her is impossible!
And if I try for one more day, I'll wind up in General Hospital!

I've gotta be here, I've gotta be there
I frankly cannot face it.
Rescue me from havoc, please, show me what is basic!
Slow me down, Lord, save this life and keep my eyes on You.
Satan can have this rat race world—

Thank God, I'm just passin' through.

**How does God want you
to respond to what He showed
you today?**

_____

_____

_____

_____

_____

_____

_____

_____

[1]James Strong, from the *Hebrew and Chaldee Dictionary* of *The Exhaustive Concordance of the Bible* (Nashville: Holman Bible Publishers, n.d.), 12.
[2]Spiros Zodhiates et al., eds., *The Complete Word Study Dictionary: New Testament* (Chattanooga, TN: AMG Publishers, 1992), 924.
[3]James Strong, from the *Hebrew and Chaldee Dictionary* of *The Exhaustive Concordance of the Bible*, 108.
[4]Spiros Zodhiates, *The Complete Word Study Dictionary: New Testament*, 1091.
[5]Ibid., 309-310.
[6]Ibid., 1351-1352.
[7]Ibid., 1283.
[8]Ibid., 929.
[9]Ibid., 152.

Week 3

Greatest of These Is Love

We talk about it. We sing about it. We praise it. We seek it, and we long for it. Love. "The fruit of the Spirit is love…." God's kind of love is foreign to us. How can we love the unlovely—not endure them, but love them? How can we genuinely desire the best, not for ourselves or our friends, but for our enemies? Love challenges us. It frightens us, and it embraces us. Ultimately only love can change us so that we become people who love.

This week we will study the foundational characteristic of the fruit of the Holy Spirit. Every characteristic of the fruit exudes love. First, we will see some components of the world's love. Then we will examine the distinctive nature of God's love. "For God so loved the world…."

Principal Questions

Day 1: How might an ongoing deprivation of your mate for inappropriate reasons be considered a unique form of adultery?

Day 2: What caused Herod and Pilate to become friends?

Day 3: Why did God choose the foolish things of the world to shame the wise?

Day 4: What does Psalm 145:8 tell us about God's anger?

Day 5: What is the relationship between the Holy Spirit and *agape*?

Day 1

Eros: Grasping Love

Today we arrive at the heart of our study: the fruit of the Spirit. Before we begin our detailed study, let's attempt to answer some rather general questions about the fruit of the Spirit. Look carefully at Galatians 5:22-23. First of all, WHAT is the fruit of the Spirit, for heaven's sake? I want to answer that question with a twofold definition. The fruit of the Spirit is—

- the supernatural outcome of being filled with the Spirit.
- the living proof that the Spirit of God dwells in us.

Often you will hear people refer to the "fruits" of the Spirit. The word is actually singular. Galatians 5:22-23 speaks of one kind of fruit with nine different qualities, each of which we will study during the next eight weeks.

Name three or four of your favorite kinds of fruit. Patience – self-control – Kindness

Imagine one, incredibly perfect fruit that combines all the best characteristics of your favorite kinds of fruit. Feature a seedless fruit like a banana, nice and crisp like an apple, bursting with the flavors of strawberry and nectarine, and....You get the idea. God is developing a fruit in His children. The fruit has the characteristics of love, joy, peace, patience, kindness, goodness, faithfulness, gentleness, and self-control.

You may see another connection when you realize the nature of the fruit. Have you ever wondered what the fruit of the Spirit has to do with Jesus? Yes, now you see. If you go looking for this incredible, wonderful fruit, you will find the best example growing in the life of the One who hung on the tree.

God has divinely inspired the first quality of the fruit of the Spirit to be LOVE. We will spend this week examining this one particular quality.

One major reason we pay such special attention to the Greek and Hebrew ← words is because our language may use one term for perhaps several words in the original text. Both the Greek and Hebrew languages tend to be more specific and focused than the English language.

We need precision in a study of the word *love*. We use the word *love* for feelings or responses to which the Greeks attributed several totally different terms. Over the next few days, we will consider the Greek words for *love* to better distinguish the kind of love in the fruit of the Spirit. Let's begin in what you may consider an unusual place. Today let's consider a word our New Testament never uses, but a common word for *love* used by the ancient Greeks—*eros*.

In Greek mythology, *eros* love was taken from the Greek belief in a "god" of ← love called by the same name. The word actually means "longing and desire." *Eros* is a selfish love; it asks "what can I get for myself?"

We can easily understand how *eros* came to be associated with sexual love. Unless sexual love is redeemed by the presence of God, it becomes possessive.

⌒Today's Treasure:

"But the fruit of the Spirit is love, joy, peace, patience, kindness, goodness, faithfulness, gentleness and self control. Against such things there is no law" (Gal. 5:22-23).

It seeks to conquer and control. Human sexuality can be a destructive force, but such was never God's intention. He created the physical attraction between a woman and a man. He did not intend selfish *eros,* but He definitely did create the longing and desire that makes up sexual love.

Read the Song of Songs (or the Song of Solomon, KJV), chapters 1 and 4. Please do not skip this reading or you will not fully understand the love expressed in the fruit of the Spirit! Have you read it? Then you may proceed. If you did not, go back. It won't hurt you and it might do you a world of good!

God repetitively uses two different Hebrew words in the Song of Songs. For example, read again 1:2 and 1:4. In these verses He employs the word *dowd* which means in this context, "My one beloved."

The term *beloved* is one I love and use often. I began to use the term in reference to the aerobic class I taught and worshiped with for many years. They were such delight to me that I began to express that joy by calling them "my Beloveds." Since then, those dear to me in the faith also have become "Beloveds." However, if I had to single out only one "Beloved," as the word in the Song of Songs suggests, it would undoubtedly be my man!

In the context of this Hebrew word, my husband is my "Dowd," my "one beloved." He is my one and only lover. I hope those of you who are married can say the same for your husband, your beloved. Try calling him that and see what wonderful things might happen!

The other Hebrew word God uses in this divinely inspired description of love is the word *rayah*. It is used in 1:9,15; 4:1,7; and 6:4 to mean "a female associate," my female love.[1] Solomon simply means "the woman of my dreams."

Precious sister, physical desire is a very important part of marriage. I don't mind saying that marriage would be pretty difficult without desire. *Dowd* and *rayah* are both specialized terms in the context of these Scriptures. This kind of love is acceptable toward only one person: your marriage partner. If you are married, God gave you this precious gift (see 1 Cor. 7:7) that you might experience great pleasure together.

As I write these words, I am aware that many of you reading them may have no physical desire for your mate. It may be that you love him dearly, but he simply has become undesirable to you. Please hear my heart and allow me to be very open with you for the sake of God's kingdom. Physical love or sexual intercourse is to marriage what prayer is to our spiritual life. Prayer is the hallmark of intimacy with Christ. Sexual desire and fulfillment are the hallmarks of intimacy with our mate. With the exception of medical or physical limitations, I do not believe healthy marriages exist absent of physical affection.

Take a moment right now to read 1 Corinthians 7:3-6 and answer the following questions:

Besides herself, to whom does the woman's body belong?

<u>her husband</u>

In the same way, to whom does the man's body belong?

<u>his wife</u>

What are the grounds for depriving each other?

_____*agreement*_____

(I just have to wonder how many evening "quiet times" this verse has spurred that might never otherwise have happened!)

What are the two reasons Paul gives for a husband and a wife to return to each other?

1.__*To Keep Satan away*__ 2.__*Prayer*_____

❧ According to these Scriptures, an ongoing deprivation of your mate for inappropriate reasons could be considered a unique form of adultery. Describe a relationship that would be the opposite of depriving your mate. (Don't worry, you won't be asked to share your response in group!)

_____

_____

Beloved, Satan is out to destroy the church, which is best accomplished through destroying the family. He is looking for a way to tempt you. If you or your mate are depriving each other, Satan is not missing the opportunity to ultimately use it against you. You have inadvertently made your marriage vulnerable to attack. Also, Paul states that by nature we lack self-control. The enemy of our flesh will attack us if we are not satisfying each other as husband and wife.

What about our third enemy, the world? The world is perpetually selling marital infidelity. A few years ago I was stunned when I read the "marquee" at a familiar hotel on a popular Houston thoroughfare which said, "Come have your next affair with us!"

I know exactly what some of you are thinking, and I understand these feelings with all my heart: *But, Beth, how can I make myself feel desire for my husband? I just don't!* Some years ago, a very godly woman gave me the best advice I've ever been given concerning this area of marriage, and it was her own personal testimony. She said, "Every single day I pray to thrill to his touch."

Dear Friend, that day I began to pray that I would thrill to my husband's touch and grow more desirable to him every single day. Prayer dramatically transformed our lives—and it can transform yours. Remember, I was a victim of childhood sexual abuse. Yet I thrill to my husband's touch. You're right in thinking you cannot make yourself feel desire. But, oh, my sweet sister, God can change your heart and give you healthy desires toward your mate. Will you let Him?

I sense the leadership of the Holy Spirit directing me NOT to identify a question for group discussion from today's lesson. I fear there may be too much temptation to share things which should rightly remain in the private places of our marriages. But by all means, share them with God! He is the ultimate marriage Counselor!

How does God want you to respond to what He showed you today?

_Pray!!_____

_____

_____

_____

_____

_____

_____

Today's Treasure:

"Finally, all of you, live in harmony with one another; be sympathetic, love as brothers, be compassionate and humble" (1 Pet. 3:8).

Day 2

Philos: Friend Love

Our first consideration this week has been sexual love, often referred to by the Greek word *eros.* God wonderfully illustrates a second kind of love to us in Scripture. This unique kind of love is called *philos,* and it is a general term usually defined as "the love one has toward a friend or companion." In fact, the word can simply mean "friend."

Look up each of the following references. What do you learn about *philos* from each of these Scriptures?

When a person has *philos* love for another, in what position does he place the friend? (Luke 14:10).

_____ higher personal position _____

How do friends respond to each other's joys/sadnesses? (Luke 15:8-9).

_____ lovingly - in "sister-hood" - yes, to All - _____

What sad fact about friends do you gather from Luke 21:16?

_____ they are still "human" - & friendship don't alway last. _____

⌀ What caused Herod and Pilate to become friends? (Luke 23:8-12).

_____ evil- _____

First, I hope you noted from Luke 14:10 that when someone has *philo* love for another, she places that friend in a high personal position. We hold our *philos* in high esteem.

Secondly, you might have noted that *philo* love is characterized by shared experience, as the joy of one becomes the joy of all. In Luke 15:9, the actual Greek term is *tas philas* which means "female friends." Obviously, her girlfriends were aware she had lost the coin and shared her distress because the moment she found it, they rejoiced with her.

I am so blessed to have such wonderful *tas philas.* I would not trade them for anything in the world. My dear friend, Johnnie, has rarely asked me HOW I was doing in the 13 years I've known her. She only asks WHAT I am doing. Do you know why? Because she knows me so well that if she learns what I'm doing, she can practically assume how I'm doing. She knows my likes, my dislikes, my idiosyncrasies, my general attitudes, and my basic nature.

Another good friend and I have coined an abbreviation we use with each other based on the fact that dear friends share things that don't make one bit of difference to another soul. We call it TFT: Trivial Friend Talk. I'll fly to the phone to call her and share something one of the kids has said, and my husband will laugh, shake his head and say, "Ya'll are so weird." Why "so weird"? Because we are *tas philas* and he can't relate!

From Luke 21:16 did you note that a friend in some cases can be capable of betrayal? The fear of betrayal should never keep us from cultivating friends; however, for the sake of our study, it is important to acknowledge that *philos* love can turn sour.

Lastly, from Luke 23:8-12, perhaps you observed that a common pursuit can make some people *philos*. A very important characteristic of *philos* is the adoption of like interests. James 2:23 tells us that Abraham was a *philos* of God. Does this Scripture infer that God and Abraham were "chums"? Hardly. It teaches us that Abraham adopted God's interests as his own.

In the case of Herod and Pilate, the common interests were evil in nature. You see, the catalyst of friendship is not always positive. Have you ever made a friend under the wrong conditions?

What were those conditions, and how did the friendship prove to be a negative influence on one or both of you?

_____ Y- _____

_____

Several Greek words are derived from the word *philos*. Read 1 Peter 3:8. Peter exhorts us to demonstrate what kind of love?

_____ kindhearted - brotherly // bl. related _____

The Greek word for "brotherly love" or "love as brothers" is *philadelphos*. It is a compound word formed from *philos* which means "friend" and *adelphos* which means "brother." In essence, *philadelphos* means "to love a friend like a brother." In particular, Peter is exhorting fellow Christians to love one another as if "blood related."

๑ In Christ, you and I are "blood relatives." How should our kinship affect our relationship?

_____ Positively. _____

_____

This Scripture, as well as many others, infers a wonderful concept. When it comes to good works and to meeting needs, we have God's permission to be partial to one another as sisters and brothers in Christ.

How does Galatians 6:10 suggest we treat fellow believers?

_____ do good - to all fellow believers _____

The word *philema* is also a derivative of *philos* and it is found in 1 Thessalonians 5:26. Did you catch it? It means "a kiss, a token of love and friendship." In our present culture, we usually hug more often than we kiss as a token of friendship. In other cultures, kissing, usually on the cheek, is a very common expression of friendship.

Philarguros, another derivative of *philos*, can be found in 1 Timothy 6:10. This is also a compound word.

What do you think *arguros* means, knowing that *philos* means "friend of, or lover of"?

lover of ... money?

(Contrary to how it appears, it does not mean "lover of a good argument," although I've known of few of those!) Do you know anyone who is a *philarguros*, a "lover of money"?

What does God say about the love of money in 1 Timothy 6:10?

root of all evil

Obviously, some forms of love are not sanctioned by God. Let's add another to this list. Take a very careful look at 2 Timothy 3:1-2. Which kind of persons does verse 2 describe? (Check one.)
- ❏ **lovers of others**
- ☑ **lovers of themselves**

The Greek word *philautos* is a compound word made from *philos*, which by now you know means "friend of, or lover of" (No, this is not the love of cars!), and *autos* which means "himself." This term in no way suggests a healthy appreciation of who you are in Christ. The term means "self-centered or selfish, an undue sparing of self with the primary concern that things be easy and pleasant for oneself. The *philautos* is one who loves his life so much that he seeks ignobly to save it."[2]

How does Jesus respond to the *philautos* in John 12:25?

He who loves life loses it, the who hates his life in this world shall keep it to life eternal

Let's recap what we've learned about love so far. *Eros* can refer to the unique love between a man and a woman. The love between friends is called *philos*. One can be a friend to persons or things. She can make friends for common good or evil and lose friends in betrayal. God invites His children to be more than friends. He wants us to love as brothers. A person can love self above all else and seek personal gain at all costs.

As you can see, to be a friend or "lover" has positive and negative aspects. We have noted everything the first quality of the fruit of the Spirit is NOT. None of the forms of love we have studied on day 1 or day 2 have been the kind of love God expresses through us via the filling of His Holy Spirit.

Many of you are familiar with the Greek word for *love* in Galatians 5:22. The word is *agape*. This divine love stands in a class all its own. In contrast to *philos*, *agape* is not a feeling or relationship based on common interests. *Agape* is propelled by the highest interest. Two individuals can agree on something—as Pilate and Herod did—and both be wrong. *Agape* always flows from what is right and best. *Agape* is not as much a feeling as it is a response. We will discover that God commands us to *agape*. He is not commanding us toward a feeling, He is commanding us to surrender to an act of His Spirit which results in obedience. Emotion may accompany *agape*, but emotion and *agape* are not the same.

Agape is not fueled by the desire of its recipient; it is fueled by the need. "For God so *[agape]* the world, that he gave his only begotten Son, that whosoever believeth in him should not perish, but have everlasting life" (John 3:16, KJV). If God had done what man desired, we would surely be lost. *Agape* means God did what humanity most needed—He pursued in us that which was highest and best. We have much more to learn tomorrow. Until then…

Day 3

Agape: Caring Love

At the end of day 2, we considered the Greek meaning of *agape*, the foundational quality of the fruit of the Spirit. In addition to a study of the Greek meaning of *agape*, God was gracious to include in His Word a beautiful discourse describing this unique kind of love.

Turn to 1 Corinthians 13. Do not let the bug of familiarity bite you! You can be very familiar with words yet quite unfamiliar with meaning. Trust God to faithfully teach you something new about His personal way of loving. As you read through the chapter, keep in mind that every use of the word *love* or *charity* (KJV) in 1 Corinthians 13 is the Greek word *agape*.

From first reaction to these verses, how do you feel about practicing *agape*? Circle as many as apply:

overwhelmed   challenged   confident

skeptical   unattainable

Remember that Paul was in the process of giving very specific instructions about the purpose and practice of spiritual gifts. He began his discourse on *agape* by illustrating its relationship with the gifts of the Spirit. The people of Greece appreciated eloquence. They loved philosophy and listened all the more if it was presented with depth and color. In fact, they might have considered a discourse most impressive if they couldn't comprehend a single word of it! Now, read 1 Corinthians 2:1-2. Paul admitted that he did not come before them with great polish and fluency. In fact, he claimed to know only one thing.

It's no wonder that the people of Corinth misused the gift of tongues! They

---

How does God want you to respond to what He showed you today?

_____

_____

_____

_____

_____

_____

_____

**Today's Treasure:**

"It always protects, always trusts, always hopes, always perseveres. Love never fails" (1 Cor. 13:7-8).

were more interested in the expression of language than the content. Paul responded to their obsession with words when he said: "If I speak in the tongues of men and of angels, but have not love *[agape],*" my words will be meaningless noise (see v. 1). He, then, referred to the spiritual gifts of prophecy, knowledge, and faith (see v. 2).

Scripture says if these three gifts express no love, I am:

_____ *nothing!* _____

Beloved, have you ever heard speakers who said all the right things but their personalities seemed as cold as ice? Perhaps they were attempting to exercise their gifts without love. I am continually sobered by 1 Corinthians 13:2 as I prepare to speak. Each time I go before the Lord and ask Him to give me a supernatural love for the people I'm teaching; otherwise, my words are meaningless.

In verse 3, Paul broadens his expression to the extreme by saying essentially, "neither material abstinence nor martyrdom would gain me a thing without love." Then, in verses 4-8, Paul provides a perfect description of *agape*.

Please complete the following two columns from the information you gleaned in these five verses:

AGAPE IS…	AGAPE IS NOT…
patient, kind, bears all,	jealous, failure,
believes, hope,	brag, arragant
endurance,	act unbecomingly

CHARACTERISTICS OF AGAPE

1. First we learn that *agape* is PATIENT. The Greek word used for this English interpretation is *makrothumia*. Basically, the word represents "a person who is able to avenge himself yet refrains from doing so."[3]

Read Romans 12:17-21. Mark the following statements correct (C) or incorrect (I).

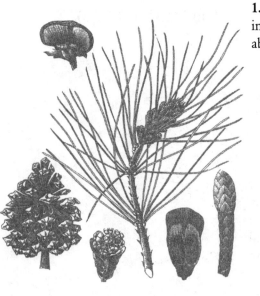

C 1. **We should make every effort to live peaceably with "everyone."**
I 2. **When we have been wronged, we should not take revenge because God is not angered by such behavior.**
I 3. **We should treat our enemies as they treat us.**
I 4. **Evil is most likely to be overcome with good.**

What response of God does Proverbs 25:21-22 add to Paul's words in Romans 12:20?

if hungery-feed your enemy / if thirsty-give drink to your enemy. He will burn w/ shame.

You will be rewarded.

2. Next, in 1 Corinthians 13 we read that *agape* **is KIND.** The Greek word for *kind* is *chresteuomai* which generally means: to show oneself "useful."[4] *Agape* volunteers to help. Perhaps poor Martha was just searching for a little kindness from Mary in the kitchen while Mary was seeking the better thing!

3. Third, Paul taught that *agape* **does NOT ENVY.** The Greek word *zeloo* means "to be zealous" and it connotes a passionate sense of jealousy.[5] Left to reap, envy always ends in some form of action. This same word is used in Acts 7:9.

> **In this verse, what act did envy or jealousy spur? (Circle one.)**
>
> murder   competition   (slavery)   fighting

One only has to scan a newspaper to find evidence that envy can kill. *Agape* never envies.

4. Fourth, we learn that *agape* **does NOT BOAST.** The Greek word *perpereuomai* comes from the root word meaning "braggart."[6]

> ✆ **Why did God choose the foolish things of the world to shame the wise? (1 Cor. 1:27-29).**
>
> He chose what is considered weak to shame the powerful.
>
> **What is the only grounds for boasting? (1 Cor. 1:31).**
>
> In the Lord.

5. Fifth, we discover that *agape* **is NOT PROUD.**

> **What negative consequences resulted from pride in the following Scriptures?**
>
> **2 Chronicles 26:16** arrogance
>
> **Psalm 10:4** pride
>
> **Proverbs 11:2** pride
>
>
>
> **Daniel 5:20** proud, stubborn, cruel
>
> **Obadiah 3 (Isn't it fun to go to a passage in Obadiah? How often do you get that opportunity?)**
>
> pride   head knowledge
>
> **Jeremiah 13:17** pride

How does God want you to respond to what He showed you today?

_____

_____

_____

_____

_____

_____

_____

Name the positive consequence that came from repenting of pride in 2 Chronicles 32:26.

did not punish the people until after Hezekiah's death.

✑ Proverbs 13:10 says "Pride only breeds quarrels." The last time you quarreled with someone, was any pride involved on your part? ☑ Yes ❑ No If so, explain.

_____

_____

By the time we are emotional enough to quarrel over an issue, pride is always involved. (Remember, quarreling and loving confrontation are two different actions.) During the early years of our marriage, my husband sometimes chose fishing over church. It upset me so badly that I could not refrain from quarreling with him about it. I hoped to make him miserable enough that he would decide instead to go to church with me. Does this sound familiar? Would you like to know what bothered me most about his absence? Having to explain why he wasn't at Sunday School.

Relief flooded my soul the day I relinquished responsibility for my husband's spirituality! It was hindering my own! He still occasionally skips church to fish, and when he does, he leaves me a note that says, "Elizabeth, Jesus loves a fisherman." I don't doubt it. Oddly enough, though, he rarely catches a thing on Sunday. Isn't God good? He's taken up the cause Himself, and He loves Keith even more than I do.

We will continue our study of *agape* tomorrow. Good work! Keep in mind your homework is an extension of *agape!* For our highest and best—keep letting Him in!

✎ **Today's Treasure:**

"Above all, love each other deeply, because love covers over a multitude of sins" (1 Pet. 4:8).

Day 4

More About Agape

Today we will continue the study of *agape* we started on day 3. We discovered that *agape* (1) is patient, (2) is kind, (3) does not envy, (4) does not boast, and (5) is not proud. Review 1 Corinthians 13:4-8.

The sixth characteristic of *agape* is that it is not rude. The Greek word for *rude* is *aschemoneo*, and it means "to behave in an ugly, indecent, unseemly or unbecoming manner."[7] We have all been around crude, obscene people. They not only expose their shame, but they also cause others to feel ashamed to be in their presence. A Spirit-filled Christian immediately senses that the Holy Spirit is offended in the presence of obscenity. When the Holy Spirit is at work in us, He bears a keen sensitivity toward that which is indecent.

Do we ever become so spiritual that we are unaffected by obscenity or indecency? Absolutely not. The destructiveness of indecency comes from the mind's tendency to replay events, words, or pictures. If we experience and replay those events often enough, we lose our sensitivity. Then the indecency appears in us.

Agape is never obscene. If we participate in the indecent or obscene, we cripple our ability to exercise *agape*. Philippians 4:8 provides excellent guidelines to ensure that the capacity to exercise *agape* is not quenched in us.

God gives us permission to enjoy many experiences as long as they provoke only certain kinds of thoughts. Which kinds?

> *good, & deserve praise, things which are true, noble, right, pure, lovely, & honorable.*

Seventh, we are reminded that *agape* is not self-seeking. On day 2 we learned about a kind of love which is "self-seeking." Second Timothy 3:2 explains that in the last days "people will be lovers of themselves." *Agape* seeks the highest and best for another. Self-seeking is the polar opposite of *agape*. Had God been seeking His own interest, He would have spared the life of His precious Son, and we would be hopelessly lost.

Eighth, *agape* is not easily angered. The fact that *agape* is not self-seeking has great impact on its ability to be slow to anger. Much of what angers us is a result of how we perceive we are personally affected by a situation.

Would you say you are: (Check one.)
❏ slow to anger   —   ❏ quick to anger

Is much of your anger based on getting your feelings hurt?
☑ Yes   ❏ No

↶ **What does Psalm 145:8 tell us about God's anger?** _____

> *is loving & merciful, slow to anger & full of constant love.*

Take a close look at the last phrase, "slow to anger and rich in love." The assumption is that we cannot be rich in love and quick to anger.

What do the following passages tell us about anger?
What key for dealing with anger do you find in Proverbs 15:1?

> *harsh answers stir up anger.*

How does your reaction affect stressful situations? (Prov. 15:18).

> *hot tempers cause arguments, patience brings peace.*

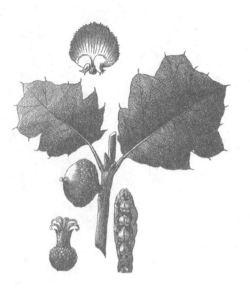

Why do you think someone who exercises self-control is greater than a world conqueror? (Prov. 16:32).

violent people decieve their friends & lead them to disaster

How does a person receive glory? (Prov. 19:11).

ignoring someone who has wronged you

How can you make life miserable for yourself and others? (Prov. 21:19).

complaining

Why is the company you keep important? (Prov. 22:24-25).

take on their bad traits (bad temper) take on their debts

Ninth, Scripture teaches us that *agape* keeps no record of wrongs. On June 27, 1993, at Shea Stadium, Anthony Young led the Mets to a record-breaking, 24-game losing streak, supplanting Cliff Curtis' record of 23 losses with Boston in 1911. The *Houston Chronicle* read: "The people asked the silliest questions: 'Don't you want the record, Anthony?' they asked, wide-eyed, as they hovered over his table. 'Wouldn't it be nice to have it? to be in the record books?'" He replied: "No, I don't want the record… Everything is over with now…I broke the record. I'm in the record books. Now that I have the record, I hope you all can leave me alone." Somehow, we humans revel in recording the failures of others.

Read Psalm 103:10-14. Give an example of God's *agape* toward you.

My father & mother

Read Hebrews 10:16-18. Which of the following best describes God's ability to forgive and forget. (Circle one.)

(superior)   excellent   adequate   poor

Praise God, He keeps no record of wrongs! Do you?

What would help you be a better "forgetter" of wrongs? (Check one.)
☑ letting God be in charge of justice and/or revenge
❑ not indulging in self-pity
☑ focusing on the future, not the past
❑ disciplining my thoughts toward the wholesome and productive
❑ other _____

The tenth characteristic of *agape* is that it does not delight in evil but rejoices with the truth.

↶ Read Psalm 119:29-32. How would your life be different if you could wholeheartedly embrace the words and attitude of the psalm?

obey - your commands - completely

David was one who experienced the pain of exposed truth, yet he knew that even as the truth hurt, freedom and gladness would soon follow.

The eleventh characteristic of *agape* is that it always protects. The Greek word for *protects* is *stego* and it means "to cover over in silence."[8] In 1 Corinthians 13:7, it simply means that love does not expose the faults of others. When we exercise *agape* toward an individual, no matter how well we know her, we would never expose her faults to others. It is the word picture of covering an individual with such a cloak of love that the fault cannot be seen. Isn't that beautiful?

First Peter 4:8 perfectly expresses *agape* in terms of helping us choose what to ignore or tolerate with grace. What does *agape* do?

love in earnest

If I am quick to notice fault and it is easy for me to expose that fault, then I am not exercising *agape*.

The twelfth characteristic of *agape* is that it always trusts. The Greek word for *trust* is *pisteuo*, which basically involves having faith in someone.[9] ←

My sin nature on its own leans quickly toward skepticism, especially when someone has disappointed me. One of the most painful things I've done was to aid in restoring a fallen sister. Some months later she said to me: "God has completely removed that temptation from me. Do you believe me?" My immediate response was, "Absolutely." I have never again considered that the situation could repeat itself because I chose to believe her. I know now that God was exercising a characteristic of *agape* through me.

Agape's thirteenth characteristic is that it always hopes. The Greek word for *hopes* is *elpizo*, which means "to expect with desire."[10] In the context of *agape*, to ← hope in someone means to trust them...to expect the best from them. Take a look at 2 Corinthians 8:22-24. Paul sent Titus to the church of Corinth with great anticipation that he would see and understand why Paul loved them as he did. Paul expected the best from them and, therefore, probably received it.

The fourteenth characteristic of *agape* in 1 Corinthians 13 is that it always perseveres. The Greek word for *perseveres* is *hupomeno* which means "to remain under."[11] In common terminology, *agape* "hangs in there." Do you enjoy long-term relationships? How easily are you discouraged in a relationship? Spend some time today thinking about that.

Finally, *agape* never fails. The Greek word for *fails* is *ekpipto*, and it means "to ← be without effect, to be in vain."[12] Perhaps, Beloved, this characteristic, more than any other, encourages us toward *agape* love. Concentrate on this truth: *agape* is never without effect. *Agape* is never in vain!

If we allow God to exercise *agape* through us, no matter how it appears, no matter what happens—whether the work of *agape* is in us as the giver, in others

How does God want you to respond to what He showed you today?

_____

_____

_____

_____

_____

_____

_____

I've arrived at a conclusion,
maybe one of life's rare finds
that there's not a lot worth salvaging
within this heart of mine.

It's ever ready to destruct
and lie above all things…
It tends to laugh when it should cry
and mourn when it should sing.

I've wasted countless hours begging,
"Fix this heart, Lord, please!"
while it stomps its feet, demands its way
and floods with sin's disease.

At last, you're able to get through
and lay it on the line:
"You must give up that heart of yours
and trade it in for mine."

So I cry out with the psalmist,
create within me, Lord
A new heart crystal clear
that only Calvary could afford.

A heart which pounds the rhythm
of heaven's metronome
and issues forth a boundless love
and beats for You alone.

I want to love that which You love,
despising what you hate
and see myself as least of these
oh Lord, retaliate

The efforts of the evil one
who seeks to make my plea
that of his own, "I'll make no move
til I've considered me."

Peel away my fingers,
finally make me understand
the power to love and please You
can't be found within a man.

So, my Lord, I bring this offering;
a stubborn heart of stone
And ask You, in its absence,
please exchange it for Your own.

as the receivers, or both—it will never be in vain. If God is calling upon you to love a very difficult person with *agape*, rejoice that your obedience will never be in vain! *Agape* is always effective!

As we close, let's review some scriptural truths: "Love is patient, love is kind. It does not envy, it does not boast, it is not proud. It is not rude, it is not self-seeking, it is not easily angered, it keeps no record of wrongs. Love does not delight in evil but rejoices with the truth. It always protects, always trusts, always hopes, always perseveres. Love never fails" (1 Cor. 13:4-8).

Are you thinking what I'm thinking? I have "loved" my children as much as I thought a soul could love, yet my love has not always been patient! I cannot say my love is not self-seeking. I want certain things from and for my children. I have not always had faith in the people I love nor have I always "hung in there." In fact, I look at this list of "nevers" and "always" and I realize I have never always done anything! What's my problem?

Go back to the origin of *agape*. John 3:16: "For God so *[agape]* the world that he gave his only begotten son." And Galatians 5:22, "The fruit of the Spirit is *[agape]*." Beloved, we are incapable of *agape*! No matter how hard we try, we cannot exercise this kind of love. We cannot love the unlovely. We cannot love those who do not love us. We cannot love those who have hurt us.

Agape is divine love. Its only origin is the heart of God. *Agape* is the love of God expressed through us to others. Actually it is a response more than a feeling. This is the way it works:

- We confront a situation in which God requires us to *agape* another person.
- We admit to Him that we lack *agape* for this person.
- We consider how God would personally respond to this person according to the Scriptures.
- We act in obedience and respond as He would.

The short- or long-term joy of obedience and the guaranteed effects (see 1 Cor. 13:8) of His choosing cause a chain reaction of feeling far greater than any fleshly love we could muster. He tenders our hearts toward the person. The relationship perseveres. Ultimately we are blessed to have been the vessel through which a holy God expressed His great love to one of His children. Nothing else is like God pouring *agape* through you.

Some years ago God convicted my heart that *agape* would be the key to my being able to forgive someone who had hurt me deeply. He called upon me to begin responding with the externals of *agape* before I ever dreamed of "feeling" them. Eventually He taught me to pray for good things to happen to this person, to express hope in him, to protect him (which, at first, was excruciating for me). Little by little, my heart began to change. And so did the person for whom I was praying. God was faithful; He set me free from one of Satan's most strangling holds on my life. Have you experienced the transforming effects of *agape* in your own life as giver or receiver?

Agape begins as a response and ends with a feeling. It may be the most difficult request God ever makes of us—and the most glorious privilege. But it is absolutely impossible without a heart transplant. I penned the words to the poem in the margin after some frustrations with my own heart. I call it "A Matter of the Heart." God has since performed a miracle in the situation which precipitated the poem. I hope the words speak to your heart.

D a y 5

Agape in Action

Today we conclude our study of the first quality of the fruit of the Spirit. Let's begin by recapping the major truths we have gleaned about *agape*.

- *Agape* is a divine capacity to love. Only God is capable of *agape*.
- *Agape* is more a response than a feeling.
- *Agape* is fueled by the needs rather than the desires of self or others.
- *Agape* is expressed through me when I surrender to the empowerment and temperament of the Holy Spirit.

Now, let's look at one remaining but major element of *agape*.

Compare Romans 5:8, 1 John 3:16, and 1 John 4:9. On the following lines, write the two factors these verses have in common. You will discover the remaining characteristic of *agape*.

Christ died for us.   Sacrifice

His love for us.   demonstration

Did you discover two common factors in the three verses? First, each referred to Christ's sacrifice. *Agape* sacrifices. Did you also note the second factor? "God demonstrates His own love for us." "This is how God showed His love among us." "This is how we know what love is: Jesus Christ laid down his life for us." *Agape* is always demonstrative! Because *agape* is more a response than a feeling, *agape* always shows. *Agape* cannot help but be expressed because that is its essence. As the expression comes, the joy and affection come!

God commands us to love as He loves. Today we will study three segments of Scripture which instruct us concerning the demonstrative nature of *agape*. First, let's look at John 17 and take a glimpse into the very intimate moment between Father and Son. I remain amazed that we are allowed to read the precious words they exchanged just before Christ's trial and crucifixion. Christ has just delivered His farewell discourse to the disciples; then He interceded for them before the Father. If you have a problem believing Christ loves you, the truth of John 17 should open your spiritual eyes.

Carefully read John 17. When you have finished, on the lines below describe specifically how Christ shows His love in each of the following verses:

John 17:6 *Christ made the Father known to the disciples. They belonged to You & you gave them to me.*

Today's Treasure:

"A new command I give you: Love one another. As I have loved you, so you must love one another. By this all men will know that you are my disciples, if you love one another" (John 13:34-35).

John 17:8 _They believe that you sent me (Christ) & He gave the Father's message_

John 17:9 _Christ prays only for the disciples who He was given by the Father._

John 17:12 _Christ kept dis. safe by the Father's name. Only the one was lost - none others._

John 17:19 _They dedicated themselves to You by my example_

John 17:22 _We are one & they were given the same glory to be One._

✳ John 17:23 _I in them. You in me. So world know you sent me & loved me & love them_

John 17:24 _I want them to be w/ me & see the glory given me bef. the world - By You!_

✳ John 17:26 _I made you known to them & shall continue/so love will be in both._

Look! Review your list! One chapter with one basic message: Father, I LOVE THEM! Notice that Jesus displays a very partial love. He is not referring to the world. He is confessing precisely the love He has for His own.

Christ demonstrated His precious, unspeakable love in at least the following nine ways. Because Christ loves us:

1. He reveals to us the Father.
2. He gives us the Father's Word.
3. He prays for us.
4. He protects us.
5. He sanctifies Himself.
6. He gives us His glory.
7. He places us in Him.
8. He makes the Father known to us.
9. He desires for us to be with Him and to see His glory.

His love for us is beyond my deepest comprehension. Without a doubt, we see that the very nature of *agape* demands demonstration.

love! **Now read Today's Treasure. John 13:34-35 tells us we'll be known as Christ's disciples by what? Write it in the margin.**

You've seen and heard this "new command" of Christ countless times, yet this may be the first time you have considered it with an increased understanding of *agape*. Let's look at another Scripture passage which will continue to instruct us in ways to demonstrate *agape*.

Read 1 John 3:11-24 and note everything you learn about the demonstration of *agape*.

love one another, give your life for your brother, action'

How can we know that we belong to the truth and set our hearts at rest in God's presence? (vv. 18-19).

Action'

Look very carefully at verse 20 and fill in the following blanks:

"For God is ___*Greater*___ than our ___*hearts, Conscience*___" (NIV).

Repeat this verse aloud several times! Do you believe God's Word? Then you must believe that God is greater than your heart. Even a heart that says: "I don't love my husband anymore"; "I'll never love my father"; "I'll never be able to love God more than myself, it's hopeless"; or "I am imprisoned by selfishness." All these phrases and more are ways in which your heart "condemns" you and convinces you that you are "only human." God is greater than our hearts!

Now read the third Scripture passage found in 1 John 4:7-21. Where is the only place you can receive *agape*? (v. 7).

God.

Be sure to notice the words which follow: "Everyone who loves has been born of God and knows God." By now you know that this verse is not referring to your "loving" neighbor who supports benevolent causes. This verse does not mean that anyone who is "loving" in the human sense of the word is born again. It is not referring to *eros* or *philos*. This is the word *agape*.

Go back and read the verse aloud, but this time substitute *agape* for the word *love*. Did you get a better sense of the verse's meaning? First John 4:7 says that anyone capable of being a vessel of God's divine love toward another must belong to Him, because *agape* is possible only through God!

Read 1 John 4:13 and 1 John 3:24. How do we know that we live in God and He lives in us?

He has given us the Spirit.

◌ **Recalling what you have learned, what is the relationship between the Holy Spirit and** *agape*?

_____

Read Romans 5:5. How has God equipped our hearts to possess *agape*?

Thru the Holy Spirit

Write the command found in 1 John 4:21.

Whoever loves God must love his brother also.

Let's conclude our study of *agape* by reading one last Bible passage: Matthew 22:36-40. So crucial is *agape* to God, that it is His foremost command to His children. First God says, *"Agape* ME." Do you realize that even the capacity to love God is completely divine and supernatural? Upon your constant request and deepest heart's desire, God will supply you with a divine, ever-growing love for Himself. Oswald Chambers said it this way: "Love is the sovereign preference of my person for another person, and when the Holy Spirit is in you, that other person is Jesus. The only lover of the Lord Jesus Christ is the Holy Ghost."[13]

Because He first loved us, we are free to love Him and to love others with the same kind of *agape* Calvary made possible. Oh, Beloved, we have been so deceived. True love is not at all blind. When we are vessels of *agape,* our spiritual eyes will be open like never before, because only true love can really see… right into the heart of God.

> And now these three remain: faith, hope and love. But the greatest of these is love (1 Cor. 13:13).

I would like to end with one last activity. Keeping in mind that *agape* is always demonstrated, "But God demonstrates His own love," how do you demonstrate your own love? A short time ago, I had a serious health problem to arise suddenly, and I was so touched to see the different ways my close friends "demonstrated" their love to me. One washed clothes, cleaned house, and carried me to the rest room. Another delivered food and made arrangements for my absence at a speaking engagement. Still another demonstrated her love to me by caring for my children. We may have various ways of expressing *agape,* but it always shows! Love never fails to be demonstrative.

In the space below, write the names of 10 people you "love" most on this earth:

_____

_____

_____

Do they know without a doubt that you love them? ❑ Yes ❑ No

↪ Remember, God both told us He loved us and showed us He loved us. How do they know you love them? In other words, in what ways are you demonstrating *agape*?

_____

_____

Is there someone God is calling upon you to *agape* that you are resisting? (Besides me, after all this homework!) ❑ Yes ❑ No

Is your heart the problem? ❑ Yes ❑ No

What does 1 John 3:20 (NIV) say? " God **_____ is greater than our** hearts conscience **."**

Are you convinced or scared it will never work? ❑ Yes ❑ No

What does 1 Corinthians 13:8 say? " Love **_____ never** fails **."**

"Love never faileth!" What a wonderful phrase that is! but what a still more wonderful thing the reality of that love: greater than prophecy—that vast forth-telling of the mind and purpose of God; greater than the practical faith that can remove mountains; greater than philanthropic self-sacrifice; greater than the extraordinary gifts of emotions and ecstasies and all eloquence; and it is this love that is shed abroad in our hearts by the Holy Ghost which is given unto us.[14]

Therefore, Dear Sister, "Follow the way of love" (1 Cor. 14:1).

[1]James Strong, from the *Hebrew and Chaldee Dictionary* of *The Exhaustive Concordance of the Bible* (Nashville: Holman Bible Publishers, n.d.), 109.
[2]Spiros Zodhiates et al., eds., *The Complete Word Study Dictionary: New Testament* (Chattanooga, TN: AMG Publishers, 1992), 1445.
[3]Ibid., 939.
[4]Ibid., 1481.
[5]Ibid., 699.
[6]Ibid., 1153.
[7]Ibid., 284.
[8]Ibid., 1310.
[9]Ibid., 1160.
[10]Ibid., 570.
[11]Ibid., 1424.
[12]Ibid., 551-552.
[13]This material is taken from *The Love of God* by Oswald Chambers. Copyright 1988 by the Oswald Chambers Publications Assoc. Ltd., and is used by permission of Discovery House Publishers, Box 3566, Grand Rapids MI 49501. All rights reserved.
[14]*The Place of Help* by Oswald Chambers. Copyright © 1989 by the Oswald Chambers Publications Assn. Ltd., and is used by permission of Discovery House Publishers, Box 3566, Grand Rapids MI 49501. All rights reserved.

How does God want you to respond to what He showed you today?

_____

_____

_____

_____

_____

_____

Week 4

The Joy of the Lord Is Our Strength

What a needed commodity! What a source of attractiveness to a broken and needy world! Joy! Joy is the second characteristic of the fruit of the Spirit. That makes perfect sense. Only love better describes the lifestyle of Christ. Only love more aptly meets the needs of our torrid age. Love melts the heart of stone. Joy touches the deepest part of that heart. We need joy, and our world needs believers who evidence the fruit of joy.

This week we will examine the wonderful fruit of joy. We will find in Scripture five key sources of joy. Some of them you will readily recognize. Some will be a surprise. Come along as we study the second characteristic of the fruit of God's Spirit. "The fruit of the Spirit is…joy."

Principal Questions

Day 1: By what "record" or "reservation" will we enter the kingdom of heaven?

Day 2: How did Paul consider everything else to compare to the "surpassing greatness of knowing Christ Jesus"?

Day 3: What two matters did Paul see as parts of "knowing Christ"?

Day 4: Why has Christ told us to "remain" in Him?

Day 5: What did Paul consider to be his "joy" and "crown"?

Day 1
Joy's Bedrock

The fruit of the Spirit is love, joy, peace, patience, kindness, goodness, faithfulness, gentleness and self-control. Against such things there is no law" (Gal. 5:22-23). Today we begin to study the second character quality of the fruit of the Spirit—JOY. The Greek word for *joy* is *chara*, pronounced with the accent on the second syllable. *Chara* is the most common word translated joy in the English New Testament. It means "joy, rejoicing, gladness—enjoyment, bliss."[1] In many ways, *chara* means "to celebrate!"

We will attempt to discover the origin of optimum joy. Scripture highlights five reasons for *chara*. This week we will consider each of the five. Today we give attention to our primary reason. For the remainder of the week, we will revel in the other four as icing on the cake! Through His words to the 72 as they returned from their mission, Christ revealed the first and foremost reason for joy.

Read Luke 10:17-20. Why were the 72 joyful?

_____

_____

According to Jesus, what was their greatest reason for rejoicing?

_____

_____

Jesus made clear the primary reason for joy among His disciples. He said, "Rejoice that your names are written in heaven."

Take a look at Psalm 51:12. What was the source of David's joy?

_____

_____

Did you notice whose joy David was concerned about? He recognized the joy was of "Thy" salvation.

Read Revelation 7:10. To whom does salvation belong?

_____

_____

Now pray. Ask God to show you the significance of the truth that salvation belongs to Him. After you have prayed, answer this question: Why do you think salvation is described as God's rather than yours?

_____

_____

_____

Today's Treasure:

"Send forth your light and your truth, let them guide me; let them bring me to your holy mountain, to the place where you dwell. Then will I go to the altar of God, to God, my joy and my delight" (Ps. 43:3-4).

You may have recognized several aspects of God's ownership of salvation. Did you note that salvation is God's to give? It is a gift of GRACE that we have the privilege to accept. The Greek word for *grace* is *charis*, which means "unmerited favor."[2]

Do you remember the Greek word for *joy*? Write it in this space.

_____

Do you see a very close relationship between *charis* and *chara*? That's because joy is an absolute assumption in grace. Joy is literally written into grace! God is telling us, "If you only understood what grace means and what you have received by way of it, you would never cease to rejoice!" Whether we ever have one external thing over which to rejoice, it is enough that we are born again! I believe the main reason we lack an awareness of joy in our salvation is because we are unaware or seldom reminded to what and from what we have been saved. In this way, we have neglected "so great a salvation" (Heb. 2:3, NKJV). We need to consistently focus on our great salvation so that our joy might be full.

You may have noted another facet of "God's salvation." Recognizing that salvation belongs to Christ helps to get us out of ourselves. Simply stated, "it's not about us." Sometimes we get so wrapped up in ourselves that we become the center of our own universe. Salvation is His. It's about Him. Following Christ breaks the stranglehold of self in our lives as He becomes the center of our universe. We decrease; He increases (see John 3:30). Joy results.

You will remember that Christ said, "Do not rejoice that the spirits submit to you, but rejoice that your names are written in heaven" (Luke 10:20). Christ linked our joy to reservations made in our names somewhere in heaven. Let's see what we can learn about the place where our names are recorded.

Read Hebrews 12:18-24 and answer the following questions:
What is the city of the living God called? (v. 22).

_____

Describe the assembly. (v. 22).

_____

Whose names are written in heaven? (v. 23).

_____

◆ Notice all the things, persons, and places believers "have come to" in the New Jerusalem. From all the items identified, which two mean the most to you personally and why?

_____

_____

Turn to Revelation 13:8. What is the record of names called?

_____

To whom does the record belong? _____

Whose names are not written in the "book of life"? _____

Now read Revelation 17:8. How long have names been written in the "book of life"?

_____

In Revelation 3:5, what does Christ say about those who "overcome"?

_____

Consider TO WHAT we have been saved as a result of the reservation Christ made for us in the "book of life."

Read Revelation 21:22-27. In your own words, describe the New Jerusalem.

_____

_____

_____

Read Revelation 20:11-15. FROM WHAT have we been saved?
(Check one or more.)
❑ being cast into the lake of fire
❑ the second death
❑ judgment according to our works

We who are saved by grace through faith have been saved from all three of the above penalties. While our works are important—we were "created in Christ Jesus to do good works" (Eph 2:10)—we will not be judged by our works. Rather, we are saved by Christ's work.

Now read 2 Peter 3:3-7, with emphasis on verse 7. Notice the phrase, "being kept for the day of judgment and destruction of ungodly men." The Greek word for *destruction* is *apoleia* which means "losing, loss, the state after death wherein exclusion from salvation is a realized fact."[3] That definition sends chills up my spine. A moment will come, at the ushering in of eternity, when every lost man and woman will be confronted with the staggering loss of his or her salvation. Remember, Philippians 2:10 says that "every knee should bow, in heaven and on earth and under the earth and every tongue confess that Jesus Christ is Lord to the glory of God the Father." The lost will suffer a horrible threefold realization: they will realize that He is LORD, that they are LOST, and that it's too LATE. Another definition of the word *apoleia* is just one sobering word: waste.[4] Their lives will have been a total waste. A life without Christ is a wasted life. All the energy, all the pain—for absolutely nothing. Praise God, with reverence, that your name is written in the "book of life."

Now let's attempt to adjust our perspective so that our joy might be full in our salvation. Read Psalm 39:4-7. How long will we be here on this earth?

_____

Now answer the following review questions.

How long will we be in heaven? _____

☙ According to today's study, by what "record" or "reservation" will we enter the kingdom of heaven?

_____

Who put our names in the book? _____

When? _____

Reread Luke 10:20. You may have many reasons, but what is the only reason you need to rejoice?

_____

First and foremost, our salvation, which assures our reservation, is reason to rejoice!

Take one last look at Today's Treasure. What does the psalmist call his God?

_____

God is our JOY. What do you enjoy most about God?

_____

_____

Lord Jesus, teach us to enjoy YOU and revel in Your great salvation even when difficulty surrounds us. Make our lives a celebration of your grace!

How does God want you to respond to what He showed you today?

_____

_____

_____

_____

_____

_____

_____

Day 2

Surprised by Joy

On day 1, we studied the origin of our joy: our salvation—the foremost catalyst of our joy! Our names have been written in the Lamb's book of life! Hallelujah! Today we turn our attention to a second catalyst of joy. As I prepared this study, I printed out every New Testament Scripture containing the word *joy* and read them repeatedly. After a while, the Holy Spirit opened my eyes to a wonderful common denominator in the many verses containing the word *joy*.

Let me give you a detective assignment. The following list of Scriptures each contain a common denominator. Try to identify what these very different situations have in common. Write your notes in the margin below Today's Treasure. You may need to read some of the verses before and after to get an idea of the context.

Matthew 13:44: "'The kingdom of heaven is like treasure hidden in a field. When a man found it, he hid it again, and then in his joy went and sold all he had and bought that field.'"

Matthew 28:8: "So the women hurried away from the tomb, afraid yet filled with joy, and ran to tell his disciples."

Luke 1:44: "As soon as the sound of your greeting reached my ears, the baby in my womb leaped for joy."

Luke 2:10: "But the angel said to them, 'Do not be afraid. I bring you good news of great joy that will be for all the people.'"

Luke 10:21: "At that time Jesus, full of joy through the Holy Spirit, said, 'I praise you, Father, Lord of heaven and earth, because you have hidden these things from the wise and learned, and revealed them to little children. Yes, Father, for this was your good pleasure.'"

Luke 24:52: "Then they worshiped him and returned to Jerusalem with great joy."

Did you discover the common element in each Scripture? Each has to do with things hidden. More precisely, each describes joy resulting from discovery. In Matthew 13:44, a man discovered a hidden treasure. In Matthew 28:8, the women discovered an empty tomb. In Luke 1:44, from the womb of his mother, John the Baptist discovered the Messiah. In Luke 2:10, the shepherds discovered the good news! In Luke 10:21, the children discovered truths. In Luke 24:52, the disciples discovered and worshiped the resurrected Lord.

Today's Treasure:

"At that time Jesus, full of joy through the Holy Spirit, said, 'I praise you, Father, Lord of heaven and earth, because you have hidden these things from the wise and learned, and revealed them to little children. Yes, Father, for this was your good pleasure'" (Luke 10:21).

The second catalyst of *chara* is discovery: the joy of discovery! Joy comes not from a random discovery. Each one of these references describes the discovery of one perfect treasure–Christ Jesus, Himself. Look back at your list. The locations and circumstances are diverse, but there are two constants: the discovery of Christ and the joy of the discoverer. So, how can we further define *chara*? *Chara* is the supernatural result which flows from the glorious discovery of our Lord and Savior in every circumstance where we wish to find Him.

Observe this precept at work. Look at that dreaded verse, James 1:2. We will consider James 1:3-4 in a future unit.

> **Let's look at a few places in God's Word where believers considered it "pure joy" to face trials. First read Acts 16:16-40, then answer the following questions.**

1. Why were Paul and Silas arrested? _____

_____

2. What had Silas done? _____

3. What was the punishment Paul and Silas received because Paul commanded the "spirit" (demon) to leave the slave girl?

_____

4. How did Paul and Silas respond to their bonds? _____

_____

5. Who heard the testimony of their prayers and singing?

_____

6. How did God respond to their praises? _____

_____

7. How was the life of the jailer spared? _____

_____

8. What was the end result of Paul and Silas's imprisonment?

_____

This occurrence was not unusual for the apostle Paul. From the damp, cold walls of another prison, Paul exhorted all believers to: "Rejoice in the Lord always. I will say it again: Rejoice!" (Phil.4:4). Through his trials Paul learned something I believe God desires for all believers to learn: the presence, purpose, and power of God is best discovered through difficulty. How encouraging to recognize that Paul did not discover the strength to leave his circumstances; he discovered the strength to stay! Because he did, places for a jailer and his entire family were reserved in the Lamb's book of life!

> ✎ **How did Paul consider everything else to compare to the "surpassing greatness of knowing Christ Jesus"? (Phil. 3:8).**

_____

Why was the loss of anything and everything worth it to Paul? Because in Christ, Paul discovered that "to know Him" was greater than any loss he would suffer. Paul's joy in tribulation was motivated by his knowledge that the "best" of God's presence, purpose, and power was undoubtedly discovered in the worst of circumstances. Let's take a last look at someone in Scripture who met earthly circumstances with heavenly responses.

Read Acts 7:54-60. What was Stephen's "condition"? (v. 55).

_____

We have already learned from our study that the fruit of the Spirit is the supernatural outcome of being filled with the Spirit. Therefore, all the qualities of the fruit were expressed in Stephen. Considering only what we have learned thus far, can you even imagine him as he stood before his accusers demonstrating a heart overflowing with *agape* and a face illuminated with *chara*? What was the source of his joy?

"Look," he said, "I see heaven open and the Son of Man standing at the right hand of God" (Acts 7:56). Stephen saw Christ, not sitting but standing on behalf of the first of many who would willingly lay down their lives for the cause of Christ. Surely, that day Stephen discovered his glorious Lord in ways he never dreamed, and the result was a joy which transcended the grave! His joy provided strength not only to live for Christ—but also to die for Christ.

Paul and Stephen set examples of joy in suffering that have since been followed by thousands throughout the centuries. To this day, Christian martyrs imitate Paul and Stephen's tenacity, as well as their joy. *Foxe's Book of Martyrs* by John Foxe records numerous testimonies of joy in the face of impending death. Just one example is a man named Ignatius who succeeded Peter as the bishop of Antioch. Upon receiving the order of his death, he wrote:

> Now I begin to be a disciple. I care for nothing, of visible or invisible things, so that I may but win Christ. Let fire and the cross, let the companies of wild beasts [which indeed took his life], let breaking of bones and tearing of limbs, let the grinding of the whole body, and all the malice of the devil, come upon me; be it so, only may I win Christ Jesus![5]

Stephen Curtis Chapman sings a song with this lyric: "What kind of joy is this: to count it a blessing to suffer?" Could it be the wonderful, unspeakable joy of discovery? Are you willing to look for Him in the midst of your struggles?

How does God want you to respond to what He showed you today?

_____

_____

_____

_____

_____

_____

☙ **Today's Treasure:**

"Though you have made me see troubles, many and bitter, you will restore my life again....My lips will shout for joy when I sing praise to you" (Ps. 71:20,23).

☙ Have you ever found Him in the midst of your struggles? If so, when and what was your marvelous discovery?

_____

_____

If you struggled with the previous question, spend some time in meditation with God. Ask Him to remind you of times when joy resulted from discovering His presence, His purpose, and His power in an entirely new way.

Could it be that if our focus is on Christ, we'll see Him transfigured before us rather than our circumstances? Hallelujah! Look for Him. He's there. Right in the middle of your circumstances—just waiting to be discovered.

Conclude by writing Jeremiah 29:13 in the space below:

_____

_____

Day 3
Restoration Joy

On days 1 and 2, we studied the first two of five major catalysts for joy. First, our reservation in heaven is reason enough to rejoice. Second, we rejoice in the pleasure of discovery as we uncover the presence, purpose, and power of Christ through all our tribulations. Today we are going to research a third catalyst of true joy, best evidenced in the Old Testament where the Hebrew words for *joy* are practically identical in definition to the Greek word *chara*. Joy is not only a response to our salvation and our ongoing discovery of the One who saved us, but also a response to restoration. Let's look at three different circumstances through which God seeks to bring restoration.

Read Psalm 71:1-24 and answer the following questions.
1. What kind of relationship did the psalmist have with God and why?

_____

_____

2. Identify the psalmist's fears. (See vv. 1,4,9-12.)

_____

3. Did you notice bitterness in the psalmist's words? ❏ Yes ❏ No

4. From what is the psalmist seeking restoration? (v. 20).

_____

5. What will be the psalmist's response to restoration? (vv. 22-24).

_____

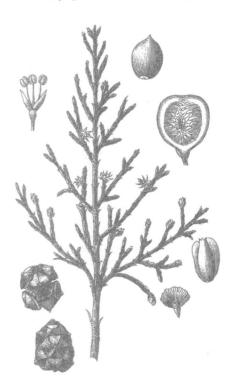

One reason God allows us to experience troubles is because He desires to reveal His joy to us through restoration. Reread those difficult words: "Though you have made me see troubles many and bitter." A consistent theme running throughout God's Word is the believer's trial resulting from God's perfect will. I am not referring to God's permissive will when we choose to go astray. I am referring to His perfect choice for us to know hardship for kingdom gain…times when He ordains difficulty in our lives.

I've experienced trials that I finally was forced to acknowledge as the absolute will of God. My life has never been easy…and I have finally confronted the fact that it probably never will be. Yet, in the same breath, I can readily proclaim that my life has been good. Part of the still-limited maturity I have gained is the result of realizing that good does not equal easy. Rarely has God removed from my life circumstances or people that force me to my knees. Many of my trials must have been ordained by Him because of the results they rendered.

Read Philippians 3:10. What did Paul say he most desired?

_____

✎ What two matters did Paul see as parts of "knowing Christ"?

The power of His _____

The fellowship of _____

I am convinced we cannot begin to really know Christ until we learn to fellowship with Him in His sufferings. The closest friends I have are those with whom I have "suffered" in one way or another. How much more my precious Redeemer? But spiritual maturity is not the only reason God sometimes chooses hardship for us.

Read 2 Corinthians 1:3-7. Are you making use of your miseries by allowing God to turn them into ministries? In what ways have you comforted others with the comfort you have received from God?

_____

_____

In retrospect, are you able to identify some purpose for your difficulty? You may be wondering, *Then, Beth, must we just accept that our lives will be lived in perpetual pain?*

Read 1 Peter 5:10. How long does Peter say we must suffer?

_____

_____

What does Peter say will follow our suffering? _____

_____

If God has ordained difficulty for you, He has also ordained restoration for you. Count on it!

Reflect for a moment. Can you cite a time when God obviously chose a trial for you? ❑ Yes ❑ No   **If so, briefly describe the circumstance.**

_____

_____

☙ Can you remember a joy which accompanied the realization of restoration? ❑ Yes ❑ No   If so, briefly describe it.

_____

Identify two more reasons for restoration. Read Psalm 85:4-7. What caused the people's need for restoration? (vv. 4-5).

_____

God seeks to restore us from the wide gulf caused by sin. In our study of what it means to "grieve" the Holy Spirit, we talked about true repentance. The most wonderful part of repentance is the blessed restoration which follows!

Review Psalm 85:6. What is the response of the restored sinner?

_____

Are you separated from God because you cannot pry yourself loose from the snare of a certain sin? I know that feeling. It is miserable. You may not be willing to give it up, but would you be willing to let Him come and take it? However painful the loss of letting go, it does not compare with the unspeakable joy of restoration.

Let's look at one last area in which God desires to bring restoration. Read Jeremiah 31:1-20. This is a chapter about restoration which follows discipline. It describes a general separation between God and His own and His deep desire and readiness to close the gap. God does not like separation.

Why does God hate to be separated from His children? (Jer. 31:3).

_____

Look carefully at Jeremiah 31:18. Discipline preceded restoration. Remember, discipline basically means "teaching." As a parent, I "teach" my children in many different ways: sometimes gently; sometimes very firmly—and in ways they don't like! Remember the words of Hebrews 12:6-7,10: "The Lord disciplines those he loves, and he punishes everyone he accepts as a son. Endure hardship as discipline; God is treating you as sons. God disciplines us for our good, that we may share in his holiness."

Look back over Jeremiah 31. Locate at least 10 promises regarding the joy of restoration. List them below.

_____   _____

_____   _____

_____   _____

_____   _____

_____   _____

Beloved, are you in need of restoration? Have you been experiencing hardship which seems to have come by God's hand and not your own? Or, have you been separated from God because of sin? Have you recently known the discipline of the Lord? Oh, my friend, if you are willing, restoration is coming! Get your tambourines ready! He is faithful who promised!

Day 4
Abiding Joy

Joy results when we realize that our names are written in heaven. Joy results when we discover the presence, power, and purpose of God in every circumstance. Joy results from experiencing complete restoration. Today the secret of joy we are sure to discover is found in John 15:1-17.

Please read John 15:1-17 and then answer the following questions.

1. Why does the gardener prune the branches? _____

_____

How does God want you to respond to what He showed you today?

_____

_____

_____

_____

_____

_____

_____

Today's Treasure:

"You have made known to me the path of life; you will fill me with joy in your presence, with eternal pleasures at your right hand" (Ps. 15:11).

2. How is the branch "cleaned"? _____

3. How does a branch bear fruit? _____

4. What is the key to effective prayer? _____

5. How can we "glorify" the Father? _____

6. How should we respond to Christ's love for us? (v. 9).

_____

7. How can we "remain" in His love? (v. 10).

_____

☙ Why has Christ told us to "remain" in Him? (v. 11).

_____

Once again we discover that the fruit of the Spirit originates in the heart and personality of God: "I have told you this so that my joy may be in you and that your joy may be complete" (John 15:11). *Chara,* just like *agape,* belongs to Christ. He is the Possessor and Giver of true joy. Fleeting moments of "happiness" may be experienced through other channels, but inner joy flows only from Christ. Through these verses, Christ teaches us how to tap into His reservoir of joy to our fill: REMAIN in Me! The Greek word for *remain* is *meno,* which means "to abide, dwell, live."[6]

What does it mean to "abide" in Christ? Let's take a look at the kind of determination required for one person to "abide" with another.

Read Ruth 1:11-18 and answer the following questions.

After Orpah kissed Naomi goodbye, how did Ruth respond? (v. 14).

_____

What vows did Ruth make to Naomi? _____

_____

Ruth, who chose to remain with Naomi, had no idea about the future. She simply knew they must be together. As we remain in Christ, our attitudes and determinations must be similar to Ruth's. To remain with Christ means to cling to Him, to refuse to be budged under pressure, to never allow loss to cause us to leave. We must be "crucified" with Him in His death (Gal. 2:20) and be raised to dwell in Him here...until we dwell with Him there.

The key to "abiding" or "remaining" in Christ is in John 15:3,7,10. Read these verses carefully. God's Word propels us to abide in Christ. When His words "abide" in us and we obey His commands with a tenacity similar to Ruth's, we abide in Him. His Word is our cling wrap, adhering us to His presence.

Chara can be lost as well as gained. No doubt many of you studying this lesson have experienced authentic joy in Christ, but, somewhere along the way, you've lost that joy. Is anyone above the risk of losing her joy? How long or how well do you have to know Christ to keep your spirit of joy? The Word of God answers those questions for us.

First Kings 17–19 relates a key story from Elijah's life. God led Elijah to confront the evil king Ahab and to declare a long period of drought. At the end of the drought, Elijah confronted Ahab and defeated the prophets of Baal at Mount Carmel. At the apparent height of his ministry, Elijah was in fear of Jezebel, ran away into the wilderness, and fell into a suicidal depression. However, God restored and recommissioned Elijah for his last years of ministry.

Read the following Scriptures and answer the questions.

1. **In 1 Kings 17:1-6, how did God relate to Elijah? (Check one or more.)**
   ❑ He allowed Elijah to live in peace and comfort.
   ❑ He provided Elijah's physical needs.
   ❑ He protected Elijah from harm.
   ❑ He gave Elijah a multitude of followers.

2. **In 1 Kings 17:7-16, Elijah left Israel and stayed in Zarephath. How did God demonstrate His presence with Elijah?**

   _____

3. **First Kings 17:17-24 relates a miracle God performed through Elijah. How would you have felt if you had been the mother?**

   _____

4. **Elijah confronted the 450 prophets of Baal in the famous "God contest" on Mount Carmel. What part of the story in 1 Kings 18:25-45 intrigues you most? (Check one.)**
   ❑ Elijah's courage
   ❑ the display by the prophets of Baal
   ❑ the simplicity of Elijah's prayer
   ❑ Elijah's persistent prayer for rain
   ❑ other _____

5. **Describe Elijah's condition in 1 Kings 19:3-5.**

   _____

6. **When God asked Elijah why he was in a cave, how did Elijah respond? (1 Kings 19:9-10).**

   _____

7. **How did God ultimately reveal Himself to Elijah? (1 Kings 19:11-13).**
   ❏ **a great and powerful wind**　　❏ **an earthquake**
   ❏ **a fire**　　❏ **a gentle whisper**

8. **Notice a very important part of God's prescription for Elijah's depression in 1 Kings 19:19-21. What did He give Elijah?**

_____

Few people have ever experienced God in the same way Elijah did, yet we see him suddenly filled with fear and depression. He was not living in sin, yet he had lost his joy. All of us are at risk of losing our joy, and there are plenty of joy quenchers available to accommodate us! Based on what we've learned from Elijah's life, let's consider circumstances which may place us in the high-risk category for losing our joy.

WE MAY LOSE OUR JOY...

1. When our outpour exceeds our intake.
We don't see evidence that Elijah was continually refueling. He was pouring out more than he was pouring in. Are you serving more than you're seeking?

2. When our talk exceeds our walk.
Certainly things did not start out this way for Elijah, but in order for him to sink to the low described in 1 Kings 19, somewhere along the way, his mouth and his heart most likely parted company. These first two points are closely related. We rarely know the exact moment that our output begins to exceed our intake, but a sure sign of lack of fuel is a talk that exceeds our walk.

3. When we become "wonders junkies."
Elijah had grown accustomed to seeing God in the midst of magnificence. He had seen God in such miraculous circumstances that he missed Him as the joy in the midst of the mundane. He looked for God in the wind, the earthquake, and the fire, but he did not find Him there. I am convinced the most intimate times we ever will spend with God will be listening to His gentle whispers. It is there that we will find true *chara*.

Please carefully and tenderly consider this point with me: rarely are you more at risk for losing your joy than when you have just experienced a spiritual "high." When God miraculously spares a life...when He supernaturally intervenes to meet your needs...when you've just experienced a revival or a retreat...anytime you've just been on Mount Carmel standing firm against the enemy, you're sitting in a dangerous place—ripe for a fall. Jesus' baptism was followed by temptation. Pray to enjoy those marvelous times, but never more than you enjoy His sweet whisper when you are all alone.

4. When we are exhausted.
What on earth would have caused Elijah to run *from* his circumstances rather than *to* his God? Surely God, Who had already worked so many miracles in Elijah's life, could have handled Jezebel! But Elijah was exhausted. He had

neglected to rest or eat. Notice God's tender care for Elijah. God created the body. He knows we cannot function well when it is neglected. Are you neglecting your rest? What about eating? In our culture, we rarely neglect to eat; however, we neglect to eat for the body's benefit. Just a little food for thought.

5. When we feel all alone.

Elijah felt as if he were the only one standing up for God, yet, by comparison, he had it easy! All the other prophets of God were holed up in caves! As you're growing in Christ, beware of feelings that tempt you to believe you are all alone and that no one else wants to serve or love God as you do. Just because someone does not share our "cause" or our personal "passions" does not set us apart. When we view ourselves as the only spiritual persons we know, we're setting ourselves up for a fall.

> ✎ Review the above list of joy cheaters. Which one have you most recently experienced?

_____

Have you allowed God to restore your joy? ❏ **Yes** ❏ **No**

When we allow God to train us so that receiving and obeying His Word becomes our "high," we will know the fullest expressions of His joy.

Look back at Today's Treasure. Where can we always find true joy and pleasure?

_____

If you've lost your joy, it's right where you left it–in His presence. Remember, He is our joy. If you've never lost it, praise Him and continue to depend on Him.

Day 5

My Joy and My Crown

Today we conclude our study of joy, the second quality of the fruit of the Spirit. After four days I still think much remains unsaid! Oh, how I pray you will consider this study as a challenge to dig deeper into the magnificent outpouring of God's Spirit! We are only scratching the surface. Before we continue with the fifth catalyst of joy, or *chara*, let's recap the first four.

On the following page, list from memory the first four catalysts of joy; take a peek at our previous studies if necessary.

How does God want you to respond to what He showed you today?

_____

_____

_____

_____

_____

_____

❧ Today's Treasure:

"Your love has given me great joy and encouragement, because you, brother, have refreshed the hearts of the saints" (Philem. 7).

Day 1: _____

Day 2: _____

Day 3: _____

Day 4: _____

✍ Which of the catalysts of joy has been most important to you in your present journey and why?

_____

_____

I never would have guessed that today's subject would be one of the five major catalysts of joy, but through my study, I am certain it is. After researching all the New Testament Scriptures which contained *chara*, I not only noticed the constant repetition of "discovery," but also I noted another common denominator in many of the passages.

Read each of the following Scriptures and answer the accompanying questions. Note those facts you discover about joy.

1. Why did Paul wish to be rescued from the unbelievers in Judea? (Rom. 15:30-32).

_____

2. Why was Paul full of joy? (Rom. 16:19). _____

_____

3. What did Paul desire to do when he arrived in Corinth? (2 Cor. 2:3).

_____

4. What was the basis of Paul's encouragement and confidence? (2 Cor. 7:4).

_____

5. What news increased Paul's joy? (2 Cor. 7:7). _____

_____

6. Why did Paul desire to remain with the Philippian believers? (Phil. 1:25-26).

_____

✎ **What did Paul call his "joy" and "crown"? (Phil. 4:1).**

_____

From the previous group of Scriptures, what common catalyst for joy did you detect?

_____

Draw lines connecting the following Scriptures to corresponding sources of Paul's joy.

1 Thessalonians 1:6	You have refreshed the hearts of the saints.
1 Thessalonians 2:19-20	You are our glory and joy.
1 Thessalonians 3:9	I long to see you so I may be filled with joy.
2 Timothy 1:4	You welcomed the message.
Philemon 7	We have joy in the presence of our God because of you.

I am so thankful that God has given me each of you. WE are catalysts of joy for one another! After we were born again, He did not leave us on earth to be loners. He wants us to bring joy to one another!

Words cannot express the joy I experience as I share this Bible study with you. As I write, I try to picture your faces before me. I imagine the faces of the many women I have encountered through years of speaking. Every word God gives me is directed to you, members of the body of Christ. My gifts are not for me; they are for you. Your gifts are not for you; they are for the body of Christ. I am unable to explain my feelings as I teach a Scripture and observe the light of understanding dawn on faces. You—each and every one of you—are a joy to me; you challenge me to dig deeper and deeper into God's Word.

My Sunday School class has been immeasurable joy to me. They pray for me, encourage me, and keep coming back 52 weeks a year in spite of this Arkansas twang. They are my joy and my crown! My pastor is another joy to me. While sitting in a worship service at my church, I am at times overwhelmed as I listen to my pastor. I thank God for His faithfulness. I also love the familiar faces of church members I pass in the halls every Sunday. My heart overflows with joy when I stoop to my knees to hug my adult friend, Selma, who is a little person at First Baptist Church. Nothing gives me greater joy than to worship with friends.

I have a dear friend who has made me feel so secure with her that together we sing praise songs from the tops of our lungs…just the two of us! JOY—the indescribable joy of the body of Christ! Even now, as I type these words, tears of joy stream down my cheeks.

Beloved, do you understand? He ordained it just this way! He does not mean for us to be autonomous! He gave us one another to enjoy!

Do you enjoy the body of Christ? ❑ Yes ❑ No

If so, what do you enjoy most?

_____

_____

If you cannot honestly say you enjoy fellow believers, what do you think is causing you to lack joy in your fellow believers?

_____

_____

If you don't enjoy the body of Christ and don't know why, ask God to reveal the reason. Then respond. My friend, this world is much too painful to bear without experiencing the joy of fellow believers!

Write Hebrews 10:24-25 in this space:

_____

_____

_____

Are you presently an involved member of a fellowship of believers? (Not just on the roll, but involved?) ❑ **Yes** ❑ **No**
Do you actually "fellowship" with them? ❑ **Yes** ❑ **No**

When was the last time you enjoyed the body of Christ? It may be that you are so busy serving that you are missing the cohesiveness of being with other adults. You can serve faithfully in the preschool department and still remain connected to the adult body of Christ. Ask God to direct you. He does not mean for you to be disconnected.

Right now, I want you to stop and think about the following question: in what ways do you think it would be dangerous, or at the very least disadvantageous, to be disconnected from other Christian adults?

Perhaps you are one who enjoys all the fellowship you can find! Look around you. Someone terribly lonely is sure to be close by. Observe carefully! They wear many masks. Some are very quiet and some are irritatingly vocal—but they share one serious problem: they feel like outsiders in the body of Christ. Ask God to make you sensitive to those who are lonely in the body of Christ. Ask Him to give you a supernatural love for them. Step out in faith and draw them in. Dear friend, how boring and mediocre our lives would be if we were surrounded only by the stereotypical persons with whom we feel comfortable. Branch out! Make friends and relationships of different colors, different economic persuasions, different backgrounds, even different denominations! Go ahead! Live a little! The body of Christ comes in all shapes and sizes. Take some risks. They will become your joy!

Conclude this study time by reading Psalm 51:12-13. How does our joy impact others?

_____

_____

How does God want you to respond to what He showed you today?

_____

_____

_____

_____

_____

_____

_____

Joy not only comes from the body of Christ, but also adds joy to the body of Christ! Our joy makes us soul-winners! Beloved, the world is frantically searching for true *chara*. If all they want is "happiness," which is an affirmative response to externals, then why can't they ever seem to achieve satisfaction? People are searching for a joy which comes from the inside. And if you've got it, you can be sure people will be asking you how they can get it! When someone asks the reason for the hope they observe in you, be ready with an answer (see 1 Pet. 3:15). Joy keepers are soul-winners!

One last assignment for this week. Enjoy the body of Christ! Find a specific way to do it and be creative—then praise God for the privilege of fellowship!

Let's recap what we've learned this week:
- Joy is the result of realizing that our names are written in heaven.
- Joy is the result of discovering the person, power, and plan of God in our multitude of circumstances.
- Joy is the result of restoration.
- Joy is the result of "remaining" in Christ.
- Joy is the result of relating God's way to God's people.

Has this week's study opened your eyes to joys you didn't even know you possessed? I hope so! I pray that people literally will see a difference in us because of all we've learned. May we be people who not only know Christ—but also enjoy Christ.

Go ahead. Count it all joy, Beloved!

[1]Spiros Zodhiates et al., eds., *The Complete Word Study Dictionary: New Testament* (Chattanooga, TN: AMG Publishers, 1992), 1467-1468.
[2]Ibid., 1469.
[3]Ibid., 246.
[4]Ibid.
[5]John Foxe, *Foxe's Book of Martyrs* (Grand Rapids, MI: Baker Book House, 1995), 19.
[6]Zodhiates, *The Complete Word Study Dictionary: New Testament*, 959.

Week 5

Peace Be with You

Proverbs 31:10 says the price of a wife of noble character is "above rubies," but Proverbs 21:9 says "to live on a corner of the roof" is preferable to sharing a house with a "quarrelsome wife." What is the difference? Peace. A popular prayer begins: "God grant me the serenity…." If you could bottle and sell peace, tranquility, or serenity, your wealth would be assured. If, however, you have peace, wealth doesn't really matter. Everybody needs it. Very few seem to have it. Peace. Let's see what the Word says about this precious commodity.

This week we will study the third characteristic of the fruit the Spirit produces in the believer. First, we will see an example of our need for peace. Then we will see how Jesus both provides and epitomizes peace.

Principal Questions

Day 1: How did Job's friends respond to his loss?

Day 2: Now that we have been reconciled to God, how does Christ present us in God's sight?

Day 3: Why did Christ withdraw into a mountain?

Day 4: What is the guaranteed outcome of "believing" God?

Day 5: What was Christ's only request of the soldiers?

Day 1

Life Without Peace

On Tuesday, October 5, 1993, the front page of the *Houston Chronicle* displayed a gigantic picture of a dead soldier. The caption read, "A body identified as an American soldier is dragged Monday through the dusty streets of war-torn Mogadishu, Somalia. The soldier was one of five Americans killed Sunday when Somali militiamen shot down two U.S. helicopters during United Nations military operations." The name was unknown, but the body was someone's son...someone's brother...someone's husband...someone's Daddy. That "someone" may have discovered his or her excruciating loss over a cup of coffee and the morning paper. Where is peace?

I confront a similar emotion each time I enter a place of business which posts the faces of children stolen from their parents. My grief for these parents extends beyond the horror I feel for those whose children have died. Parents who lose children to death at least have the minimal comfort of knowing where their children are, but for parents of stolen children, where is peace?

One of the most ancient sacred books of all times considers the vital relationship between peace and the soul.

Read Job, chapters 1–3 and answer the following:
What kind of man was Job? (1:1-5).

protective of his children

feared the Lord.

What kind of father was Job? Loving

In Job 1:6, who stood before God making petition? (Check one.)
☐ Job   ☑ Satan   ☐ Job's sons

Where had he been? (1:7). walking the Earth

What was Satan doing as he roamed through the earth? (1 Pet 5:8.)

Looking to devour someone

According to Satan, why had Job been faithful to God? (1:9-11).

God protected Job & Job have a piece of the good life.

What calamities occurred in Job 1:17-20? (Check one or more.)
- ☑ the loss of Job's livestock
- ☑ the death of Job's children
- ☑ the death of Job's servants
- ☐ the death of Job's wife

What was Job's response? _Not blaming the Lord_

What was Job's second test? (Job 2). _Sores on his body_

How did Job's wife react? (2:9). _curse God_ _But, he did not_

➥ How did Job's friends respond to his loss? (2:11-13). _did not recognize him / weeped / sat for 7 days & 7 nights not speaking - but w/ Job_

Now, reread Job 3:1-26. Write a one-sentence synopsis of Job's feelings.

no peace / no rest / never ending troubles.

Complete Job 3:25-26 by filling in the blanks.

"What I _fear_ has come upon me;
what I _dread_ has happened to me.
I have no _ease_, no quietness;
I have no rest, but only _turmoil_."

Surely God gave us Job so that in the midst of our own misery, we would always remember a man who experienced worse…and made it. He lost his livelihood, his servants, his children, and his health. After days of sitting in silence, Job spoke "out of the overflow of the heart" (Matt. 12:34) and wished aloud that he was dead. Why was he overtaken by such despair? Because buried deeply in the midst of all Job had lost was his greatest loss of all: his peace. Life is unbearable without peace.

I am no psychologist. I am no specialist. But for years I have believed that people more often take their lives from lack of peace than they do from lack of love or happiness. During my preparation for this week's study, I discovered what appears to be biblical support for such a belief.

Psalm 37:37 says, "There is a future for the man of peace."

Proverbs 14:30 says, "A heart at peace gives life to the body."

In Job 3:26, Job describes what a life is like without peace: "I have no peace, no quietness; I have no rest, but only _turmoil_."

The word *turmoil* means "commotion, restlessness, excitement, rage."[1] The same word is used of "the raging of thunder" in Job 37:2. A lack of peace manifests itself in many ways: a sleepless night filled with tossing and turning, fear that lodges itself like a pine cone in your stomach, a mind and body in perpetual motion, memories that imprison you repeatedly, unending strife, hopelessness, and the general, yet horrible, sense of being out of control.

Peace is often that "something" dissatisfied people ultimately discover they are missing. Sadder still, others never can quite put their fingers on it, living and dying in absolute turmoil. Recently I heard an interviewer ask an Academy Award winning actor who "has it all" what he still wants to achieve. His answer? "Peace of mind."

A man cannot create peace in his own soul. It is not packaged with great intellect, talent, or sensitivity. By six years of age, Wolfgang Amadeus Mozart, the Austrian composer of the 1700s, was an accomplished musician on the clavier, violin, and organ and the composer of five works frequently performed today. By the age of 14, he was commissioned to write his first serious opera, establishing what was already a phenomenal profession.

Rarely has one life held such promise; rarely has one future been more secure. But Mozart was wracked by an inner turmoil that not only stole from him length of days, but also the quality of those same days. He died a pauper at the age of 34, was buried in an unmarked grave, surrounded by only a handful of friends. He never discovered what he continually searched for between the notes on a page: peace. He was only one of millions who are much less famous and have never captured that which makes life bearable.

    ✎ Describe a circumstance of life that challenges your peace.

_____

_____

There is one who delights in the saint's lack of peace. That one can both create and capitalize on havoc. He is the same one who on countless occasions may implore God to give him access to the externals of our lives. If Job is not enough to convince you, take a look at Luke 22:31.

What did Satan desire? _permission to test_

What is Satan's descriptive name in Revelation 12:10? _____

_____ _accuser_ _____

So closely are peace and joy linked (see Rom. 14:17 and 15:13) that Satan will most certainly steal our joy if he can undermine our peace. Striving, churning, tossing, turning, bitter, burning, never learning....

"But the fruit of the Spirit is...peace" (Gal. 5:22).

Pray now, asking God to give you His peace this week in the area of your greatest need. Pray for insight and growth in God's peace.

How does God want you to respond to what He showed you today?

Think of AIDeP.

_____

_____

_____

_____

_____

_____

Today's Treasure:

"But now in Christ Jesus you who once were far away have been brought near through the blood of Christ. For he himself is our peace" (Eph. 2:13-14).

Day 2

The Price of Peace

On day 1, our Scripture reading painted a portrait of life without peace. Most of us can readily testify to at some time having been in the worst of circumstances and experiencing peace or in the best of circumstances and lacking it. Without a doubt, God's peace is paramount to spiritual, mental and emotional wholeness. For the remainder of week 5, we are going to study peace and its position of importance in the heart of God; then we will discover how this same peace is applied to the hearts of believers. The Greek word for *peace* is *eirene*, which simply means "peace of mind, tranquility."[2] Simply said, simply defined, and simply found in very few.

Throughout God's Word we see evidence that God considers names to be of great importance. He names and renames to express the essence of a person's purpose or character. Scripture teaches that God knows even the stars by name (see Ps. 147:4). It stands to reason that God chose the highest and best of names to describe the character of His one and only Son.

Complete the familiar words of the Messiah's birth announcement in Isaiah 9:6 and Jesus' declaration of purpose in Matthew 10:34.

**For to us a child is born,
to us a son is given,
and the government will be on his shoulders.
And he will be called
Wonderful Counselor, Mighty God,
Everlasting Father, _Prince_ _of_ _Peace_.**

Do not suppose that I have come to bring _peace_ to the earth. I did not come to bring _peace_, but a _sword_.

Obviously, we've uncovered a problem. Is Christ the "Prince of Peace" (Isa. 9:6) or isn't He? God uses apparent contradictions in His Word to force us to dig. Read Matthew 10:32-42 to capture the context of verse 34.

Interestingly, when I looked up the Greek word for *sword*, which is *machaira*, the Greek dictionary lists not only the definition of the word, which is "knife," but also the antonym for the word. Guess what it is? Eirene. Peace.[3] When the Word was made flesh to dwell among men, He came to bring the very opposite of peace.

In the passages you've just read, from your understanding who was He desiring to divide with the "sword"?

Satan.

What is His "sword"? (Eph. 6:17). (This is the same Greek word, *machaira*.)

_____ Sword of the Spirit. _____

Throughout Christ's earthly ministry, He accomplished exactly what He said He would. His Word divided the righteous from the unrighteous, the humble from the proud, the faithful from the unfaithful, and the genuine article from the Pharisee. His Word cut to the heart, dividing friends and families, saints and synagogues. Then—out of the blue—the issue of peace toward men emerged in Scripture.

What do each of the following verses—John 14:27, Luke 24:36, John 20:19, John 20:26—have in common?

Fear — Christ in their midst - Peace be w/ You!

Suddenly, we behold the "Prince of Peace" like a beacon in the night. What happened? Let's trace God's "way" of peace and we'll answer that question.

Read Colossians 1:15-23. Why should Christ have supremacy in all things?

1st born of the invisable God.

_____

What two things "pleased" God? (vv. 19-20).

all the fulness to dwell in Him/ Peace thru the blood.

How did God make peace? Crucifiction

☙ **Now that we have been reconciled to God, how does Christ present us in God's sight? (v. 22).**

made You his friend

How does this assurance impact your personal sense of peace?

Completely accepted in His Holy Eyes

Hallelujah! Do you see it now? What happened to usher us from the sword of division to the peace of reconciliation? The CROSS! We could not experience peace with God until the fullness of the Godhead made peace with death!

Read Ephesians 2:11-22. Write the first six words of verse 14 in this space.

For He Himself is our Peace.

93

How does God want you to respond to what He showed you today?

Thank Him.

☙ Ephesians 2:18 shares the good news resulting from the outcome of our peace with God. What does access to the Father mean to you?

Thru Christ we are able to come in one Spirit into the presents of the Father.

ACCESS to God. Can you even imagine? If such privilege has become commonplace to you, or if you simply desire a greater sense of awe to appreciate your access, read Psalm 104 aloud at this time.

I don't know about you, but this psalm makes me feel rather minuscule, and yet we, of all creatures great and small, have access. Why? Because Christ became our peace on Calvary.

I will never forget watching an evening talk show featuring the story of the parents and killer of a young college student. The killer was his best friend. The weapon was high alcohol content inside a speeding automobile. We've heard so many stories about drunk drivers and their victims. What made this particular feature prime-time viewing? The parents had forgiven the young driver…and if that was not enough, they had taken him in as their own.

This young man sat at the table in the chair which was once occupied by their only son. He slept in the son's bed. He worked with the victim's father, teaching seminars on safety. He shared their fortune and supported their causes. He spoke about the one he had slain in ways only someone who knew him intimately could have.

Why did these parents do such a thing? Because it gave them peace. The interviewer was amazed; I was amazed. I kept trying to put myself in the parents' position–but I could not. Then, as the tears streamed down my cheeks, I heard the Spirit of God whisper to my heart and say: "No wonder you cannot relate. You have put yourself in the wrong position. You, my child, are the driver."

God was the parent–who not only forgave–but also invited me to sit at His table in the space my Savior left for me. As a result, I have peace.

❧Today's Treasure:

"Peace I leave with you; my peace I give you. I do not give to you as the world gives. Do not let your hearts be troubled and do not be afraid" (John 14:27).

Day 3

Portraits of Peace

On day 2, we discovered that we cannot possibly experience the peace of God until we have peace with God. Jesus Christ took on the sins of all humanity, and in our own stead, He died on the cross to pay the penalty. His death purchased our peace with God. Throughout the remainder of this week's study, as Scripture reveals, we are going to observe the nature of God's peace and how we receive that peace. Let's begin our study by carefully reading Today's Treasure.

WHOSE peace have we been given? ___God___

How does Philippians 4:7 describe the "peace of God"?

___Surpassing all comprehension___

Now, let's combine the previous two Scriptures and see what we can learn:
• A peace exists that transcends all understanding (see Phil. 4:7).
• The world cannot give this kind of peace (see John 14:27).
• This kind of peace guards the heart and the mind (see Phil. 4:7).
• This peace belongs to Christ and is only His to give (see John 14:27).
• Christ has offered His peace to us (see John 14:27).

Before we can comprehend such peace as applied to us, let's spend two days researching how this peace looked in the earthly life of Christ. All of the following accounts are taken from the life of Christ and probably are very familiar to you. Today we will glean wonderful, fresh truths from them, specifically regarding the "peace of God, which transcends all understanding."

PORTRAITS OF PEACE IN THE LIFE OF CHRIST

Portrait of Peace #1: Luke 2:41-52
How old was Christ when He "stayed behind in Jerusalem"?

___12 yrs.___

At the least, how far away was their home? (v. 44).

___day's journey___

How long did it take Jesus' parents to find Him? (v. 46).

___3 days.___

What was He doing when they found Him? ___

___listening & asking questions.___

What was Jesus' mother's response when they found the boy? (v. 48).

___"Them" Why have you done this to us.?___

Why wasn't Jesus anxious over the separation? (v. 49).

___He was in His Father's House ...___

What feast was being celebrated in Jerusalem at the time?

___Feast of Passover.___

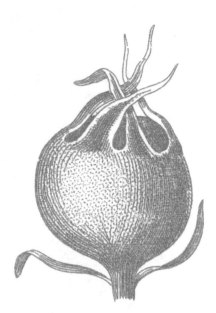

What amazed the people who were listening to Christ? (v. 47).

His understanding & His answers.

The first time Christ seized the opportunity to teach, it "just happened" to be in the temple courts where the altar of sacrifice would have been positioned during the Feast of Passover. Christ utilized a unique and effective teaching method. He used His surroundings as visual aids to teach the precepts of God in a manner His listeners could understand. The parables were perfect examples of His teaching style. Often, He also taught by asking questions, a method first mentioned in Luke 2:46. I do not believe Christ chose this specific festival by accident as the occasion during which He first revealed His "understanding" of God's Word. So important was this opportunity to teach, He remained behind at the risk of frightening His parents.

Why do you think Christ seized this particular time to teach?

(1 Cor. 5:7-8). *For Passover / 12 yrs. - manhood.*

Christ was only 12 years old. He was alone in Jerusalem for four days. (They were one day away, and it took them three days to find Him.) Where had He slept? Where did He eat? Who did He know? In most 12-year-olds, bravery dissipates quickly when the sun goes down—but not in Christ. He was all alone, yet He was found in perfect peace.

Portrait of Peace #2: John 6:1-15

Why did the people follow Jesus? (v. 2).
❏ **They thought He was the Messiah.**
☑ **They saw miraculous signs He had performed.**
❏ **They wanted a king to overthrow the Romans.**

What question did Christ ask Philip and why?

where are we to buy food for so many?

How much food could they find among five thousand people?

5 loaves 2 fish.

What did Christ command the people to do before He fed them?

sit down

Who distributed the fish and loaves? *Jesus.*

After all were fed, how much food was left over?

12 baskets.

 **Why did Christ withdraw into a mountain? (v. 15).**

Precciving they were coming for Him.

Christ took on a tremendous burden of responsibility for those who followed Him. Not coincidentally, only one person had any food in his possession. Also not coincidentally, plenty of baskets were available to gather the leftover food. Christ had perfect peace in provision. He did not fret. He did not form a committee to plan a covered-dish dinner. I see four basic steps which extended the peace of God's provision to the masses:

- He made them aware of their need.
- He took what little they had.
- He placed them in a posture to rest in His provision. He commanded them to "sit down" and fed only those who were "seated" (vv. 10-11).
- He gave them "immeasurably more" than they could "ask or imagine" (Eph. 3:20).

Christ was perfectly at peace with the needs of His followers because He had perfect confidence in His Father's provision.

According to the following Scriptures, what did Christ know about God that gave Him peace in the face of need?

Matthew 6:8 *Your Father knows your needs bef. you ask.*

Matthew 6:25-32 *Father will take care of you — do not concern yourself of your needs.*

Romans 8:32 *A Father who sacrificed His own son for us, will certainly give to us.*

How do you feel about God's promise to "graciously give us all things"? (Phil. 4:19 and Rom. 8:32).

It is a wonderful feeling — when we think about it

We will continue to see "Portraits of Peace" in the life of Christ on day 4. Until then, consider the lessons you've learned today. Do you have peace in times of aloneness, or do you tend to require the security others provide?

Is there a need you've placed before your Provider? Have you "given" Him ALL you have to offer, even if it's only a few loaves and fishes?

Are you "sitting down" in a posture of trust and sitting quietly to receive it? If so, prepare the baskets!

How does God want you to respond to what He showed you today?

Ask for others who do not understand His graciouse giving —

More Portraits of Peace

Today's Treasure:

"For the kingdom of God is not a matter of eating and drinking, but of righteousness, peace and joy in the Holy Spirit" (Rom. 14:17).

Today we continue the lesson we began on day 3, Portraits of Peace in the Life of Christ. Let's recap what we've discovered thus far—Portrait #1: Christ had peace in aloneness, and Portrait #2: Christ had peace in provision. Continue with the following illustrations of the "peace of God."

MORE PORTRAITS OF PEACE

Portrait of Peace #3: Matthew 14:22-33
Keep in mind that this account immediately follows the feeding of the five thousand.

Why did the disciples get into the boat and head to the other side?

(v. 22) _Christ made them_

Where did Christ go? _up the mtn. to pray - alone_

When did Jesus go "out to them"? (v. 25). _4th watch of the night_

Notice the length of time Christ must have prayed on that mountain! He was already there by "evening" (v. 23), and the "fourth watch of the night" would have been between 3 and 6 a.m. That's a lot of prayer!

How did Christ approach the boat? _walking on the sea_

How did the disciples react? _frightened_

Why should the disciples have no fear? (v. 27).

He told them - it is was Himself.

What were the circumstances surrounding the time Peter walked on the water? _If it is You, Let me walk_

What were the circumstances when Peter began to sink in the water?

frightened of the wind.

We see the peace of God so vividly in this wonderful account. First, we see that Christ purposely created circumstances in which He could reveal His majesty. The last place one would seek safety during a storm would be in a boat...separated from all visible signs of security! The hour of the night indicates how long they had struggled against the wind which had risen in the early evening. Without a doubt, they were at the end of their physical strength and were mentally exhausted. Notice, Christ did not run to their rescue. He walked. Just picture the contrast with me: 'Christ approaches at a nice and easy pace while the disciples are scurrying and screaming, "It's a ghost!"

According to this account as well as the Matthew 17:7 and Matthew 28:1-6 accounts, what is the only basis for fearlessness?

little faith - FAITH

We have one, and only one, reason not to fear—the presence of Christ in our circumstances; but He is more than enough reason. He was reason enough for Peter to step out on the water. As long as his focus was straight "toward Jesus," Peter remained on top of the waves, but then he began to sink. What happened? Why couldn't Peter stay afloat through the power of Christ Jesus? Because Peter switched his focus to his circumstances while Christ remained tightly focused on His destination. Then came Peter's fear...the same kind of fear that binds weights to our ankles and submerges us in the waves of surrounding circumstances.

What happened when the waves threatened Peter's life? "Immediately Jesus" (v. 31). No more walking toward Him. He was there—in an instant. I believe it noteworthy that God parted the Red Sea for Moses and the Jordan River for Joshua, but when the Master of the seas approached, He simply climbed the waves and walked. Christ didn't change His circumstances to make them bearable. He mastered them at the peak of their impossibility. Yes, Christ had perfect peace in the storm.

Portrait of Peace #4: John 11

How did Christ feel about Mary, Martha, and Lazarus?

He loved them

Which action of Christ seemed inconsistent with that love?

He didn't immediate go to Lazarus bedside

Why was Lazarus sick? (v. 4). *For the Glory of God*

Why did Christ apparently wait several more days before returning?

To show forth the miracle

For whose sake was Christ glad He was not there before Lazarus died?

Disciples' Sakes

How long had Lazarus been in the tomb? *4 days*

What happened during those four days? (v. 19).

Others came to console sisters.

How did both Mary and Martha react to Christ's absence? (v. 21,32).

angry. My brother would not have died if you had been here

It might be comforting to you "Martha" fans to know that although Mary sought the "better things," her faith also wavered in grief. She was not perfect. Are you relieved? ☑ Yes ☐ No

Exactly why was Jesus "moved"? Check your context.

He wept

✎ What is the guaranteed outcome of "believing" God? (v. 40).

Seeing the Glory of God

What effect did Lazarus' resurrection ultimately have in the circumstances which surrounded the life of Christ? (v. 45-48,57).

Seizing Christ / frightened of Him Afraid Romans would take place & nation.

Several vital truths concerning the peace of God are woven into this unique scriptural account. Christ purposefully timed His absence from Lazarus during his critical illness. Consistently through God's Word, illness and infirmity arise as opportunities for God's work. Check out John 9:1-3. Why was the man born blind?

Christ had glory in mind when He tarried so long before responding to Mary and Martha, too. Christ waited four days before He returned…long enough to accomplish at least two goals:

- A prevalent belief existed at that time that the spirit remained close to the body for three days after death. By waiting past that point, Jesus left them void of other explanations.
- He waited until a crowd had gathered at Mary and Martha's home so that many would "put their faith in him" (v. 45). Christ was peaceful in the wait. He waited thousands of years to become flesh and dwell among us. He waited 30 years to begin His earthly ministry. He waited until Lazarus was cold and decaying before He raised Him from the dead. And we must learn to wait as He does. What profit is there in the wait? (Read Isa. 64:4.)

↺ Are you waiting on the Lord right now? ☑ Yes ❑ No If so, how does this Scripture encourage you toward greater peace in the wait?

_____

_____

Last in this fourth portrait of peace, Christ experienced peace in the midst of tears. Why did Christ Jesus cry? Because He saw the tears of His loved ones (v. 33-35). He "demonstrated His own love" with tears of anguish, yet all the while His peace remained. Please understand this vital point of peace: peace means ← the absence of fear and turmoil, not the absence of pain and grief. It greatly concerns me when I fail to see those who have lost loved ones shed tears in the name of "peace." Christ, Himself, grieved over the separation of loved ones as shown here in John 11, in the garden of Gethsemane and, finally, on the cross ← as He saw His mother's pain and suffered the separation from His Heavenly Father.

We can be filled with sadness and still possess a wonderful sense of God's peace. Perhaps it is at that moment beyond all others when the peace of God transcends all understanding. God is not a proponent of emotional annihilation. But He gives us specific instructions regarding those emotions.

Fill in the blanks from Psalm 62:8.

"__Trust__ in __Him__ at all times, O people;

pour out your __heart__ to him,

for God is our __refuge__."

Our goal is not the absence of sorrow in our grieving, but rather that we refuse to grieve "as those who have no hope" (1 Thess. 4:13). Perhaps right now you are walking through a time when the obvious actions of Christ in your behalf seem inconsistent with His professed love for you. Oh, Beloved, can you see today that it is quite consistent with our Savior to:
• go for the greater glory?
• have us be void of all other explanations?
• wait until many surround us who may put their faith in Him?
If you believe Him, He will show you His glory. Guaranteed.

Throughout days 3 and 4, we have studied four portraits of peace and have come to at least the following conclusions: Christ had perfect peace in ALONENESS…in PROVISION…in the STORM…in the WAIT…and in the TEARS.

A final portrait of peace awaits us on day 5. Bask in His bountiful love today, my Friend.

How does God want you to respond to what He showed you today?

__Pray for Eastman__

__Wives.__

_____

_____

_____

_____

_____

_____

"The mind of sinful man is

death, but the mind

controlled by the Spirit is

life and peace" (Rom. 8:6).

Day 5

Prequisites of Peace

Today we complete our study of the peace of God. God's Word offers many more pictures of peace. My heart aches at the ones we must forego, but I trust God has led us to the ones beneficial for this study. Let's conclude week 5 with a final portrait of peace, to be followed by the prerequisites of peace necessary for all five of these to be applied to our lives.

Portrait of Peace #5: John 18:1-11

Where were Jesus and His disciples going and what route did they take? (v. 1).

Kidron – over the ravine

A garden

Christ and His disciples had just partaken of the last supper and were on their way to the Mount of Olives via the Kidron Valley. Both of these locations have great significance. The word *Kidron* suggests "the gloom of the valley, or perhaps to the peculiar nature of impurity connected with it"[4] The valley was a deep ravine which had been a large cemetery since before 1500 B.C. The Kidron Valley was infamous for being the center of death and the grave. The Mount of Olives is just as significant.

What future event will take place on the Mount of Olives? (Acts 1:11-12; Zech. 14:3-9).

The Ascension

God's Word is amazing, isn't it? A little child can understand it, and yet, it continues to reveal wonderful new insights. The Word often reminds me of a beautiful mosaic or an intricate tapestry. Scripture portrays truth through both clear teaching and enacted pictures. In these verses and the actions of Jesus we see one of those pictures. Christ's walk through the Kidron Valley on His way to the Mount of Olives illustrates this fact: He had to walk through the "valley of the shadow of death," placing death and the grave beneath His feet before He was able to return to the Mount of Olives as King of kings and Lord of lords, the reigning PRINCE OF PEACE! Now refer again to John 18:1-11 as we continue our study of this portrait of peace.

How did Judas "know the place"?

Christ met His disciples there often.

It frightens me just how well Judas "knew" Christ. He sat in countless intimate gatherings with Jesus. He enjoyed the privilege of Christ's teaching on numerous occasions. He witnessed the Master's miraculous power, yet Judas never accepted Christ for his own. That Christ knew who would betray Him, yet never treated Judas any differently, is beyond my comprehension.

We find proof of Jesus even-handed treatment in the disciples' puzzlement. When Christ explained that one of them would betray Him, they were mystified. Had Christ treated Judas any differently, at least 1 of the other 11 would have suspected him.

Do you see the frightening truth Judas demonstrates? Yes, it is possible to be in intimate gatherings with Christ, hear His teaching, and see His power before our very eyes—and be lost. Only at our invitation can Christ surgically open the blocked artery that connects the head to the heart.

Who accompanied Judas to the grove and how were they armed?

Cohort = 600

A "detachment" of soldiers was a cohort or *speiran* "of which there were ten in every legion" or, as in this encounter, 600 men![5]

Was Christ surprised at their arrival? ❑ Yes ☑ No
How do you know?

v. 4 He knew what was coming

What reaction did the soldiers have when Christ replied, "I am he"?

They fell after drawing back.

Isn't it odd that six hundred men fell on the ground? What made them fall? In the *King James Version*, the word *he* in verses 5 and 8 appears in italics, which means the word is not in the original text but is added for our understanding. Please read the exact translation from Greek to English as it appears in the *Interlinear Bible: Hebrew-Greek-English*. The capital letters are not mine. I am presenting these sentences exactly as they appear.

> Whom do you seek? They answered Him, Jesus the Nazarene. Jesus said to them, I AM! Then when He said to them I AM, they departed into the rear and fell to the ground. Then again He asked, Whom do you seek? And they said, Jesus the Nazarene. Jesus answered, I told you that I AM (John 18:6-8).

Jesus did not say "I am he." He said, "I AM." Now read on the following page the exact words translated from Hebrew to English in another significant encounter on a mountain. Once again, any capital letters are exactly as they appear in the *Interlinear Bible* and not used as my emphasis.

Moses said to God, Behold, I shall come to the sons of Israel and say to them, The God of your fathers has sent me to you; and they will say to me, What is His name? What shall I say to them? And God said to Moses, I AM THAT I AM; and He said, You shall say this to the sons of Israel, I AM has sent me to you (Ex. 3:13-14).

What knocked six hundred armed soldiers to their backs? The God of all creation, *El Elyon,* the Sovereign and Supreme Most High God, the God of Abraham, Isaac and Jacob, stood before them in living, breathing flesh and uttered His perfect, divine and holy Name: "I AM!"

❧ What was Christ's only request of the soldiers? (John 18:8).

_____ let my disciples go - free

How did Peter respond to the confrontation? cut the ear of

the slave off - by sword

How did Christ rebuke Peter? Put the sword away.

Shall I not drink my cup - from my Father.

What action followed the rebuke? (Luke 22:47-51).

_____ Betrayal by Judas

Now let's watch as this all comes together. Once again, as you did on day 2, read Matthew 10:34. Through His earthly ministry, what did Christ "come to bring"?

Do you remember the Greek word for *sword?* It was *machaira*. Now look back at John 18:10. Peter drew his *MACHAIRA*—the same Greek word. At this point Christ rebuked him, saying, "No more of this!" (Luke 22:51). Why "no more"? Because the time for PEACE had come. The peace of the cross.

The authorities were not taking Christ's life from Him; He was laying it down. Jesus' perfect peace in God's plan afforded Him perfect peace in His death. From the time Christ suffered, bled, died, and then rose from the dead, He has greeted us with the most liberating words known to spiritual humanity: "Peace be with you!" Praise His name. My heart pounds within me, "Lord, I want your peace!" I want peace in ALONENESS, peace in PROVISION, peace in the STORM, peace in the WAIT, peace in the TEARS, peace in Your PLAN— and even peace in my DEATH. How may I have such peace?

PREREQUISITES FOR PEACE

What made Jesus the one uniquely qualified to bring reconciliation?

(Col. 1:19-20). made Peace thru blood of the cross.

How do the verses say Jesus accomplished His task of reconciling all things to Himself?

Thru Self reconcile all thing.

You must first have peace with God before you can experience the peace of God. You receive peace with God by accepting His gift of grace on Calvary. Christ was uniquely able to bring reconciliation because He is fully God. All God's fullness dwells in Christ. He accomplished His task through the shedding of His blood on the cross.

To whom does peace belong? (John 14:27). _Us!_

What does the verse suggest should be the result?

No trouble - No fear

Recognize that peace belongs to Jesus alone. It is His—you must receive it from Him.

Read Romans 15:13 and Galatians 5:22. How does God give peace?

Thru the Holy Spirit

Christ Jesus gives us His peace through the Holy Spirit. It is a quality of the fruit of the Spirit. The filling of the Holy Spirit releases the glorious power of His peace.

Repeat Romans 8:6 aloud three times. What does the verse describe as the key to peace?

Mind set on the Spirit is Life & Peace

To what key does Isaiah 26:3 point as the mark of the person who will have perfect peace?

Steadfast of Mind

What are Paul's instructions for maintaining peace? (Phil. 4:6-7).

Do not be anxious for anything, but PRAY & be Thankful - let God know your requests. Your hearts & minds shall have Peace - guarded in Jesus Christ

A mind controlled by the Spirit, a mind steadfast on the Spirit, prayer and petition—each of these sounds like a synonym for a Spirit–filled life. The key to being filled with the Holy Spirit so that God's peace may be released within is a mind focused on Him. The peace of God sustains abundant life.

> What is the most important thing God has taught you this week about "peace"?
>
> _____ *No fear.* _____
>
> _____

In conclusion, our peace with God is translated into the peace of God through the filling of the Holy Spirit and quickened in us by a mind "stayed" on Him. As we close today, enjoy the words of this wonderful hymn. If you know the tune, sing it aloud. If not, speak the words with faith and assurance. Oh, how I love Him. Thank you for allowing me to learn of His peace with you through my preparation of this study.

LIKE A RIVER GLORIOUS

Words by Frances R. Havergal, 1874

Like a river glorious is God's perfect peace,
Over all victorious in its bright increase;
Perfect, yet it floweth fuller every day;
Perfect, yet it groweth deeper all the way.

Hidden in the hollow of His blessed hand,
Never foe can follow, Never traitor stand;
Not a surge of worry, not a shade of care,
Not a blast of hurry, touch the spirit there.

Every joy or trial falleth from above,
Trac'd upon our dial by the Son of Love;
We may trust Him fully all for us to do;
They who trust Him wholly Find Him wholly true.

Chorus:
Stayed upon Jehovah, Hearts are fully blest;
Finding as He promised, Perfect peace and rest.

How does God want you to respond to what He showed you today?

_____

_____

_____

_____

_____

_____

_____

---

[1] Spiros Zodhiates et al., eds., *The Complete Word Study Old Testament* (Chattanooga, TN: AMG Publishers, 1994), 2364.

[2] Spiros Zodhiates et al., eds., *The Complete Word Study Dictionary: New Testament* (Chattanooga, TN: AMG Publishers, 1992), 519.

[3] Ibid., 950.

[4] Ibid., 855.

[5] Ibid., 1303.

Week 6

A Composite of Peculiar Patience

Have you ever known a serene person who never passed judgment on others? How often do the failures, emotions, or outright sins of someone else ruin your peace of mind? What would it be like if you refused to allow the behavior of others to spoil your day? This week we will study the commodity called patience, a characteristic of the fruit the Spirit desires to bear in your life. Patience is inspired by mercy, devoid of condemnation, and evidence of the presence and power of our Holy God.

This week we study a distinctive form of patience called *makrothumia*. Mercy drives this patience. Because God has mercy on us, He shows us incredible patience. Because we are becoming like Him, we reflect His patience to others.

Principal Questions

Day 1: Exactly what "inspired" the endurance of the Thessalonians?

Day 2: What was God's promise to Noah, and what was the proof God gave to seal the covenant?

Day 3: What was David's attitude toward judgment after his sin of pride in 2 Samuel 24:14?

Day 4: How does God create ministry from misery?

Day 5: What percentage of our sin does God forgive?

Day 1

A Divine Hope

Through week 6 we study the fourth quality of the fruit of the Spirit: patience. Two important Greek words translate into the English word *patience: hupomone* and *makrothumia*. Both words are vital in the life of the believer, but only one is a quality of the fruit of the Spirit.

Makrothumia is the word used in Galatians 5:22, but we cannot fully comprehend its meaning apart from the word *hupomone*. For this reason, we will devote today's study to this wonderful, yet often painful, Greek word.

The word *hupomone* possesses the meaning you most often associate with the word *patience*. It means "to persevere, remain under....bearing up under. ...refers to that quality of character which does not allow one to surrender to circumstances or succumb under trial."[1] *Hupomone* is endurance in relation to "things or circumstances."[2] The word has another important component, best discovered in 1 Thessalonians 1:3. Carefully read this verse. As we will see today *hupomone* is often translated "endurance" or "perseverance" in the NIV.

🙠 **Exactly what "inspired" the endurance of the Thessalonians?**

work of faith & labor of love & steadfastness is of hope in our L. J.C.

A very strong association with hope is crucial to our understanding of the word *hupomone*. The Greek word for *hope* is *elpis,* and it means the "desire of some good with expectation of obtaining it."[3]

As you see, the Greek meaning of *hope* is much stronger than our English definition. We think of hope as a positive thought or wish toward something we might obtain. The biblical concept of hope is a positive outlook toward an expected end. Biblical hope is not focused on what might happen but what must happen. Thus we can say that *hupomone* is perseverance, endurance, and bearing up under difficult things or circumstances inspired by a beneficial expectation. Keep in mind, hope inspires *hupomone*.

Let's take a look at several examples of *hupomone*. Look up James 5:11. The NIV's English word *perseverance* is translated from the Greek word *hupomone*.

What biblical character possessed *hupomone*? *Job*

Take a quick look back at week 5, day 1. What were a few of the "situations or circumstances" through which Job persevered?

_____

_____

_____

Have you ever wondered why Job remained faithful? What in the world was his motivation? his inspiration?

Since Job possessed *hupomone*, what HAD to be his major inspiration according to the specific meaning of this Greek word?

_____

Two major "hopes" inspired the incomparable perseverance or patience of Job. We discover the first in chapter 23.

Read Job 23:8-10. When Job could not find God, in what did he take comfort? (v. 10). Be tried & coming forth as Gold - entrance Hope.

Job could not "find" God, but he knew without a doubt that God had not lost him. "He knows the way that I take." Job knew that God had not overlooked one moment of his agony, and he had HOPE in a very precious promise: "when he has tested me, I will come forth as gold."

How often, in the midst of a trial, have we all said, "I don't know how any good will ever come from this one." Yet, have we ever lost our entire fortune, all our children, and our health? In the midst of circumstances which continually testified that nothing good could ever be obtained, Job persevered, fueled by his hope that, "when he has tested me, I will come forth as gold."

The metaphor of gold holds such beautiful symbolism for our instruction. Gold is not "finished" until it reaches a point of perfect luster. The chief objective of the refiner is to bring the gold to a point of greatest reflection. The gold is not as costly for its own sake as it is for the sake of that which it reflects. It is the light which exposes its qualities.

Interestingly, the Greek word for *glory* is *doxa* which means to give a correct estimation of.[4] For instance, according to 1 Corinthians 10:31, we are "to give a correct estimation of God" in all that we "eat, drink, or whatever we do." In other words, our actions are to reflect God's actions (what they would be) in that situation. Job believed that his trials would result in his own refinement in God and God's own reflection in him. Job placed his hope in the truth expressed in Romans 8:28 long before it was ever written!

What things work together for the good of those who love Him and who have been called according to His purpose? (Rom. 8:28).

_____

The refining process is rarely comfortable, but what is OUR "HOPE" or expectation? (Rom. 8:29).

To be Christ-like

_____

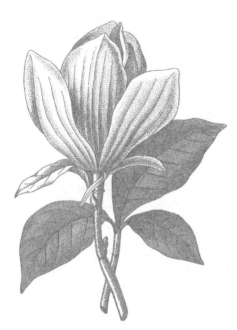

Our expectation is that we shall be conformed to the very likeness of Jesus. Like Job, in that process we can confidently depend on one thing: being made conformable is rarely comfortable. But when Christ is reflected in us as in fine gold, our glorious hopes are fulfilled.

How are we being "transformed" into His likeness? (2 Cor. 3:18).

from glory to glory

Job drew upon two hopes. He had hope in the fact that God was at work. God had not misplaced or forgotten about him. Job trusted that God would transform him. Now take a look at Job 19:25-27 to find the second "hope" which inspired Job's perseverance.

Read Job 19:25-27. In what was Job ultimately placing his hope?

glory

Glory! Although Job had never seen God, he voiced his faith that someday God would assume a bodily form and stand upon this very earth! He also knew that one day, after his old body had been destroyed, he would take on a new body and return to the earth. In that new body Job would see his God—not through someone else's eyes, but with his very own! His heart yearned for the day, and that yearning was his hope…a hope which inspired his incredible perseverance.

Job did not possess a single motivation that we don't possess. In Scripture we hold in our hands vast promises that Job never held, assuring us that God will work our pain toward perfection. We also possess written prophecy which promises us that our "Redeemer lives, and that in the end he will stand upon the earth" (Job 19:25), and in that moment we will "see him as he is" (1 John 3:2).

Let's conclude today by looking up each of the following appearances of the word *hupomone*. The word is translated in English forms of either "endurance" or "perseverance." Remember, *hupomone* is always inspired by hope.

In each of the following circumstances, record what appears to be the "hope" inspiring *hupomone*.

receive what was promised

Hebrews 10:35-36: *Do not throw away your confidence*
You need endurance—so when you have done the will of God you will

Hebrews 12:1-2: *Crucifixion.*

James 1:2-4 *encountering various trials testing produces*
endurance—Endurance—you may be perfect & completely lacking in nothing

2 Timothy 2:10 _To obtain salvation which is in JC_

ew/ eternal glory

2 Timothy 2:12 _To reign w/JC_

Without hope, no patience; without patience, no maturity; without maturity, no reflection; and without reflection, no glory.

Close with Colossians 1:27. Christ in you is the " _Hope_ ****

of _Glory_ **"!**

❧ Are you presently experiencing difficulty in regard to situations or circumstances? Based on today's study, what hopes do you possess to help you persevere through this trial?

Pray for God's guidance in those "situations and circumstances." Thank Him for the hope He has already given you.

How does God want you to respond to what He showed you today?

Day 2

Be Still, Be Filled

We learned about two Greek words translated into the English word *patience: hupomone* and *makrothumia*. We devoted the previous day's study to cultivating an understanding of *hupomone*.

From the definition you learned on day 1, please fill in the following blanks: *Hupomone* **means "to** _perservive endure_ **, remain**

inspired **,** _bear_ _up_ **under. [It] refers to that quality of character which does not allow one to**

falter **to** _situations_

or succumb under trial. HUPOMONE IS _Hope_ **in relation to things or circumstances."**

🖙**Today's Treasure:**

"The Lord is not slow in keeping his promise, as some understand slowness. He is patient with you, not wanting anyone to perish, but everyone to come to repentance" (2 Pet. 3:9).

We also found that the word *hupomone* is often translated in various forms of the words "endurance" and "perseverance" in the *New International Version*. One of the most important characteristics we learned about *hupomone* is that it is inspired by _____.

This review will help you as we consider the distinction between *hupomone*, which is biblical perseverance or endurance, and *makrothumia* which is a quality of the fruit of the Spirit. The remainder of this unit will concentrate on the study of this second word.

According to *The Complete Word Study Dictionary: New Testament*, *makrothumia* means "to be long-suffering." It means "forbearance…self-restraint before proceeding to action."[5] It is "the quality of a person who is able to avenge himself yet refrains from doing so. *Makrothumia* is patience in respect to persons while *hupomone*, endurance, is putting up with things or circumstances."[6]

While both Greek words are crucial to the understanding and obedience of the believer, they describe different qualities. In 2 Timothy 3:10 and Colossians 1:10-12, notice the way God uses the words together while making an obvious distinction between the two. Read each reference and consider the following: in both cases, the Greek word *makrothumia* is translated into the English word "patience," and the Greek word *hupomone* is translated into the English word "endurance." By using both of these words, Paul emphasized the importance of being patient in respect to persons and enduring in respect to situations or circumstances. Another very important distinction distinguishes *hupomone* and *makrothumia*. *Hupomone* is inspired by hope and *makrothumia*, or the fruit of the Spirit called "patience," is inspired by mercy.

Everywhere you discover the word *makrothumia*, you find some form of mercy. The Greek word for the kind of "mercy" present in *makrothumia* is *eleos*. The word means "mercy, compassion, active pity, with the sense of goodness in general, especially piety."[7] Scripture uses *eleos* to describe God.

Now you're about to see why this kind of "patience" is a quality of the fruit of the Spirit. When it comes to prioritizing between circumstances and people, God is obviously going to choose people. How we respond to circumstances *(hupomone)* is important, but how we respond to others *(makrothumia)* is critical.

Wouldn't you agree that to be patient with circumstances is far easier than with people? Consider why this might be true: we need to respond with *hupomone* when some circumstance or situation is trying us. We need *makrothumia* when someONE is trying us. With *hupomone* we have no one to blame! When it comes to dealing with trying people, we have someone to blame, so we need all the help we can get! Amen?

Hebrews 10:36 tells us we need *hupomone*, (or "hope which inspires perseverance") which qualifies it as something for which to pray. In other words, we should actively petition God for endurance in our circumstances, but *makrothumia* is not merely the answer to prayer. Patience is the release of the fruit of the Spirit; it is the supernatural outcome of being filled with the Holy Spirit. *Makrothumia* is impossible except when expressed by God through us.

Many of us have suffered great frustration as we have tried to practice *makrothumia* in our own strength. I pray that through this study we will learn and practice allowing the Holy Spirit to express His patience through us.

Look up and read 1 Peter 3:20. What example is this Scripture giving for the expression of God's *makrothumia* toward people?

The people during Noah's day awaiting the ark

Read all of Genesis 6. What did God "see"? (v. 5).

Can you even imagine the condition described in Genesis 6? If you are like me, you seek repentance for more thoughts than actions. I struggle far more with internals than externals. I experience days when my mind is consumed with thoughts less than "true, noble, right, pure, lovely, admirable, excellent or praiseworthy" (Phil. 4:8). I become so frustrated with myself. The area of personal victory I pursue most consistently is a mind held captive to Christ. Yet, as much as I struggle, I can joyfully say that "every inclination of the thoughts" of my heart have never been "only evil all the time." If you are born again, neither have yours. Consider what a state the world was in: the people's minds were filled with evil all the time.

How does Genesis 6:11 describe the thoughts of humans at this time?

filled w/violence - Corrupt.

How did God respond to their evil inclinations? (v. 6).

Sorry He had man - grieved in His head

The Hebrew word for *grieved* is *nacham* and it embodies the expression of drawing breath and groaning as one would do while sobbing in grief.[8] Imagine God expressing such grief. It was as if the sorrow of God took on a physical form, much like ours does when we cry. The Word of God tells us that this grief cut straight to the heart of God—and He hurt.

❧ **Considering Genesis 1:27,31, why must this observation have caused God such pain?**

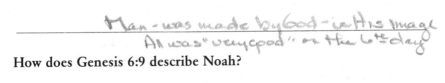

Man - was made by God - in His image
All was "very good" on the 6th day

How does Genesis 6:9 describe Noah?

Noah walked w/God

In contrast with his culture, Noah was a righteous man. Sometimes we use our society's depravity as an excuse for our bouts of unrighteousness: "If I didn't have to work in this godforsaken place…"; "If I didn't have to live with this awful man…."; "If we didn't have to live in this horrible city…"; "If I hadn't come from such a godless family…"; "If all that hadn't happened to me…"; "But Noah…."

What does Noah's example teach? *You don't need to "follow" others — Only God!*

How long would God strive with this evil generation? (v. 3).

120yrs

In addition to building the ark, what other obvious responsibility had God given Noah during those 120 years? (2 Pet. 2:5).

"preacher of righteousness" for the 7 others

Without a single convert. How often we base success and favor on visible evidence. Now read Genesis 8:15 through 9:17. This is the account of what scholars refer to as the "Noahic Covenant."

☙ In simple terms, what was God's promise to Noah, and what was the proof God gave to seal the covenant?

rainbow

Why did God wait 120 years while Noah preached righteousness? What prompted God's promise to never again flood the earth? First Peter 3:20 gives the answer: the *makrothumia,* or the PATIENCE of God! Now, the answer to this next question is crucial. God's promise was prompted out of patience, but what prompted His patience? *Mercy*

Read 2 Peter 3:9 and fill in the blanks.

"The Lord is not slow in keeping his *promise*_____**, as some understand slowness. He is** *patient*_____ **with you, not wanting anyone to** *perish*_____, **but everyone to come to** *repentance*_____**."**

Read 2 Peter 3:15 and fill in the following blanks:

"Bear in mind that our Lord's _____ *patience*

means _____ *Salvation.* _____**"!**

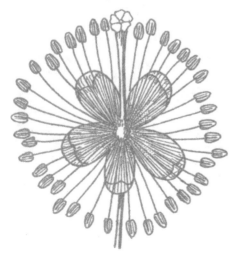

I am saved because mercy prompted God's patience. You are saved because mercy prompted God's patience. God's patience means salvation...to us and to everyone who ever believes!

Let's conclude our study today with one final assignment. Set your alarm for just before dawn tomorrow morning. Then GET UP. (I included those three words because it occurred to me that the alarm going off is not synonymous with the body getting up!) Take a chair and your Bible to the backyard (or the front if you dare!) and position yourself toward the East. Lift up the day's needs as the light begins to dawn and the sun rises. Then read Genesis 8:22, Lamentations 3:22-23, and Psalm 30:5. Meditate on the truth from God's Word that the same patience of God that ushers in the dawn every morning of your life also meant your salvation.

While the three Scriptures from above abide in your heart, write your prayer of response to God as the Sun of Righteousness rises. As the morning breaks, simply record your thoughts toward Him.

_____

_____

_____

_____

How does God want you to respond to what He showed you today?

_____

_____

_____

_____

_____

_____

_____

Day 3

Lest You Be Judged

Today we continue our study of *makrothumia*, or the "patience" toward others that results from being filled with the Holy Spirit. In His Word, God often carries us to understanding in the vehicle of contrast. For example, God doesn't just tell us what His will is for our lives; He expounds on that will by further expressing what it is not. We see this method of instruction in the concrete commands God gave Israel including both "Thou shalts" and "Thou shalt nots." Today we will see Him employ this same teaching tool as we learn more about what true patience is by studying what it is not.

What would be the polar opposite of biblical "patience"? Think again about the model of patience God displayed for us by postponing the flood for 120 years, by vowing to never again flood the earth, and by delaying the final judgment as long as possible because "it is not His will for any to perish." Can you see Scripture contrasting the two themes of patience and judgment?

An opposite practice from *makrothumia* (long-suffering toward others inspired by mercy) would be *krino* which means "to pass judgment upon, condemn, take vengeance on."[9] It means to "try" someone as if they stand accused before you in a court of law. We can see why patience and judgment are opposites: the essence of the biblical word for "patience" is the delaying of judgment.

God demonstrated that He ultimately makes a choice. He cannot judge swiftly *and* be patient. At some point, God's patience is complete and He makes judgment. Until then, the Lord is "patient" so that many may be saved. The

Today's Treasure:

"Therefore let us stop passing judgment on one another. Instead, make up your mind not to put any stumbling block or obstacle in your brother's way" (Rom. 14:13).

same rule of disposition is true within us. We cannot both judge others and be patient toward them. One cancels out the other. Therefore, if we are going to become vessels of God's patience toward others, we must also learn to be void of judgment toward others.

Today let's allow God's Word to put us to the test and to reveal if we are quenching the Spirit of patience by fanning the flame of judgment. This study is one that we probably need more than we want, but is vital to our understanding of *makrothumia*.

> **Search each of the passages below and compile a list of reasons why we must not judge one another. Imagine that you are preparing arguments for a debate team.**

Romans 2:1-4 *you condemn yourself / you do the same. Do you escape the judgement of God? Kindness of God leads you to repentance.*

Matthew 7:1-5 *"Do not judge – lest you be judged" Speck in your neighbors eye / but not your own. log in yours – speck in brothers.*

James 4:11-12 *Speaking against brother is speaking against Law. Only God is Judger of ....*

John 8:14-18 *You don't know where He came from & where He is going – Only Father & Son can judge.*

SIX REASONS WE MUST NOT JUDGE OTHERS (ROM. 2:1-5):

1. When we judge others, we cause God to be harder on us.
"At whatever point you judge the other, you are condemning yourself" (v. 1). We invite the discipline of our Heavenly Father.

2. We do many of the same things we condemn in others (see v. 1).
For example, we are quick to judge sexual sin; yet few of us have not transgressed in at least some area of sexual sin. If not physically, mentally. We often

sit on the judgment seat as if to determine and compare degrees of sin. Judgment bears hypocrisy.

3. We do not know the whole truth.

"God's judgment...is based on truth" (v. 2). We may think we have "all the facts," but we are incapable of reading minds or judging hearts.

4. We are mere humans.

"So when you, a mere man" (v. 3). I love the way Isaiah 29:16 expounds upon the temptation to switch roles with God: "You turn things upside down, as if the potter were thought to be like the clay!" We must withstand all temptation to assume God's job!

5. When we judge others, we are judging God.

Our judgment reveals contempt for the riches of God's patience. (see v. 4). To judge why God won't bring a speedy punishment to those who mock or despise Him is not our responsibility. To all of us, His long-suffering has been our salvation. Eternity is a long time; the effects are irreversible. God desires to give every chance for the sinner to say "yes." I once heard Dr. Adrian Rogers say, "Time is not nearly as important to God as timing."

6. God's judgment is always righteous. Ours is tainted by the flesh.

"When his righteous judgment will be revealed" (v. 5). Our judgment of others is colored by our attitudes, our pasts, our personalities, and our positions. Only God is the perfectly righteous Judge.

> ❧ **What was David's attitude toward judgment after his sin of pride? (2 Sam. 24:14).**

God's hands are merceful – not man's

MORE REASONS NOT TO JUDGE OTHERS (MATT. 7:1-5):

7. We risk application of the same type of judgment to ourselves (see vv. 1-2).

When I recall times I have been quick to judge, my reaction has often been tainted by my own personality and past. The same lack of mercy I've dispensed could, in turn, be dispensed to me!

8. We cannot judge the speck of sawdust in another's eye because of the planks in our own (see vv. 3-4).

We can't judge righteously because our sight is hindered by our own sin. Consider the following illustration. A precious little preschool boy was picked up by Child Protective Services after a church nursery worker discovered multiple marks and bruises on his body. After some investigation, his guardians were found picketing the rights of the unborn at an area abortion clinic. What is wrong with this picture? Why not protect the child entrusted to you first?

LET'S SEE WHAT WE LEARNED FROM JAMES 4:11-12:

9. "There is only one lawgiver and judge" (Jas. 4:12).
There's simply no room on the bench! God wrote the commands. Only He has the right to judge the infraction and punish the offender.

10. Only God has noble purpose in His judgment.
We judge to make ourselves feel righteous in comparison. Whether or not the thought is conscious, most judgments boil down to this justification: "At least I don't do that!" God's judgment is not based on His "ego." It is a practical action by which He determines the fate of all humanity.

THE FINAL REASON NOT TO JUDGE (JOHN 8:14-18):

11. Just like Christ's, our judgment would have to be completely consistent with God's. He must agree with us for our judgment to be valid.
We judge by "human standards" (v. 15) and, therefore, possess little heavenly perspective. To make a valid judgment, the second testimony cannot be our best friend or neighbor…it must be God.

> ✍ In light of the eleven reasons we've considered above, read 2 Samuel 24:14. What does this verse say to you?
>
> _Do not judge & ask forgiveness._
> _____

As we conclude, please allow me to clarify that today's study is not referring to the absence of discipline in the church or home. Some situations demand discipline. This study focuses on actions far more frequent than restoration: the quick mental and verbal judgments we make toward one another. Though God sits as Judge from a bench of awesome perfection, He has chosen to exercise "patience" toward each one of us and to delay the proceedings that would have meant our deaths. If He is patient with us and He has no sin, how patient must we be toward others with whom we share the same sin? Judgment strangles patience and grieves the Holy Spirit.

> **Would you join me in asking God for an extreme awareness of judgment? Let's petition Him for an immediate sense of conviction over the sin of judgment and our tendency to condemn.**

We have no idea how deeply imbedded this sin may be in each of us until we invite Him to expose it. This process could be painful, but if we are to be vessels through which His wonderful *makrothumia* flows, we have no choice but to cease the judgment we render toward one another. Nor do we want such judgment imposed on ourselves! Purified hearts are worth the risk of a few harsh realities. The way I see it, it's easier to be clay than the potter. Let's allow the buck to stop with God. He is the only wise Judge.

How does God want you to respond to what He showed you today?

_____

_____

_____

_____

_____

_____

_____

Day 4

Have Mercy

O n day 3 we considered an ingredient always conspicuously missing in the formula for *makrothumia:* patience is void of judgment. We learned patience and judgment are opposites and impossible to exercise simultaneously. Today we consider why no room for judgment exists where the fruit of patience abounds. The mercy that inspires biblical patience contains an ingredient which overrides the temptation to judge. Today's study will be devoted to the discovery of this crucial component of *makrothumia.*

Read Matthew 18:15-35, keeping in mind that every time you see the word *patience*, it is the same Greek word, *makrothumia*, that we've learned to be a fruit of the Spirit. Please answer the following:

What question prompted the parable?
❑ "Will you at this time restore the kingdom to Israel?"
❑ "How many times shall I forgive my brother?"
❑ "Is it lawful for a man to divorce his wife?"

How much did the servant owe the king? (v. 24). _____

What did the king do with the judgment against the servant?
❑ He canceled the debt and forgave the servant.
❑ He set up a payment plan.
❑ He had the man and his family sold as slaves.

What event immediately followed the servant's release?
❑ He threw a great feast to celebrate the king's generosity.
❑ The servant prosecuted another servant over a smaller debt.

How much did the fellow servant owe? _____

What was his request? (v. 29). _____

What was the response of the king when he received the news concerning the confrontation between the two servants?

_____

_____

The amount of money each servant owed is one of the most important contrasts in the parable. The first servant owed the king "ten thousand talents," equal to millions of today's dollars. The king canceled the entire debt and freed

❧Today's Treasure:

"Therefore, as God's chosen people, holy and dearly loved, clothe yourselves with compassion, kindness, humility, gentleness and patience. Bear with each other and forgive whatever grievances you may have against one another. Forgive as the Lord forgave you" (Col. 3:12-13).

him from his obligation. The moment the servant was released, he "found" one of his fellow servants who owed him money.

The word *found* implies strongly that the merciless servant left in pursuit of the second servant. How much did the servant owe? The equivalent of only a few dollars, yet the wicked servant showed no mercy. The parable concludes with the outraged king sentencing the merciless servant to confinement and torture until the original debt could be repaid. So vast was the debt, his torture would have been unending.

Three vital terms weave the tapestry of this parable. Let's extract them one by one and then determine the common denominator.

> **Recall the purpose of the parable. What subject was under discussion?**
> ❏ stewardship ❏ eschatology ☑ forgiveness
>
> **What specific response did both servants beg from their "creditors"?**
>
> _____ mercy _____

Both servants begged for mercy. The king granted mercy and forgiveness. The first servant responded with only judgment.

FORGIVENESS, PATIENCE, MERCY

The parable of the merciless servant is about forgiveness...a forgiveness prompted by patience, and a patience perfected by mercy. If we neglect the necessity of forgiveness, we fail to complete the portrait of biblical patience. Patience is the vessel through which God pours His mercy. Mercy is fueled by forgiveness.

Forgiveness so greatly impacts the filling of the Holy Spirit that we will devote the remainder of this week's study to the following questions and conclusions: What is biblical forgiveness? Who and what must we forgive? Why must we forgive? How must we forgive? When must we forgive?

1. WHAT is biblical forgiveness?
The Greek word most often used in the New Testament for *forgive* is *aphiemi*. It means "to let go from one's power, possession, to let go free, let escape."[10] In essence, the intent of biblical forgiveness is to cut someone loose. The word picture drawn by the Greek terms for unforgiveness is one in which the "unforgiven" is roped to the back of the unforgiving. How ironic. Unforgiveness is the means by which we securely bind ourselves to that which we hate most. Therefore, the Greek meaning of forgiveness might best be demonstrated as the practice of cutting loose the person roped to your back.

2. WHO and WHAT must we forgive?
Jesus taught us to pray: "Forgive us our sins, for we also forgive EVERYONE who sins against us (Luke 11:4). In Mark 11:25 He said: "when you stand praying, if you hold ANYTHING against anyone, forgive him, so that your Father in heaven may forgive you your sins." Jesus clearly intends that we forgive every offense no matter how painful.

My heart grows tender as I consider your thoughts at this moment. *Beth, you have no idea what has happened to me! Surely God does not mean that I must forgive this!* Do you remember the definition we learned on day 2: *makrothumia* is "the quality of a person who is able to avenge himself yet refrains from doing so."[11] Yes, God desires to pour His patience through those with every right to avenge…every right to be merciless…every right to be angry and bitter…those to whom perhaps no earthly mercy has ever been shown.

If you have the "right to be mad" or the "right to hold a grudge," you are a prime candidate for *makrothumia*. Can't you almost hear the Savior say: "Perfect choice. What better choice for one through whom to pour my mercy?" Remember, God wants to reveal Himself in us—not our rights or weaknesses.

3. WHY must we forgive? We will discover at least five reasons:
We must forgive because of the very nature of the word *aphiemi*. Frankly, it's difficult to live an effective Christian life with a body roped to your back. Can you imagine how many of us are walking around roped to a corpse? Some of us are harboring unforgiveness against someone who has long been in the grave. Is there anything heavier than "dead weight"? Well, as a matter of fact, there is: a group roped to your back. Unforgiveness is extremely habit-forming. Unchecked, it spreads from one person to another. Before you know it, you have a school-bus load of people roped to your back! You cannot be free to keep step with the Spirit when you are encumbered by the load of unforgiveness.

We must forgive because God's Word calls us to forgive.

> **Read Luke 6:37 and Matthew 6:14-15. Mark each of the following statements either true or false according to those passages.**
> __T__ God links His forgiveness of us to our forgiveness of others.
> __F__ God forgives us and does not expect us to forgive others.
> __T__ When we condemn others, we are condemning ourselves also.

It almost seems unfair to our limited minds, doesn't it? God is God, for heaven's sake! How hard can it be for Him to forgive? Why must His forgiveness rely on mine? Oh, Beloved, God presses us to cut those people loose for excellent reasons! Read on!

We must forgive for our own sakes.

> **Look again at the parable of the merciless servant in Matthew 18:21-35. Record the final punishment of each servant.**
>
> Servant 1: _turned over to torturers_
>
> Servant 2: _had him thrown into prison_
>
> Which servant was tortured? _#1 - where the lord had forgiven_

The truth is this: the one who will not forgive always suffers more than the one not forgiven. Though both servants in the parable were imprisoned by the first servant's lack of forgiveness and mercy, only one was tortured. Unforgiveness tortures the person who harbors it. I know; I've been there.

After suffering a serious degree of childhood trauma, God continually confronted me to forgive my perpetrator. I refused for many years. Would you like to know why? I was absolutely certain that my forgiveness would "make it all right," and it wasn't all right. I feared that if I forgave, he would be off the hook. I had suffered painful repercussions. I didn't realize that my failure to forgive was causing me more pain than the original offense.

Finally, God wore me down until I was forced to listen to His gentle whisper to my heart. "Beth, forgiving won't make the offense all right; it will make YOU all right." He demanded that I forgive for my own sake...so that I would not be tortured by it for the rest of my life!

"So," you may ask, "was He right?"

Oh, my Friend, without hesitation I can proclaim that next to the gift of my salvation and His Son's Spirit dwelling within me, the most wonderful thing God has ever given me is the ability to forgive. I am free. Not free from all memories—but free from all torture. Yes, He is faithful.

We must forgive so that we do not provide Satan with opportunity to take advantage.

> ❧ Read 2 Corinthians 2:10-11. In what ways do you think Satan takes advantage of you when you won't forgive?

Satan is scheming - makes things look worse.

I particularly enjoy the way the *King James Version* says it, "Ye forgive any thing...lest Satan should get an advantage of us: for we are not ignorant of his devices." Few things exist in life that Satan can take advantage of more effectively than unforgiveness. It extends an open invitation for him to infiltrate circumstances and spark memories to fan the flame of bitterness.

Satan will stop at nothing to broaden the wedge unforgiveness drives between us and our Savior. Why? Because He knows that it is impossible to be filled with the Spirit and filled with unforgiveness. Only Satan wins in the war of unforgiveness. When he sees a rope, he sees an opportunity to hang us.

We must forgive because we are not the only ones bound by the rope of unforgiveness. If we refuse to forgive, we tie God's mighty hands from "working all things together for good." He will not bring personal good to you from your pain if you do not release Him through your forgiveness. Why? Read Romans 8:28. This verse applies to those who love Him enough to be called according to His purpose. Christ has a purpose in the pain you've suffered or He never would have allowed it. Until you surrender to His purpose in the specific matter at hand, He cannot work it for your good. Do you know what that means? It all happened in vain—for absolutely nothing.

How does God want you to respond to what He showed you today?

_____

_____

_____

_____

_____

_____

_____

122

❧ **How does God create ministry from misery?** (2 Cor. 1:3-7).
(Check one or more.)

☑ **He comforts us and leads us to share His comfort.**

☑ **Because we have been through suffering, we have opportunities to share Christ and His comfort.**

☐ **Faithful Christians do not have to suffer pain or heartache.**

I had no idea the ministry God would grant me through my misery. When I am speaking, the mere mention of my abuse results in a line of women waiting for me when I'm finished. They most often ask why God allowed those things to happen to me knowing that I was going to work for Him. I look down that line of women and respond, "For you." God has slowly but surely ushered me to a place…a glorious place…where the body of Christ has become worth my pain. How did such a miraculous transformation occur? Somewhere along the way, I began to realize some of what it means for me to be worth His suffering.

Ask God to help you let go of any unforgiveness and allow Him to minister to others through your misery.

Day 5
A Clean Slate

Let's review the basics we've learned thus far: two Greek words translate into the English word *patience*. *Hupomone* is the capacity to bear up under things or circumstances and is inspired by hope. *Makrothumia* is the quality found in the fruit of the Spirit. The word means "long-suffering in respect to persons" and is inspired by mercy. Mercy is fueled by forgiveness—the focal point of our study.

Yesterday we reached the following conclusions:

• Biblical forgiveness means to cut someone loose, to set someone free.

• We must forgive everyone and everything.

• We must forgive because:

The burden of unforgiveness is too heavy to carry.

God wants to continue to forgive us.

God does not want us to be tortured by unforgiveness.

Satan takes tremendous advantage of unforgiveness.

God can be released to work the situation to our good.

❧ Let's begin today's study by discovering one more reason to forgive. What does unforgiveness do? (Eph 4:30-32).

Frees You ← Greeves the H.S.

❧ Today's Treasure:

"Here is a trustworthy saying that deserves full acceptance: Christ Jesus came into the world to save sinners—of whom I am the worst. But for that very reason I was shown mercy so that in me, the worst of sinners, Christ Jesus might display his unlimited patience as an example for those who would believe on him and receive eternal life. Now to the King eternal, immortal, invisible, the only God, be honor and glory for ever and ever. Amen" (1 Tim. 1:15-17).

We must forgive because we have been forgiven! Not coincidentally, the foremost writer God inspired to pen His exhortations toward forgiveness was the apostle Paul.

According to Today's Treasure, why did Paul consider himself to be the perfect choice?

Most sinner - patience shown to him through J.C.

How might a lost man or woman, having lived their entire lives immersed in sin, find encouragement in the relationship between Christ and the apostle Paul?

because he had rec'd - he was capable of giving

Through Paul, Christ displayed His unlimited *makrothumia!* As a result, He often displayed His unlimited patience toward others through Paul. Paul was capable of extensive forgiveness because he had received extensive forgiveness.

Read Luke 7:36-50. Fill in the following blanks:

"But he who has been forgiven little **loves** little" **(v. 47).**

In your own words, write what you believe this verse means:

_____

_____

Because I was saved as a small child, every major sin I have ever committed has been as a redeemed temple of God's Holy Spirit. I despise the depth and frequency of my sin, but I am aware that my salvation did not simply BEGIN as grace—but daily PERSISTS by grace. We have been called to forgive because we have been forgiven. Now, for question four.

4. **HOW do we forgive? Knowing now what biblical forgiveness IS, whom and what it is FOR, and why it is so crucial, how do we do it?**

Colossians 3:13 tells us exactly HOW to forgive. We are to forgive

Put on Love = Perfect bond of unity.

Therefore, to ascertain how we are to forgive others, we must discover how God forgives us.

Judge → Patience

Look up the Scriptures below and record what you learn regarding God and His blessed forgiveness.
What percentage of our sin does God forgive? (Ps. 85:2-3; 1 John 1:9).
❑ 66%   ❑ 85%   ☑ 100%

Notice how Ephesians 4:31-32 exhorts us to do exactly the same!

What does God do with our forgiven sins? (Ps. 103:12).

Removes them — as far as the East from the West.

Mark the following true or false. (Ps. 130:3-4; Jer. 31:34).
_F_ God keeps a record of all our sins.
_T_ God forgives completely.
_T_ God chooses to remember our sin no more.
_F_ We must atone for our sin by living a good life.

The first characteristic we learned about God's forgiveness is that He forgives all (confessed) sin and covers all (confessed) sin. If you have a heart full of godly sorrow, He is no longer angry nor is He plotting wrath in your behalf.

Second, He removes our sin from us as far as east is from west. His desire is that we have no monuments and reminders of our past sins. Every single moment He sees the scars on His Son's side, hands and feet. That is enough. Accept the fact that your sins have been transferred to the Savior.

Third, God keeps no written record of wrongs. (Sounds like *agape*, doesn't it?)

Fourth, God keeps no mental record of wrongs. He not only erases the record of the sin, but He also erases His memory of the sin. He doesn't mentally replay our sins against Him as we tend to do when others sin against us.

If you are like me, you're thinking, *Only God can forgive like that!* You are absolutely right. But when you are filled with the Spirit of His precious Son, you become a vessel for the miraculous! Through the supernatural work of the Holy Spirit, you can indeed forgive anything and everything. This truth brings us to our last question concerning forgiveness:

5. WHEN must we forgive?
Oh, Beloved, now. God desires for you to be free. For your sake, forgive. It all begins with willingness. If you can't admit that you are willing, confess to Him a willingness to be willing!

Perhaps you are harboring a 30-year-old hurt and have allowed Satan to convince you that it's far too late for forgiveness. Perhaps you have allowed anger and bitterness to become your life's focus, and you wonder what would motivate you each day if God removed it? You may even be scared of what you might become. Trust Him. What do you have to lose but imprisonment, torture, and warfare? Time is so precious. Refuse to allow the enemy another moment's victory.

I feel the leadership of the Holy Spirit directing me to another passage concerning a very important element of forgiveness. I did not plan this one.

How does God want you to respond to what He showed you today?

_____

_____

_____

_____

_____

_____

Read Matthew 5:23-24 very carefully. At this very moment, any one of us may be a stumbling block to someone else who is harboring unforgiveness toward us. Just as I have done in the past, you may have refused to ask forgiveness from someone harboring something against you because you believe you are innocent. Notice God never mentions the validity of the ill feelings someone may have toward us. He simply says, "Go to them and reconcile yourself."

Does anyone hold anything against you? "Make up your mind not to put any stumbling block or obstacle in your brother's way" (Rom. 14:13). I, or you, may BE that stumbling block. At first consideration, there is every likelihood that we will respond with a blank. Let's not risk delusion. Let's ask God to reveal the names of any whose hearts are hindered because of us. We may not learn the reasons until we are obedient and confront them. A brief warning: you may receive no satisfaction from them. They may not want to forgive you. Or, they may never admit there is a problem. Remember, the satisfaction of obeying God is paramount. Do everything you can to hasten your brother or sister's forgiveness. Fruit will result.

As I began this study of patience, I had no idea of all that would be involved in the basic quality we so often speak of lacking. But, the truths we've discovered have been there all along. God desires for us the supernatural result of being filled with the Spirit…vessels honored to be chosen to pour forth His grand and glorious mercy. The patience He desires to extend to others is the same patience that meant the salvation of our souls. "Bear in mind that our Lord's patience means salvation" (2 Pet. 3:15)!

Read James 5:7-9. Conclude this study with a time of prayer concerning the passage. Pray for God's patience as you daily face and overcome the struggles and strifes of life.

May He walk through that door very soon. Until then, patience, my Friend.

---

[1]Spiros Zodhiates et al., eds., *The Complete Word Study Dictionary: New Testament* (Chattanooga, TN: AMG Publishers, 1992), 1425.
[2]Ibid., 939.
[3]Ibid., 570.
[4]Ibid., 478.
[5]Ibid., 939.
[6]Ibid.
[7]Ibid., 564.
[8]Spiros Zodhiates et al., eds., *The Complete Word Study Old Testament* (Chattanooga, TN: AMG Publishers, 1994), 2339.
[9]Ibid., 889.
[10]Ibid., 299.
[11]Ibid., 939.

Week 7

The Kindness and Goodness of God

Would you rather be known as a kind person or a good person? How do these two elements relate to each other? How has the kindness and goodness of God made an impact on your life? Kindness and goodness are complementary aspects of the fruit of the Spirit. Without kindness, goodness becomes harsh and self-righteous. Without goodness, kindness becomes indulgent tolerance. Only the Holy Spirit can balance and grow these essential qualities in our lives.

This week we will study and compare the kindness and the goodness of God. We will seek to understand how these characteristics of God and elements of the character of Christ may be ours as the Spirit develops His fruit in our lives.

Principal Questions
Day 1: What name did Hagar "give" God?
Day 2: What assurance do we have that God will never forget His children?
Day 3: Is it possible to cause another person to sin?
Day 4: What are we to guard and how are we to guard it? (2 Tim. 1:14).
Day 5: How did Paul's actions demonstrate *chrestotes*? (1 Thess. 2:6-8).

Day 1

A Nurturing Parent

"But the fruit of the Spirit is love, joy, peace, patience, kindness…"

Today we proceed to the fifth quality of the fruit of the Spirit: kindness. The Greek word for *kindness* is *chrestotes* which means "tender concern for others. It has nothing to do with weakness or lack of conviction," rather it is "the genuine desire of a believer to treat others gently, just as the Lord treats him."[1] *Chrestotes* "is the grace which pervades the whole nature, mellowing all which would be harsh and austere." The term possesses the "harmlessness of the dove." In precise terms, *chrestotes* is a tender heart and a nurturing spirit.[2]

By this time you have already discovered that each quality of the fruit of the Spirit is absolutely divine. They are impossible goals for the unbeliever, yet attainable—but not automatic—graces for the true believer. They are manifestations of the Father Himself through the yielded or Spirit-filled child of God; therefore, before we can comprehend its application to us, we must learn what each quality looks and acts like in the heart of God.

Today we are going to seize the blessed invitation to gaze into the tender heart of God. I am convinced that many believers are far more knowledgeable in the areas of God's sovereignty and judgment than they are His tenderness and kindness. You can know Him well as Lord yet never truly relate to Him as Father. Even now my heart is overflowing at the mere thought of introducing some of you for the very first time to the *El Shaddai*, the Father of sufficiency, our God, the nurturing Parent.

Begin your study today by reading Genesis 16:1-15 and answering the following:
What was Sarai's first problem? (v. 1).
❑ alcoholism ☑ childlessness ❑ she was a shrew

How did she attempt to solve her problem? Hagar - the
_____
maid
_____

_____

What was Sarai's second problem? (v. 5).
❑ Hagar remained childless ☑ Hagar despised Sarai

Mark the following true or false.
_T_ Sarai caused Hagar's departure by mistreating her.
_F_ The angel of the Lord found Hagar under a broom tree.
_T_ The angel of the Lord instructed Hagar to return to her mistress.
_F_ Hagar and Sarai became friends.

Today's Treasure:

"Let not the wise man boast of his wisdom or the strong man boast of his strength or the rich man boast of his riches, but let him who boasts boast about this: that he understands and knows me, that I am the Lord, who exercises kindness, justice and righteousness on earth, for in these I delight" (Jer. 9:23-24).

What promise accompanied the angel's instruction? *return to mistress: sub*

mit

☼ **What name did Hagar "give" God?** *Beer-lahai-roi*

How did the angel's prophesy describe Hagar's son Ishmael?

His hand will be against everyone & theirs

against him. He will live to the East. Too many descendants.

Notice that after all the scheming and resulting repercussions, Sarai still did not achieve the son she desired. Will women ever change? We are still the "fixers" in the family…the problem solvers…the peacemakers…God's "helper of the household." After all, He is so busy. As a result, we've helped ourselves to many a disaster. God-sized problems don't fit women-sized hands. (Just for reference, they don't fit guy mitts either.)

> **Now read Genesis 21:1-21 and answer the following:**
> **In spite of Sarah's sin, how did God "fix" her problem?**
>
> *Issac.*

What caused Sarah's anger at the feast in Isaac's honor?
❑ **Hagar scorned Isaac.**
☑ **Ishmael was mocking.**
❑ **Abraham loved his first son more than his second.**

I believe Sarah was at a decided disadvantage. Remember, she weaned Isaac "that day" which tells me that everyone was having a good time—except Sarah! No wonder she was in such a bad mood!

> ☼ **How do you suppose Abraham felt when he followed God's command and sent Hagar and Ishmael away?**
>
> *Heart-broken*

Why did Hagar distance herself from her son?
❑ **She feared for her life.**
☑ **She could not bear to see him die.**

What did God tell Hagar to do? *Hold his hand*   *Gen. 21 • v17.*

He will become a nation

This story so tenders my heart, I can hardly read it. Long before Christ drew a woman to a well, God drew a well to a woman. God's heart broke at the sight of this mother and son confronting the frightening prospect of death. The mother's heart was so broken that she distanced herself from her only child because she was afraid he would die before she did. A mother's biggest fear.

The boy must have been very weak; his mother "put" him under a bush, and he made no attempt to follow her. Probably, she positioned him carefully under a thorn bush to keep the wild animals from preying on his dying body. Then the mother began to sob. Doubtless her wails were heard by the boy "nearby," because Scripture records that he remained under the bush and cried as well. Then God unleashed His loving kindness. He refreshed and restored both mother and child; in the place of an absent father, God vowed to abide with the boy as he grew.

As we reflect on the encounter between God and Hagar, it seems we witness not only the compassion and sympathy of God, but also the empathy of God. He could relate to her pain and need, so He responded to Hagar as a loving God and as a fellow parent.

Might this have been the response of a Father who knew one day He also would face the intense pain of separation? Did God anticipate the torment of watching His only Son suffer…the agony of knowing He'd turn His back on His child as He died? This was a Father who proudly proclaimed, "This is my Son, whom I love; with him I am well pleased" (Matt. 3:17)! He was also a Father about whom Christ would say, "You loved me before the creation of the world" (John 17:24) and moments later cry "Abba, Father….Take this cup from me" (Mark 14:36) and hours later, "My God, my God, why have you forsaken me?" (Matt. 27:46).

Surely the physical pain paled in comparison to the agony of two broken hearts. As I consider it, I am again overwhelmed at my unworthiness for such a cost. No, I do not believe the Father simply responded to Hagar as God, although that would have been enough. He responded as a divine parent with the power to intervene. Too tender was His heart to stand by passively.

God knows the intense pain of intense love. If you are a parent, you have already experienced fear, vulnerability, and pain. And the Father hasn't missed one second of your parenthood. If you have a child who is rejected by his peers, God knows how you feel. If you have a child who is not beautiful to look upon, He knows how you feel (see Isa. 53). If you have a child who has been betrayed by her friends, He knows how you feel. If you have a child who has begged you to "fix" something you could not fix, He knows how you feel. If you have a child who is suffering, He knows how you feel. If you have a child who is dying, He knows how you feel. If you have buried a child, He knows how you feel. He's been there, too. However, there is one big difference. He could have changed every bit of it. But He didn't. For you and me.

If you're a hurting parent right now, allow God to open your eyes as He did Hagar's so long ago. Let Him refresh you at the well of the Living Water. Like Hagar, your child may be totally restored to you. Or, like the trusting, but brokenhearted mother named Mary, you may have to let your child go. God loved no mother on earth more than the one He chose for His Son. Yet she was unable to hold Him in her grasp for as long as she wished. You who are richly loved, do not give up. Once you've had a true glimpse of God's tender heart, you will begin to understand that if the Savior says "no" to a crying parent, it is because He's saying "yes" to eternal kingdom profit.

> **Conclude today's study by reading Isaiah 12:2-6. In the space below write a letter to the Father. Tell Him how you feel about His kindness and unfailing goodness.**

_____

_____

_____

_____

_____

One last assignment for today. You probably know a mother who needs some encouragement. Right this moment, give her a call, send a thoughtful card, or drop by with a favorite snack and chat. Let her know you're praying for her—then do it. She'll be blessed and so will you!

Day 2

Cords of Kindness

On day 1, God revealed glimpses of His tender heart through His compassion and commitment to Hagar and Ishmael. Remember, Ishmael was not the child of promise, yet God's heart was so tendered by his situation that He raised him up to be a mighty nation. If God shed such grace on Ishmael, how tender would His heart be to His own holy nation, the people chosen for His name? Today we will delve further into the *chrestotes* of God, touching His tender heart and His nurturing Spirit. The four segments of Scripture in today's study will lead a willing traveler straight to the heart of God.

1. READ DEUTERONOMY 7:6-9 AND RESPOND.

> **Which of the following represent reasons God chose Israel?**
> ❑ Because they were a mighty nation.
> ❑ Because they were the fewest of all peoples.
> ☑ Because they were a holy people.
> ❑ Because they were His treasured possession.

How does God want you to respond to what He showed you today?

_____

_____

_____

_____

_____

_____

Today's Treasure:

"I led them with cords of human kindness, with ties of love" (Hos. 11:4).

131

Fill in the blanks. "The Lord your God has ___chosen___

you out of all the peoples on the face of the earth to be his

___possession___, his ___People___" (7:6).

2. READ ISAIAH 49:14-16 AND RESPOND.

✎ Have you ever felt forgotten by God? ☑ Yes ☐ No If so, when?

_____

_____

Who will forget her child before God will forget His?

_____ nursing mom. _____

✎ What assurance do we have that God will never forget His children? (v. 16).

___has inscribed us on his palms. of His Hands___

The Hebrew word for *engraved* is *chaqaq* and it means "to hack."[3] This Hebrew word was used for the act of cutting or chiseling laws into tablets of stone, yet I believe God applies it to the cutting of His children's names into the very palms of His hands, arguably the most tender place on the human body. This passage paints a wonderful picture—the engraving of the names of the redeemed in the broken body of Jesus. The names carved into the hand of God were written by the precious blood of His Son! One thing is certain: a nursing mother will forget her child before God will forget His own, because their names are never any farther than the tender palm of His hand.

3. READ ZEPHANIAH 3:14-17 AND RESPOND.

Fill in the blanks from verse 17. "The Lord your God is

___in___ you, he is ___a warrior___ to save. He will

take great ___joy___ in you, he will ___exult___ you

with his ___love___, he will ___rejoice___ over

you with ___shouts of joy___."

The context which leads to this precious portrait of God's tender heart and nurturing Spirit is the calming of a child's fears by his father (see vv. 15-16).

These verses beautifully illustrate that blessed moment in which God's throne becomes a rocking chair and He pulls His fretting, fearful child into His arms and says, "It's OK, I'm right here."

What does it mean to be "quieted with His love"? If you are a mother, you have quieted a child with your love countless times, rocking the child, and all the while whispering, "Sh-h-h-h. Mommy loves you." How does God "rejoice over" His children "with singing"? This is the precious picture of a parent savoring the moment as His child's frame finally rests in His arms to the tender melody of a lullaby.

Oh, Beloved, do you know God as parent? Do you allow Him to nurture you? Do you take Him your fears and your fretting and allow Him to hold you in His arms and cover you with His love?

When we first adopted Michael, he had just turned four. Almost immediately we noticed two unusual things about him. First, his body was out of proportion. The child was absolutely darling, but as I undressed him the first night to get ready for bed, I could see that his head, hands and feet were much too big for his tiny torso. This observation, as well as the fact that he was just plain sickly, motivated me to schedule a complete physical for Michael with our doctor.

At the doctor's office, he came to me privately and said that Michael had at the least been emotionally neglected, if not abused. The shape of his body testified that adequate affection had been withheld from him. I was appalled!

The second unusual thing I noticed about Michael was that he never cried. Even as blood streamed down his knee from a fall, he would stand as stiffly as a board, clinching his fists. His former guardians had bought into the theory that to touch a crying child would only spoil him; therefore Michael had learned to totally isolate himself when in pain. I could not bear to watch his response when he was hurt, so I began to hold his body as tightly as I could every time he stiffened, and I would say, "Cry, sweet baby, just CRY!"

In spite of all the mistakes we made, within 18 months the doctor confirmed that Michael's body was in perfect proportion. Not only had he learned to cry, he had also learned to laugh! Why? Because of the wonder working power of God, our Healer.

When we received Michael, we believed our adoption to be permanent. But after seven years he returned to his birth mother who now is better able to care for him. We will always love him as our own, but we had to let go and let God love him apart from us.

We must learn to let God love us as His children. Dear Ones, let Him soothe your feelings when they're hurt, your fears when they're raging, and your spiritual knees when they're bleeding. You will never grow in Christ to maturity and wholeness until you do. You can't know Him only as the Sovereign Judge. You must also know Him as the nurturing parent—or your growth will be stunted.

Let's conclude today's study with a last look at the tender heart of the Father.

4. READ HOSEA 11:1-4 AND RESPOND.

Do the first two verses sound vaguely familiar? I've had a child or two respond to me exactly the same way! Isn't it good to know that rebellious children are not necessarily the result of poor parenting? I'm certain we all know some godly parents who have walked through crisis after crisis with rebellious children.

Look carefully at verses 3-4. Fill in the blanks. "It was I who taught

Ephraim to _walk_ **, taking them by the** _arm_ **;**

but they did not _know_ **it was I who** _healed_ **them."**

Can you imagine what the home movies might have been like of Father God teaching His children to walk? How does Scripture say He led them?

by arm

How were these cords tied? _bonds of love._

Imagine God teaching His children to walk by gently stretching a cord between Himself and them, then tying the cords securely at each end so the children will not get lost. The cords were kindness—the tenderness of God's heart—and the ties which bound them together were His love. Don't miss an important part of this Scripture: the *chrestotes* or nurturing of God was their healing, whether or not they recognized it as such!

Reread the end of verse 4. There aren't many things sweeter than watching a Daddy feed his baby. This bonding experience is portrayed so typically as God "bent down to feed" His children. Just picture it! Can you almost see Him opening His mouth as He tries to get the child to open hers—just like we do?

Complete Psalm 81:10 below:
"I am the LORD your God, who brought you up out of Egypt.

Open _wide_ **your** _mouth_ **and I will** _fill_ **it."**

Oh, Beloved, can you relate to Him as Father? Scripture is filled with evidences of God's *chrestotes,* of His tender heart and His nurturing Spirit. Are you wondering if these marvelous Old Testament passages can be applied to you?

What does 1 John 3:1 reveal to you about our Father's love for us?

We are called Children of God.

Do you allow God to nurture you? Do you understand that He takes great delight in caring for you? Can you relate more readily to His sovereignty and severity than His tender mercies? Were you more comfortable with the study on day 1 in which He related to us as heavenly parent to earthly parent than you were with today's study in which He related to us as heavenly parent to earthly child? I challenge you to grasp this truth: we will never be successful as parents to our children until we are successful at being children to our Heavenly

How does God want you to respond to what He showed you today?

_____

_____

_____

_____

_____

_____

_____

Father. Developing a healthy parent/child relationship with God can be difficult, but an unwillingness to even try will result in poor spiritual health and disproportionate growth.

Perhaps you grew up with a harsh, unloving parent or a parent you could not trust. Few of us have experienced the kind of parent God wants to be to us. How do you begin? Next time you are hurting, or fearful or anxious, don't call your husband or a friend, and don't take it out on your children—go to the Father! Immediately! Tell Him how you feel and all that has happened. Ask Him to quiet you with His love. Be bold—and ask Him to reveal His love in some obvious way. Ask Him to minister to you and HE WILL. Try a little tenderness. As it was with our Michael, it may be just what the doctor ordered!

Day 3

A Tenderhearted Savior

Today we will take a peek into the tender heart of Christ—a heart He no doubt inherited from His Father. Not coincidentally, this Son who has been nurtured with love and tenderness also knows how to administer love and tenderness. He invites us through His Word to behold the *chrestotes* of Christ in His tenderness toward children, His tenderness toward Israel, and His tenderness toward the individual.

PART ONE: CHRIST'S TENDERNESS TOWARD CHILDREN

1. **Read Matthew 18:1-9.**
   What question provoked Christ's call for the child?

   Who is the greatest in Heaven?

   How did Christ illustrate the "greatest in the kingdom"? _____

   unless you become like a child.

   Reread verse 5, then compare it to Mark 9:36-37. What additional information does Mark 9:36 give us regarding Christ and the child?

   But, Him who sent me.

Christ must have had such a gentle touch. He could just as easily have healed by thought alone, but so often He chose to touch. For example, He touched the blind man that he might see (see Matt. 20:32-34). He touched the dead child that she might live (see Mark 5:41). Christ "demonstrated" *agape*: "He took her by the hand."

~Today's Treasure:

"Let the little children come to me, and do not hinder them, for the kingdom of heaven belongs to such as these" (Matt. 19:14).

↪ Is it possible to cause another person to sin? (Matt. 18:6).
☑ Yes ☐ No

What did Christ say about the one who causes a child to sin?

"heavy millstone" hung around his neck

Beloved, we must take responsibility for every sin we commit; but Scripture proves that we can be weaker in some areas of sin because of the influence of others. Reread verses 7-9. What is Christ's warning? Get rid of the things in your life which are causing you to sin BEFORE you take a chance on causing someone to stumble!

2. **Read Matthew 19:13-15.**
   Why were the children brought to Christ? (Choose two.)
   ☑ for Jesus to bless them
   ☑ for Jesus to lay His hands on them
   ☐ for Jesus to heal them
   ☐ for Jesus to pray for them

   Who rebuked those who brought children? _disciples_

   Why do you suppose Christ responded to the disciples as He did?
   ☐ He was tired and grumpy from a long day.
   ☑ He saw an opportunity to teach them about the kingdom.
   ☐ He loved the children and desired to bless them.

As I see the tenderness Christ held in His heart for children, I wonder sometimes if He did not consider time spent with children as the closest thing to heaven on earth! The second response is true, but I believe the third hits closer to Jesus' motive. I also believe this verse substantiates what most of us have believed by faith: children who die go to heaven. If He received them so readily while on this earth because of the tenderness of His heart, how could He possibly bar their entrance to the very kingdom He described them as representing? To do so would be completely contrary to His character.

PART TWO: THE TENDERNESS OF CHRIST TOWARD ISRAEL

Read Matthew 23:37-39.
Christ longed to respond to His people from the tender heart beating within Him. Have you wondered about the image of Christ with "wings"?

   Read Psalm 91:1-4. Choose the word that best describes the purpose of wings in the passage.
   ☑ protection ☐ reward ☐ comfort ☐ correction

Christ desperately wanted to protect Israel from future pain, persecution, and separation. He had a place for them right in the warmth of His side, but they refused His tender heart and nurturing Spirit. In turn, they forfeited His protection. Jesus desires to respond to us out of that same tenderness of heart, to hold us close, and to shield us from harm. How sad that we, too, often refuse.

PART THREE: THE TENDERNESS OF CHRIST TOWARD THE INDIVIDUAL

Wouldn't you love to know every detail of Christ's 40-day trek on this earth between His resurrection and His ascension? I would! This must have been a period of time designated for priorities! Can you imagine attempting to prepare this group of people for your absence?

Read 1 Corinthians 15:1-8. To whom did Christ appear during those 40 days?

Cephas & then, 12 disc. 500 at one time
James then, all the apostles & Paul.

Forty days—just short of six weeks! Those transitional days must have whizzed by. This was Jesus' last chance to look a few people straight in the face and say, "I'm alive." Search the Scriptures with me and behold the tender heart of Christ as He handpicked the several people to whom He would appear.

1. **Read John 20:1-18.**

   What did Mary see when she looked into the tomb? _2 angels._

   Who first asked her why she was crying? _angels._

   Who asked her the second time why she was crying? _Jesus._
   (The Greek word translated *crying* in verse 15 means "wailing," which is a loud expression of grief.)

   Who did she think Christ was? _gardener_
   I can almost hear Him say, "No, my Father is the Gardener, I am the Vine."

   How did Christ identify Himself to her?
   ❑ **He asked: "Don't you recognize me?"**
   ☑ **He called her by name.**
   ❑ **He showed her the nail prints.**

   What did she say to the disciples after she took them the news?
   I have seen the Lord vs. 18

Consider with me some possible reasons why Christ allowed Mary to be the very first person to see Him as the resurrected Lord.

What do the following Scriptures tell you about Mary Magdalene:

Mark 16:9 _Had been possessed by 7 demons_

Mark 15:40-41 _A "groupee"_

Mark 15:46-47 _At his side - tomb._

Mary Magdalene's heart was broken. She owed Jesus her life and her sanity. She had experienced life firsthand in the web of the evil one. Yet, she had also experienced true deliverance. After being set free from her sin, Mary devoted her entire existence to her Deliverer. She did not deny herself the pain of watching Him die, nor did she leave Him until the stone was rolled into place. Suddenly He was gone. Unlike many others, Mary did not lament lost opportunities, nor a seemingly forfeited kingdom. Her grief was simple. She missed Jesus. So, why did He appear first to her? I believe the answer is because Mary's Lord, and ours, is tenderhearted.

2. Read John 20:24-31.
We don't know where Thomas was when Jesus appeared to the other disciples. We only know he missed the appearance. His emphatic announcement to his fellow disciples forever marked the twin as "Doubting Thomas."

What did Thomas need before he would believe?
☑ **eyewitness testimony**   ☐ **to see Jesus for himself**

How soon did Christ appear to Thomas? _8 days_

What were Christ's words to Thomas? _Peace be w/you._
Reach & see. vs 27.

How did Thomas respond?
☐ **He touched Jesus to be sure.**
☑ **He cried out "My Lord and my God!"**

As soon as Christ entered the room, He immediately confronted Thomas with the truth. Obviously, this appearance was made especially for one man. Let's gather a little background on that man.

What was Thomas ready to do with Christ? (John 11:14-16).
Lazarus.

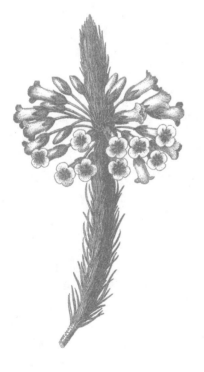

What a strange mix of loyalty and pessimism. Oddly enough, Thomas never doubted Christ would die. He doubted the most important part of all—that He would rise from the dead and live again! Christ had lived and ministered with these men for nearly three years. In John 17:6-19, He professed His deep love for them to His Father. Why did Christ want to reveal Himself to Thomas? Because our Savior is tenderhearted.

3. Reread 1 Corinthians 15:7.
Christ appeared to James. According to verse 5, this James was not one of the twelve who had seen Him. This James is the one mentioned in Matthew 13:55.

Who was he? _____ brother. _____

What does John 7:1-5 tell you about Jesus' brothers?
☑ **They did not believe in Jesus.**
❏ **They feared for Jesus' safety.**
❏ **They hoped Jesus would show Himself as the Messiah.**

Every time Scripture mentions the half brothers of Christ, they appear in the same order: James, Joseph, Simon, and Judas. The Bible usually lists names of children in their birth order. Most likely James was the son of Mary born next after Jesus. If Jesus was like most big brothers, James was His pride and joy.

Christ probably taught James how to play games, how to fish, how to climb trees, and how to run races. Jesus surely rescued James from many near misses, and late at night giggled with him under the same covers.

The young men grew to adulthood and were separated by unbelief. Jesus was forsaken by all His brothers, but I wonder if the loss of this James hurt most.

"Then he appeared to James." What might that conversation have been like? The tears well in my eyes at the thought: "My brother, my LORD!" To what did this intimate encounter lead? Read Acts 1:12-14 and see for yourself.

More to the point may be to ask: why did Christ appear to His brother? Because He is tenderhearted and He loved him.

Do you have lost family members? Jesus' experience with his brothers shows that He knows just how you feel. His heart is tender to yours as well.

Christ appeared to those who needed Him most: a mourner, a doubter, and a mocker. And out of His tenderness came belief. We've considered several examples of Christ's tender heart.

    ❧ Which example of Christ's heart reminded you most of a way He has dealt with you in the past and why?

_____

_____

_____

_____

How does God want you to respond to what He showed you today?

_____

_____

_____

_____

_____

_____

_____

Day 4

His Goodness

On days 1 and 2, we studied the *chrestotes* or tender heart and nurturing Spirit of God toward Hagar and Ishmael, the nation of Israel, and believers in Christ. On day 3 we witnessed the *chrestotes* of Christ and His tenderness toward children, His nation, and some individuals. Today we are going to examine the next quality of the fruit of the Spirit. Goodness is best understood when considered, compared, and contrasted with the quality of kindness. "But the fruit of the Spirit is love, joy, peace, patience, kindness, goodness" (Gal. 5:22).

The Greek word for *goodness* is *agathosune*. It means "benevolent" and "active goodness." *Agathosune* "is more than *chrestotes*, [which is] gentleness, kindness, a mellowing of character. It is character energized, expressing itself in...benevolence, active good. There is more activity in *agathosune* than in *chrestotes*. *Agathosune* does not spare sharpness and rebuke to cause good in others. A person may display his *agathosune*, his zeal for goodness and truth, in rebuking, correcting, or chastising."[4] Already you may see some obvious differences, but Scripture will prove to us that the two words share a strong relationship.

In Matthew 10:16, Jesus told the disciples: "I am sending you out like sheep among wolves. Therefore be as shrewd as snakes and as innocent as doves." Day 1 introduced the quality of kindness as having the "harmlessness of the dove." Today we will begin to see that a large part of goodness is being "shrewd as snakes."

The qualities of kindness and goodness differ in their employment in the believer but they "pair up" to make us both shrewd and innocent. During the next two days, we will carefully consider selections of Scripture which emphasize both the fifth and sixth qualities of the fruit of the Spirit: kindness and goodness.

Read Ephesians 2:1-10 and mark the following true or false.
We were dead in our transgressions and sins...
_T_ **when we were gratifying the cravings of our sinful nature and following its desires and thoughts.**
_F_ **when we followed the ways of this world and of the ruler of the kingdom of the air.**
_T_ **when we were by nature objects of wrath.**

Who is at work in those who are disobedient? _Satan_

Being disobedient means (v. 3): _lusting_

the cravings of our sinful nature and following its _desires of the flesh_

and _of the mind_ .

When did God make us alive with Christ? (vv. 4-5).

Made us alive tog. w/ Christ

Why did God make us alive with Christ?

His great love

What is our present position? (v. 6).
❑ forgiven of our sins and destined for heaven
❑ chosen to be accepted in the beloved
☑ seated with Him in the heavenly realms

How does God "show the incomparable riches of his grace"? (v. 7).

In kindness towards us in J.C.

vs. 10 **What kind of works were we created to do?** _Good. "His workmanship"_

In this Scripture, God speaks vividly of kindness, *chrestotes*, and goodness, *agathosune*. He clearly instructs us that His *chrestotes* to us is the vehicle by which He shows us the "incomparable riches of his grace." In other words, God's tenderness toward us—the soft spot in His heart for us—and His desire to care for us and nurture us are all ways He expresses His grace to us.

Why is grace required? Reread verse 5. "We were dead in transgressions!" How could He have had *chrestotes* toward us when we had done nothing whatsoever to endear us to Him? Reread verse 7. Because of Christ Jesus! Through the death of His Son, the payment for all sin was satisfied; therefore, God's heart toward us was ushered from a state of wrath to a state of tenderness.

We have considered our purpose for remaining on this earth after salvation. Verses 8-10 express our purpose. Notice the repetition of the word "works" in verses 9 and 10. He's driving home this crucial point: we have not been saved by our works—we have been saved for His works!

What Kind of Works Have We Been Saved to Do?

We've been saved to do GOOD works. This is the word we are studying today—the sixth quality of the fruit of the Spirit. Reread the definition for *agathosune* on the previous page. We have not only been called to the attitude or disposition of *chrestotes* or kindness, but also to energize that character into acts of good or acts of beneficence. Specifically, God is saying, "You're here to do some good—kingdom good on carnal ground." We've been saved to fulfill an assignment God issued in advance.

What is the common denominator between Romans 8:29-30 and

Ephesians 1:5,11? _by grace / circumcision. "Predestined/ Chosen/ Called"_

First Peter 2:9 tells us that we are a "chosen generation" (KJV). All four of the above Scriptures tell us that in Christ we have been predestined. Ephesians 2:10

tells us that our works were assigned in advance. In combination, all these verses tell us that we are not extra baggage. God did not save us so that we could look attractive on Sundays. He saved us and left us here because He has work to do—very specific work. He has a mission to accomplish for kingdom gain in every generation—all planned in advance and perfectly timed.

In His sovereignty, God has chosen to do His work through us. If we miss our ministry, we will miss our entire purpose in remaining here.

In light of an increased awareness of your purpose, read Matthew 25:14-30 and ask for a fresh understanding of God's perfect Word.

Who has gone on a "journey" and entrusted His property to us?

_____Jesus_____

Compare Matthew 25:15 to 1 Corinthians 12:7-11. What is the same in both situations? What is different?

Same	Different
Master	
spiritual gifts	actual abilities
	Spirit/as He wills.

Did you note that in both passages the Master is the Giver? However, in the parable, the servants received gifts "according to their abilities." In Paul's explanation of spiritual gifts, we receive the opposite. We receive gifts not based on our abilities, but abilities based on the common good—just as the Master chooses.

If we had only the parable, we might be tempted to say, "Look at all that God has entrusted to me; I must have great abilities." But once we understand spiritual gifts, we say instead, "Look at all God wants to do to benefit those He loves and to glorify Himself."

What will bring the words, "Well done, good and faithful servant" from the Master?
❑ great accomplishment   ☑ performance
❑ faithfulness   ☑ results

Look carefully at Matthew 25:21,23. What are the two results of fulfilling our purpose?

1. _praise - in charge of ..._

2. _joy_

What could be greater than a word of commendation and the trust of increased responsibility?

Do you consider Matthew 25:29 to be fair? ❑ Yes ❑ No
Why or why not?

I'm for the underdog / I think I
understand the lesson though.

One day I will see my Savior face to face, and in His hands He will hold the assignments which were prepared for me in advance. Oh, how I pray I will hear Him say that I completed each one in the course of my lifetime. Don't you desire the same?

This week take a good look at the faces around you—at the rich and poor, miserable and happy, those who drive next to you, the neighbor getting her mail, other parents at your child's ball game, the victims on the news, the criminals on the news. Look at their faces. This is your generation. Your turn. We've said it before, but can we say it enough? We've been called to _agathosune_...to do a little good. Or, a lot of good. How much we do depends on our obedience.

∽ What are we to guard and how are we to guard it? (2 Tim. 1:14).

Thru the S. — treasures entrusted
to you.

∽ Are you doing too many things to do any ONE thing well for Christ? ❑ Yes ❑ No If so, what can you do about it?

In what ways can you "guard the trust" God has given you personally?

Pray, Study

_D a y 5_

No Pain, No Gain

Today we conclude our study of _chrestotes_ and _agathosune_, kindness and goodness, which are qualities of the fruit of the Spirit. Let's begin today's study by reading Titus 3:1-8. Look for forms of the words _kindness_ and _goodness;_ then answer the following questions:

How does God want you to respond to what He showed you today?

_____

_____

_____

_____

_____

_____

_____

❧Today's Treasure:

"Those who have trusted in God may be careful to devote themselves to doing what is good. These things are excellent and profitable for everyone" (Titus 3:8).

Check each of the following terms that describe the nature of the unredeemed human according to verse 3.

- ☑ disobedient
- ☐ loving
- ☐ full of wisdom
- ☑ malice and envy
- ☑ deceived
- ☑ enslaved by all kinds of passions
- ☐ foolish
- ☑ hated and hating one another

What happened when the KINDNESS and LOVE of God appeared?
- ☐ We responded to His love by changing our behaviors.
- ☑ He saved us because of His mercy.
- ☐ We were transformed into His likeness.

WHO did He generously pour out on us? _H.S - thru O.Savior_

Because of God's kindness and love to us, what must we be careful to devote ourselves to doing? (v. 8).

Engage in good deeds.

Notice in Paul's letter to Titus, he actually defined the word *good*. Fill in the following blanks taken from verse 8:

"These things" (that are good) "are ___good___ and

___profitable___ for everyone."

Take a moment to look back at a very important part of the definition of GOODNESS as a quality of the fruit of the Spirit. (See the beginning of day 4.) Fill in the following blanks:

"*Agathosune* does not spare ___sharpness___ and ___rebuke___ to cause good in others. A person may display his *agathosune*, his

zeal for goodness and truth, in ___rebuking___, ___correcting___,

or ___chastising___."

Please understand this important fact: that which is good, profitable, or beneficial is not always fun, easy, or pleasant. The purpose of this quality of the fruit of the Spirit is to do or bring that which is most beneficial, whether or not it is that which is most popular. *Agathosune* means going for the good.

A perfect example of *agathosune* is found in 2 Timothy 3:16-17. What four methods does the Word of God use to equip us for GOOD work? (v. 16).

1. _profitable for teaching_   3. _correction_

2. _reproof_   4. _training in righteousness_

Does God's Word always tell you what you want to hear? Are His words to you always pleasant? Do you always welcome them with open ears? Surely not. Yet, have you ever found His Word to be misleading? Has He ever tried to harm you with His Word? Certainly not.

God's Word is always for the purpose of bringing good. Just like God, His Word prioritizes GOODNESS over GLADNESS because God knows that goodness ultimately brings gladness!

Through the quality of *agathosune*, we are to adopt the same objective: the good of the kingdom, or what I call "kingdom profit." *Agathosune* is always profitable. Sometimes it is pleasant and profitable; other times it is painful and profitable. But the emphasis on the profit will always outweigh the importance of the pain or pleasure.

Thankfully, the Word is replete with examples of the profitable as also pleasant. Many of Jesus' sermons, virtually all of His miracles, His healings, or the times He raised the dead are examples of actions both pleasant and profitable. However, for the sake of understanding the sixth quality of the fruit of the Spirit, we must consider examples when the profitable was the painful. Each of the following events in Scripture qualifies as a "good work."

Read each of the following examples, and describe the profit ultimately proceeding from the painful events and circumstances.

Matthew 21:12-13 _Stopped the temple from being "Robbers Den" & brought it back to "House of Prayer"_

2 Corinthians 12:7-10 _for when I am weak - I am strong! Pg. 1121_

Acts 8:1-4 _Saul's behavior seemly unrulely -_

Acts 18:5-6 _Paul began testifying to the Jews, that Jesus was the Christ - They resisted & he shook his garments & went to the Gentiles_

Matthew 27:50-51 _Jesus yielded his spirit - but was truely revealed as the Son of God - earthquakes, tombs openned._

No, the good is not always the easy. At times we may be called upon to deliver a painful exhortation or confrontational rebuke. At such moments Satan can have a field day if we do not deal carefully with this matter of *agathosune* or good works. We cannot excuse sharp tongues and self-righteous attitudes in the name of good works.

Remember, love, joy, peace, patience, and kindness precede goodness! God has a very good reason for so often coupling kindness and goodness in His

Word. Kindness provides the safeguard for misguided "goodness." You see, *chrestotes* or kindness, is all about the disposition. He wants us to have a disposition of "tenderheartedness" and a Spirit eager to nurture.

> ✎ **How did Paul's actions demonstrate *chrestotes*? (1 Thess. 2:6-8).**

_____

_____

Sometimes people are just not willing to receive and respond to *chrestotes*. The people of Christ's day demonstrated the reality of such resistance when He said, "O, Jerusalem, Jerusalem… how often I have longed to gather your children together, as a hen gathers her chicks under her wings" (Matt. 23:37). Sometimes the pain of confrontation is necessary to bring profit.

This duel role of kindness and confrontation need not be confusing. If you are a mother, surely you are tenderhearted toward your child. Your disposition as a mother is tenderness, but sometimes your child will not respond favorably to tender guidance. On those occasions, you may find that you must activate profit through pain! Thus, a few hard words or a brisk swat on the behind may be in order! What keeps the normal mother from "abusing" her unruly child? Her disposition of tenderness toward that child. A tender heart of love! Do you see it now? The disposition of kindness safeguards the dispensing of *goodness!*

In this concept we see a major reason why God only entrusts the fruit of the Spirit to those filled with the Spirit. You must be yielded to God to be a proper vessel of confrontational goodness. Self cannot be involved because self must be crucified for the Spirit to be freed in you; therefore, goodness is never a personal issue, nor a personal platform, nor for personal gain. It is never the means by which we take up for ourselves or pamper our opinions. Remember, good works are always appointed, never assumed! Oh, Beloved, I pray we have all learned today that *agathosune*, or a zeal for the good, is a trust. And we cannot be trusted to do good works until the Word of God does its good work in us. If we cannot accept the teaching, rebuking, correcting, and training of God's Word in our own lives, then we cannot be vessels of teaching, rebuking, correcting, and training in other lives. Oh, God, help us to know the difference.

> ✎ **Can you think of a time when you were either the object of kindness and goodness through a loving rebuke or the vessel of such kindness and goodness to another?** ❏ Yes ❏ No
> **If so, did good come of the confrontation?** ❏ Yes ❏ No

If you are discussing this question in a small group, be very careful not to share confidences about another person.

How does God want you to respond to what He showed you today?

_____

_____

_____

_____

_____

_____

_____

_____

---

[1]John F. MacArthur, *The MacArthur New Testament Commentary Galatians* (Chicago: The Moody Bible Institute, 1987), 168.
[2]Spiros Zodhiates et al., eds., *The Complete Word Study Dictionary: New Testament* (Chattanooga, TN: AMG Publishers, 1992), 1482.
[3]James Strong, from the *Hebrew and Chaldee Dictionary* of *The Exhaustive Concordance of the Bible*, (Nashville: Holman Bible Publishers, n.d.), 43.
[4]Spiros Zodhiates et al., eds., *The Complete Word Study Dictionary: New Testament* (Chattanooga, TN: AMG Publishers, 1992), 63.

W e e k   8

Keep Believin'

Faith. Many people struggle continually to have more of it. They groan and they strain like a woman in labor. They think: *If only I had more faith my prayers could be answered.* Have you ever considered the relationship between *faith* and *faithfulness*? Faith is not an action; it is a response. If we strive to have faith, we may be miserably disappointed. But if we learn to trust in His faithfulness, we of all persons may be most blessed. Come along on a journey to faithfulness. As we revel in His faithfulness we will grow and develop in our own.

This week we explore faithfulness as a characteristic of the fruit the Spirit grows in our lives. Because our God is infinitely faithful, and because He lives in us, we too can be characterized by faithfulness.

Principal Questions
Day 1: In Moses' farewell address, what words did he use to describe God's faithfulness?
Day 2: What does Hebrews 11:6 specify that we are to believe?
Day 3: What did God tell Paul through an angel in Acts 27:23-24?
Day 4: Which piece of the whole armor of God does faith represent?
Day 5: What is Jesus Christ called in Revelation 1:5?

Faith That Abounds

Today's Treasure:

"The Lord is faithful to all his promises and loving toward all he has made" (Ps. 145:13).

This week we will explore the seventh quality of the fruit of the Spirit: FAITHFULNESS. Really look at the word *faithfulness*.

What words, phrases, or biblical names come to mind as you consider the word *faithfulness*?

_____

_____

The Greek word for *faithfulness* is *pistis* and it means "firm persuasion, conviction, belief in the truth, veracity, reality or faithfulness."[1] It carries the idea of giving someone credit. An English synonym of the word, oddly enough, is reality. Think about it: you focus your deepest faithfulness on those things that are most "real" to you. Doesn't that make sense?

In a nutshell, faithfulness is believing the reality of a sovereign God. Keep in mind that the seventh quality of the fruit of the Spirit does not describe the faith through which we are saved. Yes, we believe in God and on Christ. But, beyond believing in Him and on Him, do we simply believe Him? in the day-to-day demands of living? in the home? in the workplace? in the crisis? Do we believe who He is and what He says?

I want so desperately to be faithful. I believe you do too; but we will never believe God until we allow ourselves to discover that He is believable!

Today we uncover a very important truth: the degree of our faithfulness is the direct result of our regard for God's faithfulness. Let me explain. When the words *faithful* or *faithfulness* describe God in the Old Testament, they are the Hebrew words *Aman* or its derivative *Emunah*. These two words carry the ideas of firmness, steadiness, sureness, steadfastness, faithfulness, trust, honesty, safety, and certainty. So what does faithfulness mean when it is applied to God? The faithfulness of God is His believability! What does faithfulness mean when it is applied to us? Look back at the definition of *pistis*. The faithfulness of the believer is his belief in God's believability!

Do you see the crucial relationship? Faithfulness is resting in His certainty, being persuaded by His honesty, trusting in His reality, being won over by His veracity…being sure that He's sure and believing He's worth believing.

Does God claim to be believable? What does God's statement that He is "abounding in love and faithfulness" mean to you? (Ex. 34:1-6).

_____

_____

148

The Hebrew word for *abounding* is *rab*. It means "abundant...exceedingly, full, great."[2] It refers to both quantity and quality! Therefore, the faithfulness you are about to discover in God is not applied to His children in modest portions, but is "exceeding abundantly above all that we ask or think" (Eph. 3:20, KJV)! Keeping such liberality in mind, search the following Scriptures. Note how each defines or describes God's faithfulness.

To how many generations does God promise to remain faithful? (Deut. 7:9).
❑ 7   ❑ 12   ❑ 10   ❑ 100   ❑ 1,000

✍ **In Moses' farewell address, what words did he use to describe the faithfulness of God? (Deut. 32:3-4).**

_____

_____

Which of the following are areas of God's faithfulness? (Ps. 33:4).
❑ His thoughts   ❑ His words
❑ His actions   ❑ His plans

Read Psalm 111:7-8. In what area of your life do you most need God's trustworthiness?

_____

_____

How long will the Lord's faithfulness last? (Ps. 117:2).
❑ all day   ❑ forever   ❑ many years

✍ **Read Lamentations 3:22-23. How has God shown compassion to you recently?**

_____

_____

Read Psalm 145:13. Which phrase in the verse means the most to you at this time in your life? Why?

_____

_____

God has told us that He is faithful based on three major characteristics. He is certain, true, and enduring, as is everything about Him. For instance, His Word exists, His Word is truth, and His Word will last forever. God could not be faithful without certainty…for He must be dependable. God could not be faithful without truth…for He must be trustworthy. And God could not be faithful without endurance…for He must persist.

Let's take a look at another important Scripture passage which describes perhaps the pinnacle of God's faithfulness. God employed the Hebrew word *aman* in these passages as well, but it is translated into a different English word.

Read Isaiah 22:20-24. See if you can guess which word is translated from the Hebrew word *aman* meaning "faithful."

_____

This fascinating passage combines many images that Scripture uses to describe the Messiah. God's immediate reference in these passages is to Eliakim, God's replacement for the one who had been in charge of King Hezekiah's household. I believe that His ultimate and prophetic reference had to be to His one and only Son, Jesus Christ. You see, Eliakim's authority would end, but God will grant to Another the everlasting fulfillment of these promises. Note the following parallels between Isaiah 22:20-24 and other messianic passages.

1. **The name *Eliakim* means "God will raise up."**
    Read Jeremiah 23:5-6. Who will God ultimately "raise up"? (Check one or more.)
    ❑ a "righteous branch" from the lineage of David
    ❑ one who will save Judah and Israel
    ❑ one who will be called "the Lord Our Righteousness"

2. **"I will clothe him with your robe and fasten your sash around him and hand your authority over to him." (Isa. 22:21).**
    How was the Son of man dressed? (Rev. 1:13).

    _____

    What has been given to Jesus? (Matt. 28:18).

    _____

3. **"He will be a father to those who live in Jerusalem and to the house of Judah" (Isa. 22:21).**
    The Messiah will be called, "everlasting _____" (Isa. 9:6).

4. **"I will place on his shoulder the key to the house of David" (Isa. 22:22).**

    Where will the "government" be? (Isa. 9:6).
    ❑ Washington   ❑ Tel Aviv   ❑ on His shoulders

    Where will He reign? (Isa. 9:7). _____

    _____

5. "I will place on his shoulder the key to the house of David; what he opens no one can shut, and what he shuts no one can open." (Isa. 22:22).

   Compare Revelation 3:7 to Isaiah 22:22. In the verse printed above, circle the words John quoted from Isaiah.

6. "I will drive him like a peg into a firm place" (Isa. 22:23). The Hebrew word for *peg* is *yathed,* and it means "nail." Now read this portion of Isaiah 22:23, inserting the word *nail* instead of peg.

   What did God do with "written code, with its regulations, that was against us and that stood opposed to us"? (Col. 2:13-14).

   _____

Now you have reached the English word translated from the Hebrew word *aman*. It is the word *firm*. Did you guess it? Consider the meaning of this verse again from the standpoint of the Hebrew words: God drove him like a "nail" into a "faithful" place–a certain place, a true place, an enduring place. The verse points to that "place" where the sins of humankind were nailed once and for all–the cross of Calvary.

7. "He will be a seat of honor for the house of his father" (Isa. 22:23).

   What "seat of honor" will God give to His Son? (Luke 1:30-33).

   _____

8. "All the glory of his family will hang on him: its offspring and offshoots–

   all its lesser vessels" (Isa. 22:24).

   What "came" to Christ through us? (John 17:9-10).
   ❑ multitudes   ❑ suffering   ❑ glory   ❑ joy

   What does He give us in return? (John 17:22). _____

Beloved, conclude today's study by reading 2 Corinthians 1:18-22. Because God is faithful, He said yes to us in Christ. He is the culmination, the embodiment of God's inconceivable faithfulness! Jesus Christ is God's guarantee.

One last thing: why did He put His Holy Spirit in us? Do you see it? Remember the meaning of God's faithfulness? It is His guarantee! His "absolutely"! His "YES"! God expressed His faithfulness to us in Christ, and Christ expressed His faithfulness to us in the Holy Spirit. Only through His Spirit can we, in turn, express our faithfulness to Him.

"The fruit of the Spirit is love, joy, peace, patience, kindness, goodness, FAITHFULNESS."

How does God want you to respond to what He showed you today?

_____

_____

_____

_____

_____

_____

"And without faith it is impossible to please God, because anyone who comes to him must believe that he exists and that he rewards those who earnestly seek him" (Heb. 11:6).

In closing today, what is something God has graciously done in your life to show Himself "believable" to you?

_____

_____

Pray now thanking God for the ways He makes Himself "believable."

Day 2

Those Who Believe

We began by studying the faithfulness of God and the greatest revelation of His faithfulness in Christ. Scripture proclaims His abundant faithfulness to us. Can we take Him at His Word?

How do we know God is faithful? (Num. 23:19). Choose one or more.
❏ **God is not a man nor a son of man.**
❏ **God does not lie nor change His mind.**
❏ **God always acts on His spoken words.**
❏ **God makes promises that He cannot or will not fulfill.**

Today let's turn our attention toward the faithfulness of God's people. One chapter in Scripture, above all others, extols God's faithful servants.

Read Hebrews 11:1-39 thoroughly and list the names of every man or woman cited as heroes in the "Hall of Faith."

_____

_____

_____

Did you find all of these: Abel, Enoch, Noah, Abraham, Isaac, Jacob, Joseph, Moses' parents, Moses, the people, Rahab, Gideon, Barak, Samson, Jephthah, David, Samuel and the prophets, women, others?

What is the definition of _faith_? (Heb. 11:1). _____

_____

Every one of the faithful was honored by God for having believed what they could not see over what they could. Don't miss the fact that verse 3 testifies to the faithfulness of all who believe that "In the beginning God created." Look closely at the verse. God is saying that by His sovereign choice, there will never be conclusive evidence to prove to all humankind that He is the Creator. He has ordained that some questions remain unanswered to force the issue of faith.

Our study today centers on the faithfulness of one man whom God used to shed some much needed light on the practice of faith. In a few short verses, God tells us volumes about the life of a man named Enoch.

Read Hebrews 11:5-6 again. List every detail you find in the verses.

_____

_____

Just how significant is it that Enoch "pleased" God? Let's find out. Read Revelation 4:11. Look carefully at the words, "and by your will they were created." The Greek word translated as *will* is *thelema* which is "not to be conceived as a demand, but as an expression or inclination of pleasure towards that which is liked, that which pleases and creates joy....it signifies His gracious disposition toward something. Used to designate what God Himself does of His own good pleasure."[3] Perhaps, then, the *King James Version* says it best, "For thou hast created all things, and for thy pleasure they are and were created."

God created us to bring Him pleasure; therefore, when we read that Enoch "was commended as one who pleased God," we realize that He fulfilled his calling. It seems that Enoch had so enraptured God that God raptured him!

Are you still searching for your calling? Are you still wrestling with your purpose on this earth? Our calling is to please Him—to wake up every morning saying, "Yes, Lord," then live through the day to discover His questions. What was it about Enoch's life that pleased God so vividly?

Note every detail concerning Enoch in Genesis 5:18-24.

_____

_____

What points did you record? Was it that Enoch "walked with God; then he was no more, because God took him away"? The only evidence we can uncover in a life set apart as one who pleased God is that He walked with God. Now, remember, Enoch was listed in Hebrews 11 for his faith.

✍ Why does it take faith to walk with God? _____

_____

_____

Enoch walked with God. And that is what God calls each one of us to do. Second Corinthians 5:7 says, "For we walk by faith, not by sight" (KJV). What kind of faith motivates a person to "walk with God"? Look back at Hebrews 11:6. God seizes the opportunity to tell us something very important about faith while He is on the subject of Enoch.

This Scripture reveals that faith is an absolute necessity in the life that pleases God. If we are faithless, we are not fulfilling our calling to please Him. The moment the church was born, the Book of Acts referred to Christians as "believers." We were called believers long before we were called Christians. The term means "the faithful" or "those who believe God." If we refuse to keep believing God after salvation, He has no pleasure in us. Love for us? Yes. Pleasure in us? No.

> ✎ **What does Hebrews 11:6 specify that we are to believe? (Check all that apply.)**
> ❑ **that He will answer a specific prayer**
> ❑ **that He exists**
> ❑ **that He will conquer evil**
> ❑ **that He rewards those who earnestly seek Him.**

First the passage demands that we believe that God "exists" or that "He is." We must believe that God lives. Then it says we must believe that He is a rewarder of those who earnestly seek HIM.

Do you ever tire of riding the roller coaster of faith? of being up one day and down the next? of believing Him one minute and not the next? We can exercise our faith in God in one of two ways. One leaves us at the mercy of life's constant ups and downs. The other is the key to steadfast faith—the way off the roller coaster to begin walking with God and practicing a faith that can't be "greatly moved" (Ps. 62:2, KJV). Every believer falls into one of these two categories on the basis of her answer to one simple question: do you base your faith on what God does or who He is?

FAITH BASED ON WHAT GOD DOES

A person with this kind of faith lives by the unspoken motto: I believe God as long as He does what I ask. Her faith is built on how often and how well God answers prayers. Such "faith" depends on results and is fueled by sight.

Faith in what God does is your ticket to ride a roller coaster that ascends the hill during times when God's activity is obvious and then barrels down the hill the moment God seems inactive. The process never stops.

What is wrong with basing your faith on the obvious works of God? on what He's doing? Aren't His works wonderful according to His Word? Absolutely!

What does Isaiah 55:8-9 tell us about God's plans and actions?

_____

_____

What about those times when God does not work according to your requests or expectations? What about those times when He obviously allows your loved one with cancer to glorify Him through restoration in heaven and not on earth? What happens to your faith when a child dies? If your faith is based on what God is doing, you are in for the scariest ride of your life.

We will rarely be able to perceive God's actions, though they will always and ultimately be wonderful. They are beyond our earthly understanding. In the times when He seems inactive, He may be accomplishing more than ever! You see, a "what God does" faith is really not faith at all. Although it is focused on God, it is still born in the realm of the obvious, or that which is seen. The faith of the faithless says, "If God is not obvious, He is obviously not God."

FAITH BASED ON WHO GOD IS

Genuine faith walks steadfastly with God for the pleasure of His company not for His results. Enoch exercised this kind of faith–based on God's existence and His desire to be sought. God does not call upon us to seek His works. He calls upon us to seek His heart!

Why is faith based on who God is a faith not greatly moved? Because it focuses on a God not greatly moved! It increases our understanding of His ways. Prioritizing Who He is will help us more accurately interpret what He does.

We must prioritize who God is over what He does for another crucial reason.

How much does Jesus Christ change from day to day? (Heb. 13:8).

_____

You see, what God appears to be doing changes constantly from our perspective. He may heal one person while He calls the other home. He may be glorified in the poverty of one and the riches of another. He will likely exalt you one year and humble you the next. Our entire lives are lent to change. But who He is will never change. As He reveals Himself to you, His heart remains the same. In the midst of a society where the only thing you can count on is that you can't count on anything, God is your guarantee. His faithfulness flows from who He is. To please Him, our faithfulness must do the same.

I cannot begin to recall the times I have survived based on my limited understanding of who God is. At times when I could not understand what He was doing, why He had permitted some of my experiences, or why He had allowed my friend's child to die of cancer, I continued forward with these words: "God, I can't understand why You're doing this. But I know that, unlike me, Your actions cannot be inconsistent with Your heart, and I know Your heart is loving, good, and faithful. Somehow, some way, somewhere all these things are for good. If I could just know You better through this, that is all the good I need."

As we conclude you may be wondering, "So, is it wrong to ever expect God to move in an obvious way?"

Oh, Beloved, if we could just comprehend that a faith based on who God is frees Him completely to show us what He can do! It's all a matter of focus. Right motives invite real miracles!

How does God want you to respond to what He showed you today?

_____

_____

_____

_____

_____

_____

_____

🍃 Today's Treasure:

"Faith comes from hearing the message, and the message is heard through the word of Christ" (Rom. 10:17).

Day 3
A Painful Deliverance

On day 2, we learned that a steadfast faith focuses on who God is and frees Him to show us what He can do. Today we are going to observe that kind of faith in action. You see, true faith always takes action. You will remember that the basic meaning of *pistis* is believing God. This is the perfect time to share another portion of the definition of the word: "a technical term indicative of the means of appropriating what God in Christ has for man, resulting in the transformation of man's character and way of life."[4]

In simple terms, faith transforms character. It shows! You may not always be aware of another person's absence of faith, but you will quickly be aware of another person's presence of faith! Our Christian character is dramatically dictated by our measure of faith. Read Acts 27:1–28:10, then answer the following:

What did Paul's eyes tell him about the voyage? (Acts 27:10).

_____

To whom did the centurion listen? _____

After the gentle south wind turned into a mammoth "northeaster," what did they do with the ship? (Acts 27:14-19).

_____

Describe the condition of the boat and the crew when Paul spoke. (Acts 27:21).

_____

_____

What did God tell Paul through an angel? (Acts 27:23-24).
❑ God would spare the lives of everyone on the ship.
❑ Half of the passengers would drown.
❑ The stock market in Rome would go up 12 points.

On what basis did Paul become certain of the future of the voyage? (Acts 27:25).
❑ a vision in the night   ❑ confidence in the sailors' skill
❑ faith in God   ❑ a break in the weather

What was Paul's warning in Acts 27:26? _____

_____

On what day did Paul encourage the crew to eat and be strengthened?
❏ day 3   ❏ day 14   ❏ day 27

How many were on board? _____

What did they do after they finished eating? _____

_____

What did the crew "decide" to do? (Acts 27:39; compare v. 26).

_____

Why weren't the soldiers allowed to kill the prisoners?
❏ The soldiers were busy saving themselves.
❏ The centurion wanted to spare Paul's life.

What kind of reception did the crew receive in Malta? (Acts 28:1-2).

_____

_____

TRUTHS LEARNED FROM PAUL'S SHIPWRECK ACCOUNT

1. Feelings or perceptions cannot be the basis of faith even in the most Spirit-filled life.

Compare Acts 27:10 and 27:24. Notice that Paul's discernment was not entirely accurate. What He thought was going to happen and what actually happened were two different things. His feelings were biased by what he could see.

Although they experienced plenty of discomfort, no loss of life resulted as Paul had suspected. One reason many people feel "disappointed in God" is because they treated their feelings as fact. However, as we will see, Paul's feelings were not so convincing that he was deaf to the facts.

2. Faith comes from listening!

Read Today's Treasure again. Notice that faith became an issue once the Word of God was spoken. Before He heard from God, Paul did not assume that all would go well. In fact, he assumed exactly the opposite.

Paul also did not assume that every promise God had ever made in history would be applied to him in his moment of need. The Word of God overflows with many wonderful "blanket" promises, continually true to all of us (i.e. He will never leave us; He will return for us; He will work things for our good), but many of God's promises are for particular times, situations and people.

God's Word is always true; God always keeps His promises, but He reserves the right to apply His Word as He sees fit. We must seek His heart to know if a particular assurance is ours to claim in a particular moment. But once God provides His Word to claim, the immediate burden of belief falls into action.

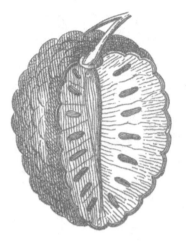

Paul chose faith. Everything he could see and feel screamed death and disaster, but Paul's greatest reality was what he could not see.

If you know God has directly applied His Word to your situation, then believe! If you are not sure, keep seeking Him until you are. The most certain way to know God is to know His Word! Paul had a steadfast faith in the midst of a rocky ride because He listened and responded to God's Word! God is perfectly capable of speaking over the wind and the waves. He may calm them as He did for His disciples, or He may lead you through them as He did Paul. Either way, keep listening—then take Him at His Word!

3. God's deliverance came through the ship running aground!

Look at Acts 27:26. God promised to deliver them, "Nevertheless, we must run aground." Deliverance does not mean ease. It may be simple and painless, or, God's deliverance in your life may be one of the most excruciating things you ever experience. God has "delivered" me from my childhood trauma, but that deliverance was extremely painful. Difficulty does not necessarily mean disaster. Heavy winds and raging seas don't always mean you're on the wrong course. It may mean you're right on target. Believer, celebrate the fact that you can sometimes "run aground" on the island of God's will for your life! Perhaps He couldn't get you to your destination any other way, and, like Paul, you may run aground for the sake of the crew on board with you!

4. God always has a destination in mind when He delivers.

God has a place of kindness, warmth, and welcome. A place where, once you have been faithful to who He is, He will show you what He can do. Malta was a place of miracles, a place of healing, and a place of supplication. The waters may be rough, and we may have to toss a few things overboard to keep from sinking, but, if we believe, God provides deliverance even in the midst of "Plan B." If only we would release God from our preconceived notions of what a miracle should be! Our eyes would be opened to so much more! All it takes to behold a miracle is seeing God do something only He can do!

I am so thankful to know that during times when we might have overlooked sound advice and headed straight into a storm, it is still possible to run aground into God's will. Listen and believe.

How does God want you to respond to what He showed you today?

_____

_____

_____

_____

_____

_____

_____

  ✍ Describe a time when God let you "run aground" into His will.

_____

_____

Close your study today with a prayer walk. Take a stroll down the street, to the park, or just around the yard. As you walk, talk to God. Thank Him for the times He has led you into His will in spite of your plans. Express your heart to Him. I wish I could be there with the two of you!

Day 4

Fight the Good Fight

Sometimes keeping the faith requires a fight. Have you noticed? At times, the evidence of what we can see stacks up so high against the assurance of what we can't that a lifelong faith crumbles in a moment. How can we "fight the good fight of the faith" (1 Tim. 6:12) so that we can live a life pleasing to God? Today's study will be devoted to answering this important question. First, let's determine why keeping the faith is such a fight. Read Ephesians 6:10-18.

> ✍ **Which piece of the whole armor of God does faith represent?**
> ❏ **belt**　　　❏ **breastplate**　　　❏ **shield**　　　❏ **helmet**

What is its purpose? _____

_____

The actual shield from which Paul drew this parallel was called a *thureon*. It was a plank of wood, 4 feet long and 2½ feet wide. (Take a moment to picture a shield in those proportions.) It was overlaid with linen and leather which were usually treated with a substance that extinguished flaming arrows.

The Greek word translated *in addition* is *epi*, which "marks an extension or spreading out upon or over something, a stretching or spreading out in various directions, distribution over."[5] *Epi* implies "above" or "over" the rest in Ephesians 6:16. The word suggests how the shield relates to all the other parts of the armor of God.

In a flesh-and-blood battle, the shield was the piece of equipment that covered all the others. Roman warriors were so adept at working the shield that their other pieces of armor were rarely hit. The shield was specifically designed to extinguish the enemy's flaming arrows. Without it, the warrior was terribly vulnerable. The other pieces of armor might keep the warrior from being penetrated by an arrow, but they were not designed to protect him from burning arrows. That was the job of the *thureon*.

God designed our faith to be exactly the same kind of protector. When we are convinced that God is believable and we respond to Him in faith, practically nothing can get through to us. But when our faith diminishes, our shield begins to drop, and we are immediately vulnerable to the enemy.

Satan will stop at nothing to get us to lower our shield of faith so he can wound and burn us. He stacks up tangible evidence in opposition to God's assurances. He delights in doubts and lies. He studies our weaknesses and then aims where we're vulnerable. His priority job description is to keep us from believing God…first, for salvation, and then for completion.

Today, we examine two of Satan's most effective weapons for weakening our hold on the shield of faith. Read and compare Mark 4:35-41 and Hebrews 11:23,27 to discover Satan's first weapon for weakening our faith.

❧**Today's Treasure:**

"I have fought the good fight, I have finished the race, I have kept the faith. Now there is in store for me the crown of righteousness, which the Lord, the righteous Judge, will award to me on that day—and not only to me, but also to all who have longed for his appearing" (2 Tim. 4:7-8).

What was present in the lives of those with no faith but absent in the lives of those with much faith?

❑ power   ❑ fear   ❑ guilt   ❑ hope

God included healthy fear in His creation. We are wise to fear poisonous snakes; Scripture tells us to fear God. Those are appropriate types of fear, but wise fear often gives way to destructive fear. Where great faith lives, destructive fear cannot live. Where great fear exists, no faith can survive. Fear is the arch enemy of faith. Very simply, we often are too scared to believe God. To increase our vulnerability to a full-fledged attack, Satan hesitates at nothing to create an atmosphere where fear abounds. He takes advantage of our fear of disappointment, our fear that God might not "prove" His love to us, and our fear of humiliation before others.

Second Timothy 1:7 tells us that "God has not given us a spirit of fear, but of power and of love and of a sound mind" (NKJV). Destructive fear is a product of the power of darkness, and Satan will strive to turn your doubts into fears and fears into panic. But remember—we have a recourse.

    ❧ Read Psalm 3. Describe a time when God has been a shield about you, your glory, and the lifter of your head.

_____

_____

_____

God's Word teaches us that we must be aware of our battle with invisible principalities, but we need not be afraid. An incident from Elisha's life demonstrates the perfect reason why fear is unfounded in the life of the believer.

Read 2 Kings 6:8-20. Why was Elisha's servant afraid?

_____

What were Elisha's words to him? (6:16).

❑ "Thy rod and thy staff, they comfort me."
❑ "Don't be afraid. Those who are with us are more than those who are with them."
❑ "Fear not, for behold I bring you tidings of great joy."

What did God do for Elisha's servant? _____

_____

When God opened the servant's eyes to the unseen world, what became visible to him?

_____

How many chariots might the servant have seen? (Ps. 68:17).

_____

Fill in the following blanks from Isaiah 50:9 and Romans 8:31.

"It is the Sovereign LORD who _____ me.

Who is he that will _____ me?"

"If God is _____ us, who can be _____ us?"

Oh, Beloved, we have nothing to fear. The pitiful powers of this world are nothing compared to the armies in heaven fighting on our behalf. Fear cripples faith, but never forget—just as quickly, faith cripples fear. Whether fear or faith prevails depends on the commander we're saluting.

Read Mark 6:1-6 to discover Satan's second weapon which weakens our faith.

Answer the following questions.
Where were Jesus and His disciples? (v. 1) _____

What was the people's response to Him? (v. 3) _____

_____

Fill in the blanks: "Only in his _____, among his relatives

and in his own _____ is a prophet without _____" (v. 4).

What was the result of their lack of faith?
❑ **They could not understand that Jesus was their Messiah.**
❑ **Jesus could do few miracles.**
❑ **Jesus was amazed by their lack of faith.**

Casual familiarity is another weapon Satan uses against us in our fight to keep the faith. Sadly, some of those who've known Christ the longest have witnessed His power the least.

Being near a brand-new Christian is exciting. They possess such childlike faith, almost an innocent audacity, and are unafraid to ask God anything! He says it; they believe it. That's all there is to it! New believers are often so engrossed in who Christ is that they seldom impose limits on what He can do.

However, those of us who have been around a while are masters of limitation. Often we practice safe boundaries that keep us from being disappointed and others from being doubtful. Mark 6 makes it clear that you can know Christ for a long time and still not know Him well. Those who truly know Him never stop inviting Him to reveal His awesome presence. They don't try to close Him in a single ring. They call on Him as the Lord of hosts, the Commander-in-Chief of the royal army, Who, in the flash of a sword, readies the heavenly hosts to battle in their behalf.

How does God want you to respond to what He showed you today?

_____

_____

_____

_____

_____

_____

Today's Treasure:

"Jesus Christ, who is the faithful witness, the firstborn from the dead, and the ruler of the kings of the earth. To him who loves us and has freed us from our sins by his blood, and has made us to be a kingdom and priests to serve his God and Father—to him be glory and power for ever and ever! Amen" (Rev. 1:5-6).

Remember, Satan will use our fears and our familiarities against us. Never stop growing; never stop knowing; and He'll never stop showing.

Really think about today's study. Which has most hindered your faith recently: fear or familiarity? Explain.

_____

_____

_____

Take time to pray. Thank God for His limitless power. Ask Him for the faith to trust Him more fully in the situation you just described.

Day 5

He Is Faithful

We began this week studying God's faithfulness or believability. Next we examined faithfulness as it is appropriated to man. We learned that keeping the faith is sometimes a fight and that Satan's primary strategy is to destroy faith by provoking doubt and fear. Perhaps, like me, you can relate to a father who stood just one obstacle away from his son's healing.

Read Mark 9:14-32. What specific words in verses 22 and 23 revealed the father's lack of faith?

_____

Read Daniel 3:17-18 and note the contrast in their attitude toward deliverance as compared to the father in Mark 9. Beloved, I am convinced that faith sometimes means knowing God can, whether or not He does.

He always can, my Friend! If He chooses not to, He has greater glory in mind. Never let the enemy convince you that God is not able to do anything He pleases! Sometimes when I'm offering up my pitiful petitions, my heart becomes convicted as if God is saying, "Come on! Challenge me today!"

Nothing is impossible for our God! You have not confronted a dilemma too big for Him to handle.

Why couldn't the disciples drive out the evil spirit?

_____

_____

Convicting, isn't it? How often do we attempt God-sized tasks on man-sized strength? Without prayer, we can forget it!

What was the father's plea in verse 24? _____

_____

Have you ever felt like this precious father? "I believe! No, I really don't believe. But I want to believe. Please help me believe!" I certainly have! We're not alone. The disciples experienced it at times, too.

Write Luke 17:5 in this space. _____

_____

Christ responded to the disciples' pleas in a miraculous way. He placed the Spirit of the One who had walked BESIDE them for three years INSIDE them for the rest of eternity. Beloved, the very *pistis* of Christ, Himself, is in you by way of His blessed Spirit. The supernatural capacity to believe God is immediately activated the moment we are filled by the Holy Spirit.

If you are born again, you possess the ability to believe God. Ask Him to flood you with His Spirit in the matters at hand so that the faith of the very Son of God will be released in you through the fruit of the Spirit!

We will conclude week 8 by considering the faithfulness of Christ just as we began with the faithfulness of God. We must understand that our belief is sandwiched and secured between the shields of their believability.

Reread Today's Treasure. What is Jesus Christ called in Revelation 1:5?

_____

Remember, when the word *pistis* is attributed to God or to Christ, it is referring to their "believability," their reliability, their guarantee. The Greek word translated *witness* is *martus* and it means "a witness. One who has information or knowledge of something, and hence, one who can give information, bring to light, or confirm something."[6] A witness is one who testifies.

In the context of Revelation 1:5, the term "faithful witness" tells us that Christ is the living testimony of God's believability! How true that is. Through the Lord Jesus Christ, God the Father has more than proved Himself. In countless ways the Father has offered "proof" that He is believable through Christ. Today, we are going to single out just one. But, it is a major one!

What is the test of the one true God? (Isa. 41:21-24; 44:6-8).

_____

One reason we know that our God is the one and only is because of His incomparable record of fulfilled prophecy. Only the true God can foretell that which is to come and then bring it to pass! Out of literally hundreds of prophecies which have arrived at their "time," every single one has been fulfilled exactly as God said, down to the most minute detail. In fact, the closest length of time between the major prophecies and their fulfillment was 200 years. Amazing! God is batting a thousand. No other "god" holds His record. More glorious still is the fact that at least 61 of God's many prophecies were foretold and perfectly fulfilled during the earthly life of His one and only precious Son!

Take a moment to read the following prophecies and their fulfillments. Then describe the subject and circumstance of each one:

Micah 5:2–Matthew 2:1 _____

_____

Psalm 78:2–Matthew 13:34 _____

_____

Zechariah 9:9–Luke 19:35-37 _____

_____

Zechariah 11:12–Matthew 26:15 _____

_____

Psalm 22:16–Luke 23:33, John 20:25,27 _____

_____

Psalm 22:18–John 19:23-24 _____

_____

Psalm 34:20–John 19:33 _____

_____

Amos 8:9-10–Matthew 27:45 _____

_____

Amos 8:10 says it will be a "time like mourning" for whom?

_____. **Awesome.**

Now, consider this. From the journal *Science Speaks*, Peter Stoner offered the following calculated figures: if you take only 8 prophecies (which I randomly chose above) out of 61, the probability of all 8 being fulfilled is 1 in 10 to the 17th power. He illustrates it this way: take 10^{17} [or 100,000,000,000,000,000] silver dollars and lay them on the face of Texas. They will cover all of the state two feet deep. Now mark one of these silver dollars and stir up the coins. Blindfold a man and send him out to pick up the marked silver dollar. The chance that he will pick up the right one is 1 in 10 to the 17th power.

If we add 40 fulfilled prophecies to the 8, the chance would be 1 in 10 to the 157th power![17] Just imagine 157 zeroes! Yet all 61 were perfectly fulfilled just as God said they would be! That's no fluke. That's a God who is believable. And His Son is the faithful witness who testifies that His Father can be trusted. God has proven Himself believable through the prophecy He has fulfilled in the life of His Son. Jesus Christ is the literal embodiment of the believability of the entire Godhead to us (see Col. 2:9)!

A few prophecies remain to be fulfilled. They all basically concern one issue.

Read the following Scriptures and describe how each passage could provide assurance in your life.

John 14:1-7 _____

_____

Acts 1:9-11 _____

_____

1 Thessalonians 4:13-18 _____

_____

Beloved, HE'S COMING BACK.

I can't tell you how many people along the way have asked if I really believe He'll return to earth in bodily form. Not long ago, a man said to me: "I can believe He is the Son of God, that He was born of a virgin, that He died and rose again, and that He sits on the right hand of God. But if you expect me to believe that a trumpet's going to blow and we are going to meet Him in the air, you're crazy, woman!" I looked at him and said: "Mister, it doesn't matter if you believe it or not. If you're born again, when that trumpet blows, you're out of here...and we'll discuss it in the air."

Before we conclude this week, I want you to recognize one thing above all others about faithfulness.

◑ What do Romans 3:3-4 and 2 Timothy 2:13 say to you in light of all we've learned about "faithfulness"?

_____

_____

_____

How does God want you to respond to what He showed you today?

_____

_____

_____

_____

_____

_____

God is faithful whether or not we believe Him! He will do what He promised! Others may ask us: "Do you still believe in fairy tales? Do you really think Prince Charming is going to carry you away on a white horse? Do you really believe everything is going to be all right?"

Take a look at this:

> I saw heaven standing open and there before me was a white horse, whose rider is called Faithful and True....His eyes are like blazing fire, and on his head are many crowns. He has a name written on him that no one knows but he himself. He is dressed in a robe dipped in blood, and his name is the Word of God. The armies of heaven were following him, riding on white horses and dressed in fine linen, white and clean....On his robe and on his thigh he has this name written:
> KING OF KINGS AND LORD OF LORDS
> (Rev. 19:11-16).

He said it. I believe it. Not because I'm faithful. Because He is. So, until He shouts…

Keep Believin'!

_____

[1]Spiros Zodhiates et al., eds., *The Complete Word Study Dictionary: New Testament* (Chattanooga, TN: AMG Publishers, 1992), 1162.

[2]James Strong, from the *Hebrew and Chaldee Dictionary* of *The Exhaustive Concordance of the Bible* (Nashville: Holman Bible Publishers, n.d.), 106.

[3]Zodhiates, *The Complete Word Study Dictionary: New Testament*, 721.

[4]Ibid., 1163.

[5]Ibid., 620.

[6]Ibid., 947.

[7]Josh McDowell, *Evidence That Demands A Verdict: Volume 1* (Nashville: Thomas Nelson Publishers, Inc., 1972), 167.

Week 9

Gentle Giants

We live in a world filled with people who cannot make certain distinctions. They push and shove. They fear that to give in means to lose. They fear that if they don't fight for their rights they will become the hole in the proverbial doughnut. Into such a world steps the eighth characteristic of the fruit of the Spirit–*gentleness*. This character trait denotes a life surrendered to real power. It pictures a person able to express calmness in the storm. Only a gentle giant can stand before Pilate with no need to defend Himself. Jesus both pictures and epitomizes the gentle giant.

This week we will examine the wonderful Greek word *praotes*, translated as *gentleness* in the fruit of the Spirit. We will see in this quality the aspects of submission, humility, and teachability. We will observe a fleshing out of Paul's great observation: *when I am weak, then I am strong* (2 Cor. 12:10).

Principal Questions

Day 1: What were some of the ways Paul had to suffer for Christ's sake?

Day 2: What evidences do you see suggesting John the Baptist's humility?

Day 3: What was Balaam's response to the words spoken by the angel of the Lord?

Day 4: What was the proper way to carry the ark of God?

Day 5: What was the obvious text of Christ's teaching?

Sacrificial Submission

❧Today's Treasure:

"As for me, I am in your hands; do with me whatever you think is good and right" (Jer. 26:14).

Today we begin our study of the eighth quality of the fruit of the Spirit: gentleness. I think you will discover that this marvelous word encompasses several intimate traits we require as maturing believers.

The Greek word translated *gentleness* is *praotes*. Observe a detailed description of this word:

> meekness, mildness, forbearance. Primarily it does not denote outward expression of feeling, but an inward grace of the soul, calmness toward God in particular. It is the acceptance of God's dealings with us considering them as good in that they enhance the closeness of our relationship with Him. However, *praotes* encompasses expressing wrath toward the sin of man as demonstrated by the Lord Jesus....This meekness does not blame God for the persecutions and evil doings of men. It is not the result of weakness...but the activity of the blessedness that exists in one's heart from being actively angry at evil....That virtue that stands between two extremes, uncontrollable and unjustified anger, and not becoming angry at all no matter what takes place around you.[1]

Carefully review the definition of *praotes*. Circle the word or phrase that most clearly communicates to you. Underline any words or phrases that you do not initially understand.

In layman's terms, *praotes* describes the complete surrender to God's will and way in your life. The term basically means to stop fighting God. It is quite the opposite of weakness. Meekness or gentleness is the power and strength created from submitting to God's will. Gentleness is responsibility with power.

We cannot comprehend the word *praotes* without studying several of its very important components: submission, humility, teachability, and teaching ability. We will study each of these ingredients this week; however, today we will consider the foundation of submission, without which *praotes* does not exist.

Do you sometimes "fight" God? If you're not comfortable admitting to an occasional wrestling match with God, do you fight with Him more covertly by demanding amendments or clauses to make His will more bearable? Do you ever lock your arms across your chest and pat your foot, waiting for Him to propose a solution you like better than the one He has already presented?

As God pushes and prods you along, with a mind set on finishing that which He started (see Phil.1:6), do you grab for every doorknob, tree limb, or mailbox to keep from going His direction? or, at least His speed? Does He have to fight you practically every step of the way in your maturing process?

Praotes describes the resting of resistance to God. It begins with that word we love to hate–submission. I think of the submissive spirit of *praotes* this way: when the wind of God's will blows, *praotes* prevails when I let go of every object of security, resist grabbing on to anything that would hold me back, and ride the wind wherever or however it takes me. *Praotes* is riding the wind of God's will and setting sail toward the remote island of intimacy.

The following Scripture passages describe lives given over to the will of God even when the prospect seemed dismal. For each of these individuals, to endure pain and suffering in the will of God was far better than to risk ease outside His faithful hands. These examples paint a portrait of *praotes*.

Read John 21:15-19 and answer the following questions.

What command did Christ give Peter? _____

What words of prophecy did Christ speak about Peter's future?
❑ "You will will receive power when the Holy Spirit comes on you."
❑ "When you are old you will stretch out your hands, and someone else will dress you and lead you where you do not want to go."
❑ "You will be my witness to the ends of the earth."

What did Jesus predict would ultimately happen to Peter? (v. 19).

_____

Coupled with John 21:15-19 and your understanding of *praotes*, how does Acts 2:14-36 reveal the quality of "gentleness" in Peter?
❑ He spoke with great compassion.
❑ His submission to Christ gave him great courage to speak.
❑ He became an effective preacher by listening to Jesus.

In *Foxe's Book of Martyrs*, John Foxe writes that, according to the ancient historian, Hegesippus:

> Nero sought matter against Peter to put him to death; which, when the people perceived, they entreated Peter with much ado that he would flee the city. Peter, through their importunity at length persuaded, prepared himself to avoid. But, coming to the gate, he saw the Lord Christ come to meet him, to Whom he, worshipping, said, "Lord, whither dost Thou go?' To whom He answered and said, "I am come again to be crucified." By this, Peter, perceiving his suffering to be understood, returned back into the city. Jerome saith that he was crucified, his head being down and his feet upward, himself so requiring, because he was (he said) unworthy to be crucified after the same form and manner as the Lord was.[2]

That, my Friend, is the submissive spirit of *praotes*.

Now read Acts 9:1-16 and answer the following questions.

What question did Jesus ask Paul in verse 4? _____

_____

Who had Paul actually been persecuting? (v. 1).

_____

What do verses 1 and 4 tell you about Christ's attitude toward Christians being persecuted?

_____

What was Paul's holy calling? (v. 15).
❑ to carry the name of Jesus before Gentiles and Israelites
❑ to begin churches in distant lands
❑ to be the apostle to the Israelites
❑ to suffer for His faith and die a martyr's death

What was Christ going to "show" Paul? (v. 16).

_____

✍ What were some of the ways Paul suffered for Christ's sake? (2 Cor. 6:4-5 and 11:24-28).

_____

_____

Read Philippians 3:3-11. What did Paul's sufferings mean to Him?

_____

Look back at the definition of *praotes*. What qualities of "gentleness" can be seen in our glimpses of Paul's life?

_____

_____

In *Foxes' Book of Martyrs,* John Foxe also writes:

Paul, the apostle, who before was called Saul, after his great travail and unspeakable labours in promoting the Gospel of Christ, suffered also in this first persecution under Nero. Abdias, declareth that unto his execution Nero sent two of his esquires, Ferega and Parthemius, to bring him word of his death. They, coming to Paul instructing the people, desired him to pray for them, that they might believe; who told them that shortly after they should believe and be baptised at his sepulchre. This done, the soldiers came and led him out of the city to the place of execution, where he, after his prayers made, gave his neck to the sword.[3]

PRAOTES—PURE AND SIMPLE

We may reason that perhaps the sufferings of Peter and Paul were made a little easier because they knew of them in advance, yet what does God's Word tell us in Acts 14:22 and John 16:33 about our own futures?

Can we submit to God's will knowing what is ahead, just like Peter and Paul? Although we have been given equal warning, we so often respond with shock and doubt. And what about those times when our suffering results from our lack of submission to God's will? Can we then submit to the painful process of letting Him work our lives back into His will?

I was meditating on the complicated definition of *praotes*. I read it over and over again, and continued to pray the words, "Teach me, my Father. Teach me." Then Melissa, 11 years old at the time, called from the bathroom upstairs, "Mom, I need you."

I had really believed I was finished with family responsibilities for the evening. All the children were either in their beds or getting ready for bed, and my husband was out of town. I hated to break my train of thought because I was so desiring to hear a word from God about *praotes*. Hesitantly, I walked upstairs to see what she needed, asking God to help me when I returned to remember where I was in my studies.

Melissa sat in the bathtub, drenched from head to toe, and said: "I've got a problem—a big problem. Last week I found a small knot in the back of my hair, and I tried to get it out with the brush. It hurt so much that I quit. Every day it's gotten bigger and bigger and now look!" In the back, nearly all of her very thick, long hair was in one huge knot. The knot was so big and so tight I could not imagine any other solution but scissors; yet I would have had to cut her hair to the scalp. I could not believe the mess.

I sat down beside her, asking God for patience *(makrothumia, of course!)*, and began to brush—one hair at a time! I tried to hold her hair as tightly as I could so that she would not feel it pull, but finally the knot was too close for me to fit my hand between it and her head. The tears streamed down her cheeks.

I asked, "Do you want me to stop?" "No, Mommy. If you do I'll never get it out. Keep brushing." It took us many minutes to get through those tangles, and those minutes seemed like hours. Totally submitted to untangling the mess she was in, she rested her head in my lap and endured the pain. Her tears were not those of resistance. They were tears of submission: knowing that the end was worth the means.

Afterward I sat down, held her, and explained how to avoid getting her hair into another mess like that. But I assured her that if she did, we'd get through it, tears and all.

I tucked Melissa in, walked down the stairs and thought, *Now, let's get back to praotes!* Then I felt the Spirit of God say to my heart, "My child, that was *praotes*." Is your life in a tangled mess, my Friend? Have you allowed certain situations to go unchecked for too long? I've done the same thing. Rest in His faithful care, cry when you must, and allow Him to comb out the tangles until you're free. Hold on to nothing except Him. He is the only One who can help. At last, Beloved, submit.

How does God want you to respond to what He showed you today?

_____

_____

_____

_____

_____

_____

_____

🐾 **Today's Treasure:**

"Remind the people to be subject to rulers and authorities, to be obedient, to be ready to do whatever is good, to slander no one, to be peaceable and considerate, and to show true humility toward all men" (Titus 3:1-2).

☙ Can you recall a time when you submitted to God's will while He untangled your mess? ❑ Yes ❑ No
If so, how do you feel He dealt with you?

_____

_____

Day 2
Selfless Humility

On day 1, we studied submission, the foundation of *praotes*, or gentleness. Because gentleness basically means "to cease fighting God," a submissive spirit toward His will for our lives is priority. Without another vital aspect of the eighth quality of the fruit of the Spirit, however, we will fight a losing battle as we seek to submit to God and the earthly authorities He ordains over us. The second aspect of *praotes* is humility.

Reread Today's Treasure. In this passage, the Greek word *praotes* is translated into the English word *humility*. Throughout today's study we are going to search for understanding regarding one of God's very important commands.

Read each of the following Scriptures. Check off each one after you have read it and note the result of humility in each instance.

❑ **2 Chronicles 7:14** _____

❑ **2 Chronicles 34:27** _____

❑ **Ezra 8:21-23** _____

❑ **Proverbs 6:3** _____

❑ **James 4:10** _____

❑ **1 Peter 5:6** _____

The list could go on and on. I'm sure you noted the common command in each verse: humble yourselves! We can all think of times when God has humbled us, yet He demands that we humble ourselves. Throughout our series we've observed the cost of pride. None of us wants to be arrogant or full of pride, but how can we stimulate humility in ourselves?

The Greek word often translated *humble* is *tapeinos*. It is a word which basically means modesty toward self and "piety toward God." *Tapeinos* encompasses the idea of arriving at a correct estimate of ourselves. It results from emptying ourselves of self. Those with authentic humility, or *tapeinophrosune,* are those who practice aggressive confession, thus developing a deep realization of... unworthiness to receive God's marvelous grace.[4] Looking back over these definitions carefully, you will find that humility is the correct estimation of ourselves which results from a correct estimation of our God.

Let's examine the life of a person who literally fleshed out these definitions. Scripture tells of a man who knew the key to Spirit-filled humility and practiced the art of humbling himself throughout his earthly life. His name? John the Baptist. The text? John 1:6-35.

Read John 1:6-35 and answer the following questions.

What did John the Baptist "not fail to confess" (v. 20)? _____

_____

What did John the Baptist say about himself? _____

_____

Upon seeing Jesus, by what name did John call Him?

_____

☞ What evidences do you see suggesting John the Baptist's humility?

_____

_____

Read Matthew 11:11. What was Christ's opinion of John the Baptist?

_____

Now read Luke 1:5-17. What was the angel's prophecy concerning this special baby's future? (vv. 15-17).

_____

_____

Only one man in all of history was chosen to be the forerunner of the long-awaited Messiah. God intervened miraculously in this precious child's behalf. He grew to be a man revered by the King of kings, Himself! If any man had reason to be proud, it was John the Baptist.

Yet read his words in John 3:30 and write them in the space below.

_____

John the Baptist possessed what may be unmatched humility. Several crucial factors fanned the flame of humility in this unique individual. First, don't miss the significant words of the angel, Gabriel, in Luke 1:15. John was filled with the Holy Spirit from birth! What impact would the Spirit's filling have on John's perspective of God and self? The supernatural outcome of being filled with the Spirit certainly included humility—an element so abundant in the quality of gentleness! Humility comes from being filled with the Holy Spirit. The more John poured himself out, the more the Holy Spirit poured Himself in!

A second factor stirred humility in the life of John the Baptist. Read Luke 1:26-45. What did Elizabeth call the baby inside Mary's womb? (v. 43).

_____

God had intervened in the pregnancies of both women, yet did Elizabeth view their experiences as equal? ❑ Yes ❑ No Why?

_____

_____

The second factor fanning the flame of John's humility was his mother's humility! As you can see, Elizabeth was a woman who humbled herself before God and others. From his birth John had observed an example of humility.

The third factor influencing John's humility was the teaching he had received. Elizabeth knew Jesus was the Christ child. He was her "Lord." She taught her son to know Him as He really was.

Now let's see if we can apply these principles as methods through which to humble ourselves. How did John the Baptist become such a humble man?
- He was filled with God's Spirit.
- He learned humility by example.
- He honored Christ.

Beloved, John had not one single opportunity to humble himself that we do not have!
- We can pray continually to be filled by the Spirit, and we can meet the necessary requirements for God to answer that prayer.
- We can adopt men and women of the Bible as models and surround ourselves with those who are Spirit-filled, as examples of humility.
- We can cease fraternizing with proud and arrogant people.
- We can pray for a continuous conviction of sin and the same ready spirit of repentance that John possessed.
- We can study continually who Christ is from God's Word; we can be dramatically transformed by what we find.

Humility is one of the supernatural results of being rightly related to God.

A Hebrew word often translated into the English word *humble* in the Old Testament is *kana* which means "to bend the knee."[5] Humility does not mean self-hatred and abasement. On the other hand, false humility is nothing more than another form of pride. According to Colossians 2:18 and 23, false humility does nothing but mislead others and disqualify us for genuine rewards. True humility is born on bent knees. Matthew 2:1-12 contains a perfect example of an authentic discovery of Christ which resulted in true humility. The encounter of the Magi with the Christ child resulted in humility from the Magi.

How did their humility show? (v. 11).

_____

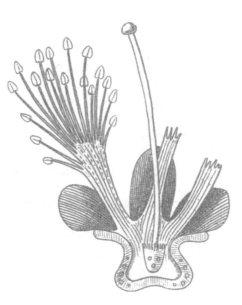

So, you ask, how do we humble ourselves? Seek Him and you'll find Him. Find Him and you'll find yourself...bowing down before Him. And you will not be able to resist giving Him back your every treasure.

I cannot describe to you how strongly I feel about the need for sometimes assuming a literal posture of humility before God in prayer. We often talk about having the right attitude of heart, but sometimes the heart is ushered to a greater humility when we literally get down on our knees and humble ourselves before God. I believe it's even appropriate to get down on our faces before God in our private time with Him when we realize we've allowed pride to erupt in our lives. Physical posture can have a great impact on spiritual stature!

A few last words. Sometimes the hard part is not in humbling ourselves before God...we know He's greater than we are! Sometimes the hard part is in humbling ourselves before others!

What are we commanded to do in Philippians 2:3?
❑ **Love God with all our heart, mind, soul and strength.**
❑ **Consider others better than ourself.**
❑ **Pray without ceasing.**
❑ **Possess faith like a grain of mustard seed.**

I really want you to give this some thought: how can we truly begin to esteem others as better than ourselves? I'm not looking for a certain predetermined answer. Identify several concrete ways we can provoke right attitudes in ourselves toward others and be comfortable esteeming them as higher than ourselves.

↪ What are your ideas for esteeming others? _____

_____

_____

_____

How does God want you to respond to what He showed you today?

_____

_____

_____

_____

_____

_____

_____

I hope you listed some specific ideas, but in general, when we are in a right relationship with God, our own sins will seem like planks and the sins of others as specks. You can trust Him on that one! Are you beginning to see just how important the filling of the Holy Spirit is to us? He is the key to the victorious Christian life!

A Teachable Spirit

Today's Treasure:

"Therefore, get rid of all moral filth and the evil that is so prevalent and humbly accept the word planted in you, which can save you" (Jas. 1:21).

On days 1 and 2, we studied two very important components of the eighth quality of the fruit of the Spirit–*praotes* or gentleness. They were submission and humility. We will devote the next two days to a third aspect of *praotes*. Read James 1:19-25. Just as it is used in Today's Treasure on day 2, the word *humbly* (or *meekly)* in James, chapter 1 is the English translation of the same Greek word for *gentleness* in the fruit of the Spirit.

Which of the following are God's commands in James 1:21?
❏ **Accept God's Word.**
❏ **Speak the truth in love.**
❏ **Turn away from evil.**

Another way of saying "humbly accept the word planted in you" is "be teachable!" "Receive instruction!" My sweet grandmother once commented about my brother's ability to play the piano, "He sure took to his learnin', didn't he?" The question today is, "Did we?"

The third aspect of gentleness is teachability. Are you willing to be taught, my friend? Anxious to learn? Do you have a teachable spirit? Let's consider the answers to those important questions as we take a look at differing degrees of teachability in God's Word.

Read Acts 18 and answer the following questions.
What had been Paul's relationship with Priscilla and Aquila in Corinth? (v. 3).

❏ **pastor**   ❏ **coworker**
❏ **employee**   ❏ **cousin**

How far did Priscilla and Aquila accompany Paul? _____

_____

After Paul had departed Ephesus, what Alexandrite entered the city?

_____

How does verse 24 describe Apollos?_____

_____

What and how did Apollos teach? _____

_____

What did Priscilla and Aquila do for Apollos? _____

_____

How do you think Priscilla and Aquila acquired their knowledge? (vv. 2-3).

_____

What did Apollos do with the instruction of Priscilla and Aquila? (vv. 27-28).

_____

What a wonderful example of the teachability of *praotes!* Paul had been faithful to receive the knowledge the disciples offered him after his conversion (see Acts 9:17-19). That which he learned, he no doubt passed on to Priscilla and Aquila, the Jews from Italy with whom he stayed. The couple traveled to Ephesus with Paul; then after he departed, they had the opportunity to hear a vibrant young preacher named Apollos. The man had passion. He spoke as a man who speaks only from his heart's overflow. Everything he knew, he handled with truth and accuracy...he simply did not know enough.

Sadly, some of the most "unteachable" people on earth are teachers. Some consider the commentary of others to be an insult aimed at their lack of knowledge. This was not the case with Apollos. He who had been faithful with little was found faithful with much. He took everything he learned from Priscilla and Aquila and went on to become such a dynamic teacher of truth that some equated him with Peter and Paul (see 1 Cor. 1:12).

What is the true sign of teachability? Being obedient to what we are taught, we "humbly accept the word planted in you, which can save you. Do not merely listen to the word....Do what it says" (Jas. 1:21-22).

Have you ever suddenly and unexpectedly realized that somewhere along the way your spirit had closed to anything new? Have you ever been concerned that anything new you might learn would refute the old? Have you ever been confronted by the fact that something you had believed all your life about God was inaccurate? Can you recall a specific example? How were you confronted with the truth?

How did you receive the instruction when confronted with truth?

_____

_____

The remainder of today's study is devoted to one tendency about which we'd all agree: our teachability most often depends on our teacher. If we respect the teacher, we might accept the teaching. If we don't, we dump it. Let's allow God's Word to speak to prejudiced pupils.

Read Numbers 22:21-38 and answer the following questions.

What did Balaam's donkey see?
❑ the tracks of the Israelite army
❑ the angel of the Lord blocking their path
❑ thousands of chariots of fire leading the way

How did she respond? _____

_____

How did Balaam react? _____

_____

Where did the donkey see the angel of the Lord the second time and how did she respond?

_____

How did Balaam react a second time? _____

_____

Where did the angel of the Lord stand the third time, and how did the donkey respond?

_____

_____

And Balaam's third reaction? _____

_____

What did God do with the donkey after her third beating?
❑ He killed the donkey with a bolt of lightning.
❑ He set the donkey free from her cruel master.
❑ He opened the donkey's mouth to speak.

Why did God oppose Balaam? _____

_____

Second Peter 2:15-16 lends added insight. What grievance did God

have with Balaam? _____

_____

What would have happened if the donkey had not turned away from the angel of the Lord?

❑ The angel would have killed Balaam.

❑ The angel would have killed the donkey.

❑ The angel would have killed both Balaam and the donkey.

🖎 **What was Balaam's response to the words spoken by the angel of the Lord? (v. 34).**

_____

_____

What was God's final instruction to Balaam? _____

_____

How did Balaam finally respond to instruction? (v. 38). _____

_____

_____

🖎 **Have you ever had a stubborn period like Balaam's when you refused to listen to God?** ❑ Yes ❑ No **If so, briefly explain.**

_____

_____

Numbers 22 clearly demonstrates God can use anything or anyone as an instrument of His instruction. He can oppose a donkey through a prophet or a prophet through a donkey. He can deliver His message to us in any form He wishes. When we are proud, rebellious, and insist on our own way, the chances are good He'll use a donkey! Unlikely teachers have a two-fold purpose: to bring humility and instruction. Often we will learn no other way.

Whatever happened to Balaam? Last I saw of him, he was riding off with an "I Pause for Donkeys" bumper sticker on the back of his beast. Not a bad idea. Beloved, let's work on having a more teachable spirit. God often wants to do "a new thing" in our lives, but we resist Him (see Isa. 43:18-19).

I have a wonderful friend named Marge Caldwell. She is beloved by many women who have heard her speak through the years. She absolutely amazes me. She would not appreciate my telling her age, and you would never believe it if I did, but she is still studying and allowing God to teach her new things when others have long since written their own eulogies. I get a kick out of watching her in our new contemporary worship service at church. She claps, sings, and sways with the best of them. Teachability! *Praotes!*

Sometimes we don't mind something new, we just don't like the vehicle God's using to drive us to that new place. A precious part of *praotes* is being willing and anxious to learn, regardless of who He chooses as our unlikely teacher. As my grandmother would say, "Child, let's take to our learnin'."

How does God want you to respond to what He showed you today?

_____

_____

_____

_____

_____

_____

_____

179

A Learning Experience

"It was good for me to be afflicted so that I might learn your decrees. The law from your mouth is more precious to me than thousands of pieces of silver and gold" (Ps. 119:71-72).

Today we continue the subject matter we confronted on day 3—the teachability of gentleness, the eighth quality of the fruit of the Spirit. Yesterday we considered the necessity of teachability, regardless of who God chooses as instructor. Today we will consider teachability, regardless of what God chooses to instruct. We will examine learning through our circumstances. Let's take a good look at how the "man after God's own heart" responded to difficult circumstances.

Read 1 Chronicles 13 and answer the following questions.
What was David's great desire at this point in his reign? (v. 3).
❑ to be recognized by the kings of surrounding lands
❑ to return the ark of God to a place of prominence
❑ to have a son to reign after him

Why did the whole assembly agree? (v. 4). _____

_____

How does verse 6 describe the ark? _____

_____

How did they move the ark of God?
❑ carried by priests
❑ floated on a barge
❑ on a cart pulled by oxen

What kind of celebration accompanied the transport of the ark?

_____

What happened when the ox stumbled, and what was God's response?

_____

_____

How did David react to God's judgment? (vv. 11-12).

_____

_____

God, in a very literal sense, rained judgment on David's parade. David reacted with great fear and anger. From our feeble understanding and limited points of view, it almost seems that God responded unfairly to David and Uzzah–but there is more to this story.

Read 1 Chronicles 15:1-15 and answer the following questions.
What were the new instructions for transporting the ark of God?

_____

Why had God's anger broken out against them on the first attempt?

_____

_____

☙ **What was the proper way to carry the ark of God?**
(v. 15; Ex. 25:13-15 gives the original instructions.)

_____

Why were seven bulls and seven rams sacrificed? (1 Chron. 15:26).
❑ **as a sin offering for those who carried the ark**
❑ **because God had helped the Levites who were carrying the ark**
❑ **to reward the priests and Levites who sanctified the temple**

So all Israel brought up the ark of the covenant of the Lord with shouts, with the sounding of rams' horns and trumpets, and of cymbals, and the playing of lyres and harps (1 Chron. 15:28).

Why did God's anger break out against the Israelites the first time? Because David was a man similar to many others. He wanted maximum results with minimum instruction. He made an executive decision without consulting the Chief Executive.

Why was God's favor on the Israelites the second time? Because, when all else failed, David checked the manual! He went to God's Word. Yes, David's first reaction was fear and anger, but he dealt with his emotions by going to God's Word. There he found instruction.

God's actions may appear harsh until we remember this was the hand-picked king of God's chosen nation and reigning representative of the lineage of the Messiah. Israel's security depended on David's obedience to God's Word. God would not allow compromise for His divinely-chosen king. The man after God's own heart made this experience his standard by which he measured all future difficulties.

David accepted tragedy and failure as a challenge to search God's Word. We would be wise to do the same. Oh, the trouble we could avoid! In my opinion, the words of Psalm 119 provide the most beautiful apologetic in the entire Old Testament for abiding in God's Word. I've chosen a few references which teach the value of turning to God's Word during difficult circumstances.

๑ Read Psalm 119:28. How has God's Word strengthened you in the past, or how might you be strengthened in the future by His Word?

_____

_____

Read Psalm 119:67. Have you experienced affliction as part of learning to obey God's Word? ❏ Yes ❏ No If so, explain.

_____

_____

Write your own paraphrase of Psalm 119:71.

_____

_____

Read Psalm 119:92. Have you ever known a person who exemplified the words of this verse? ❏ Yes ❏ No If so, describe that person.

_____

_____

Read Psalm 119:147. In what area of your life do you need to put your hope in God's faithfulness and promises?

_____

_____

Which one of the above Scriptures has come alive in your personal walk with Christ? In other words, can you testify to any one of the Scriptures from personal experience? If so, explain below.

_____

_____

_____

Beloved, we miss one of the most crucial purposes of difficult circumstances if we do not accept them as invitations to get into God's Word! If we miss their purposes, we miss God's instruction; thus, we often inadvertently sign up for the same class again!

What do the following verses tell us about instruction?
How do you "accept instruction from His mouth"? (Job 22:22).

_____

Why does Proverbs 4:13 say we should lay up God's Word in our hearts?
❑ God blesses obedience.
❑ Scripture memory builds wisdom.
❑ His instruction is life.

Fill in the blanks: "He who scorns _____ will _____ for it, but he who respects a _____ is rewarded" (Prov. 13:13).

Read Proverbs 16:20. Which of the following examples more accurately describes the prosperity and blessing promised in the verse?
❑ God gives material blessings to those who obey Him.
❑ A person with godly character tends to succeed and achieve prosperity.
❑ A person who listens to God grows to love and trust Him more.

Read 1 Thessalonians 4:8. Choose the best answer.
The motivation for obedience is grounded in:
❑ reward—God promises to do good things for those who obey.
❑ relationship—the issue is rejecting the person of our giving God.

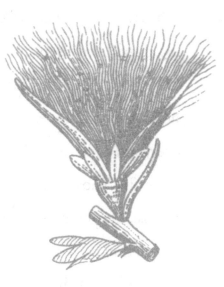

To miss God's Word in our circumstances is to miss God. To miss God is to miss the point.

Many modern-day "Davids" still look for what God has to teach them through their tribulations. I saved a story from the obituary section of the *Houston Chronicle*. A portion of the article reads: "Robert William Lillard, age 7½, began his eternal life with Christ on Friday, November 5, 1993. Bobby fought a seven-year battle against a disease called primary hyperozalurea or "oxalosis." Though hospital stays were numerable and recuperation at home seemed a way of life, Bobby's spirit was never broken. His courage and perseverance, despite his suffering and disappointments, were Christlike qualities that his family will admire the rest of our lives. We thank God for entrusting him to us and we pray his mission was fully accomplished. Bobby's love of life touched all who knew him. His family will be forever grateful."

Beloved, that is gentleness. Submission, humility, and teachability in the hardest test of life: the loss of a deeply cherished child. No, their son was not theirs to keep, but the cherished things God revealed to them through his life and death belong to them forever (see Deut. 29:29). It's all they have left; but it's enough when it has to be. "Hold on to instruction…for it is your life" (Prov. 4:13).

How does God want you to respond to what He showed you today?

_____

_____

_____

_____

_____

_____

_____

Today's Treasure:

"And the Lord's servant must not quarrel; instead, he must be kind to everyone, able to teach, not resentful. Those who oppose him he must gently instruct, in the hope that God will grant them repentance leading them to a knowledge of the truth, and that they will come to their senses and escape from the trap of the devil, who has taken them captive to do his will"

(2 Tim. 2:24-26).

Day 5

The Ultimate Teacher

Through this week's study, we have considered three aspects of the Greek word *praotes*, "gentleness" in the fruit of the Spirit. We have considered the priority of submission to the will of God in the life of the believer. We learned submission means "to stop fighting God." We explored humility, without which submission could not exist. It takes true humility to arrive at the conclusion that His work, will, and way in our lives is always preferred over our own, no matter how it may sometimes seem. We noted that a teachable spirit is a necessary component of gentleness. Today we will conclude week 9 by studying one last vital application of *praotes*: gentleness in teaching.

Reconsider the definition of the word *praotes* from day 1, giving special attention to the words, "Strength of character revealed in meekness of manner." *Praotes* is "responsibility with power." The person possessing *praotes* is the gentle giant: the embodiment of the pure, unadulterated power of the Holy Spirit and one who knows what to do with it. God's teachers are not called to wield the Word of God like a baseball bat. The Sword of the Spirit is to injure Satan, not the body of Christ.

The words *exhort* and *injure* are not synonyms. We must learn to use the weapon of our warfare carefully. The truth that we have been given is a trust… and one which must be passed on to others. We will focus on three commands regarding instruction. We will discover 1) that we must teach, 2) what we must teach, and 3) how we must teach. First, let's consider God's command that His people must be taught.

What two all encompassing commands did Christ leave with His disciples? (Matt. 28:19-20).

You may be surprised to learn that "go" is not a command in the Great Commission. The first command is "disciple all nations." To disciple them, we will have to go. The second command is "teach." The Greek word for *teach* is *didasko* and interestingly, the first part of the definition is "to know." The second part of the definition is to "instruct by word of mouth…to tutor…advise…to teach."[6] The definition of *didasko* is clear: we cannot teach what we do not know. "To know" means to accept by fact and experience.

Notice an important distinction God draws in His Word in Acts 15:35 and 28:31. What two activities are obviously distinct from each other?

The Greek word for *preach* is *euaggelizo* which specifically means "to proclaim the good news." To preach is "to evangelize."[7] Clearly, the emphasis of "preaching" is most often "the lost," and the emphasis of "teaching" is most often "the saved." Both are absolute necessities in the New Testament church. The body of Christ is in desperate need of sound teaching–teaching that matures us in Christ. How important is it that we deepen our knowledge of God's Word?

What do each of the following Scriptures tell us about the value and necessity of teaching in the body of Christ? Read Paul's prayer in Philippians 1:9-11. Match the following phrases according to the words of the apostle.

___ filled with righteousness   a. and be pure and blameless

___ you may discern what is best   b in knowledge and depth of insight

___ your love may abound   c. that comes through Jesus Christ

    How do you suppose knowledge and depth of insight results in love that abounds?

_____

_____

How does being "able to discern what is best" relate to being "pure and blameless until the day of Christ"?

_____

_____

In what way does being "filled with the fruit of righteousness" come through Jesus Christ?

_____

To which of the following does 2 Timothy 2:15 compare the teacher?
❏ an athlete who plays the game with maximum effort
❏ a manager who supervises the work of others
❏ a craftsman who does the job with care and thoroughness

What does Hebrews 6:1 say about the need to mature in our teaching and learning?

_____

_____

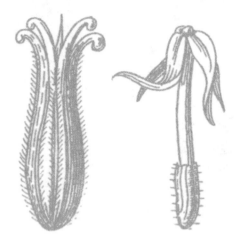

These are only a few of the many exhortations in Scripture that instruct us to continually grow in our knowledge of God's Word. The Word is our offensive weapon against Satan and our outward encouragement toward righteousness. We need teachers who correctly deal with the Word of God and use their wisdom to help us apply it to our daily lives.

What kind of teacher is God looking for? Look carefully at Today's Treasure. God seeks servants who are able to teach. He does not need egomaniacs who revel in the power. In fact, nothing in the actual position of teaching invites boasting at all! First Timothy 4:1 tells us that demons are teachers!

God is searching for servant-teachers. The Greek word for *servant* is *doulos* and it means "a slave, one who is in a permanent relation of servitude to another, his will being altogether consumed in the will of the other…one bound to serve."[8] This definition is the perfect introduction to the second command of God in regard to teaching.

God not only commands that His people be taught, He also has specific requirements as to what they should be taught. The term *teacher* occurs 58 times in the New Testament. Forty-one of these refer to Jesus Christ. He is the ultimate teacher: the teacher's Teacher. We are to teach as He taught.

 ✎ **What was the obvious text of Christ's teaching? (John 8:28-29).**

_____

We can glean from these passages a very important rule of thumb for teachers: God's teachers cannot simply teach what they please. Even Christ taught only from the Words of His Father! Remember the meaning of the word *servant*? The teacher-servant is consumed by the will of the other! Teachers must refrain from using the podium as a platform for their personal opinions and crusades. I am not at all sure our opinions matter in the least. God's teachers are bound to God's opinion, the only one which truly matters. Like Christ, we may teach God's Word in many ways, including modern-day parables, testimonies, and current applications. However, for three very important reasons, the basic text should be God's Word.

What did Jesus say God's Word is and does? (John 17:17).

God's Word is_____

God's Word does _____

Only God's Word is the absolute truth! Only God's Word can sanctify believers. He is the only One in existence who can be taken at His Word. Even teaching materials from the most excellent expositors of our time fail to reach the same high standard as the Word of God. Unfortunately, many contemporary "teachers" focus on man's experiences and then apply God's Word as an afterthought! Student, beware! Many times I've warned those who listen to me teach never to take me at my word, but always to measure my words against His! If it doesn't match, don't accept it!

Finally, God has specific commands regarding how we are to teach.

What does Titus 2:7-8 have to say about the lifestyle of a teacher?

_____

_____

How are godly teachers to deal with opposition? (2 Tim. 2:25).

_____

What is to be our attitude about sharing Christ with others? (1 Pet. 3:15).

_____

What morsel does Proverbs 16:21 add to our teaching?

_____

God commands that our teaching comes from "an inward grace of the soul" that He refers to as "gentleness"...teaching with humility...with an attitude of submission...with an awareness of our own sins and a forgetfulness toward the sins of the flock...leaving condemnation to God and conviction to the Holy Spirit. God's teacher is the vessel while God's Word packs the punch. Does gentleness mean weakness?

Conclude today's study by reading the familiar words of John 13:1-17.

I don't know of many lessons stronger than the one Christ taught from His knees. He is the Gentle Giant.

We are all called to teach in one form or another—as a witness, as a living testimony, as a mother, as a neighbor. As we do, may we remember how God's Word is best served—with a pitcher and a towel.

You may not think of yourself as a teacher, but if you really analyze the responsibilities God has given you at home, work, or church, you'll probably discover that you do teach—in some style or position. How can you apply today's study truths to your own "teaching positions"?

How does God want you to respond to what He showed you today?

_____

_____

_____

_____

_____

_____

_____

[1]Spiros Zodhiates et al., eds., *The Complete Word Study Dictionary: New Testament* (Chattanooga, TN: AMG Publishers, 1992), 1208.

[2]John Foxe, *Foxe's Book of Martyrs* (Grand Rapids, MI: Baker Book House, 1995), 12-13.

[3]Ibid., 13.

[4]Spiros Zodhiates, *The Complete Word Study Dictionary: New Testament*, 1365-66.

[5]James Strong, from the *Hebrew and Chaldee Dictionary* of *The Exhaustive Concordance of the Bible* (Nashville: Holman Bible Publishers, n.d.) 56.

[6]Spiros Zodhiates, *The Complete Word Study Dictionary: New Testament*, 450-51.

[7]Ibid., 668.

[8]Ibid., 483.

Week 10

The Crucible of Self-Control

Last but not least we consider the final component of this wonderful fruit the Spirit develops in the lives of His children. The final characteristic is self-control. Any woman or man is a mighty warrior if he or she has self-control. Any person without self-control is either an accident looking for a place to happen or a slave in chains. Only through the self-control developed by the Spirit can we ever fulfill the promise of Jesus: *Then you will know the truth, and the truth will set you free* (John 8:32).

In this final week together we will examine self-control. We will see examples of men who had it and men who did not. We will discover principles for growing in self-control, and we will end our time with a look at a day lived in the self-control of the Spirit.

Principal Questions

Day 1: Why do we need self-control?

Day 2: What was the difference between Daniel's attitude toward the king's food and Samson's attitude toward the honey?

Day 3: What happens when we attempt to serve both God and money?

Day 4: What type of person is never at fault in what he says?

Day 5: What does God do for the "blessed" person?

Day 1

That's Enough

The headline on the front page of the *Houston Post* read: "Violent youths would as soon kill you as look at you." Newspapers and tabloids overflow with headlines and articles about the drug-related deaths of popular young actors and rock stars. From the abuse of power to the abuse of substance, one theme is crystal clear: our society is in a corporate crisis caused by individual indulgence. Lack of self-control kills self respect, friendships, marriages, careers, and ministries. Not one of us can boast that we've always avoided its clutches.

How wonderful it would be if salvation and self-control were simultaneous, but they are not. The believer's struggle for self-control is ongoing, but, praise God's powerful name, He makes it available and attainable!

Today we begin our study of the ninth and final quality of the fruit of the Spirit. How appropriate that the list of qualities began with love and ends with self-control. Love keeps us afloat, and self-control keeps us anchored. Love lends us liberality, and self-control provides the boundaries within which love can be unleashed.

The Greek word for *self-control* is *egkrateia* which means "continence, temperance, self-control."[1] It means "restraining passions and appetites."[2] The antonym or opposite of *egkrateia* is *akrasia*. It means "excess, self-indulgence."[3] Today we consider just how important self-control is to the believer in Christ.

How do you feel about this topic of self-control? (Check one or more.)
❑ **Dread—I don't even want to think about it.**
❑ **Excited—I want to learn more about living a self-controlled life.**
❑ **Confused—I thought we were supposed to be Spirit-controlled.**
❑ **Condemned—I feel guilty every time I even think about the topic of self-control.**
❑ **Other** _____

Perhaps your thoughts are like those of someone else in God's Word. Read Acts 24:22-27. Notice that the subject matter of Paul's sermon to Felix and Drusilla was "faith in Christ Jesus" (v. 24), but it was expressed in a three-part outline.

Record each "part" of the outline below.

1. _____

2. _____

3. _____

❧Today's Treasure:

"Like a city whose walls are broken down is a man who lacks self-control" (Prov. 25:28).

Mark each of the following descriptions of Felix' reactions to Paul's sermon either true or false.

___ **Felix feared because of Paul's words.**

___ **Felix sent Paul away.**

___ **Felix tried to have Paul executed.**

___ **Felix said he'd see Paul at a more convenient time.**

The ancient historian, Josephus, described Felix as a man of lust, pride, greed, and selfish ambition. If the sermon topic had been announced in advance, he would have "conveniently" missed this service! There is never a "convenient" or comfortable time to consider the issue of self-control. No doubt each and every one of your toes will feel stepped on before this week is complete. I suspect you'll have moments when you may want to shelve it like Felix and say, "That's enough for now," but now is exactly the time God has chosen for you and for me.

We're going to learn to turn those four negative words from the mouth of Felix into four positive words from the mouth of God, because self-control is knowing when to say, "that's enough for now." Beloved, we are desperate for self-control, and in its absence, we are drowning in self-defeat.

Which of the following most clearly states the key to self-control found in 1 Corinthians 6:12?

❏ **I will choose to be free in Christ rather than to be captured by my desires.**

❏ **I have freedom in Christ, so I do not have to live by rules.**

❏ **Since I am free in Christ, I can do what I want.**

Look back over those last few words carefully: "I will not be mastered by anything." The Greek word for *mastered* is *exousiazo*. It means "to be ruled by or be under the power of, to be in bondage to." Its root word is *exousia* which means "authority, right and power."[4]

The key to self-control is the refusal to allow our enemies (the flesh, the world, or Satan) to rule or hold us captive in any way. What does "self" have to do with the issue of "control"? Christ has given us the victory over our flesh, our world, and our accuser. Only self can re-extend authority to one of these three enemies. They cannot presume authority over us. In the life of a believer, they can rule only where they are invited.

Self makes the choice over the issue of control. The Spirit-led self holds the power of five key words: "no," "yes," and "not right now." Self-control is as much about saying "yes" and "not right now" as it is about saying "no." Sometimes self-control is not about "what?" but "how much?" and not "when?" but "why?" Self-control is an issue of mastery, of authority, of boundaries.

☙ **Why do we need self-control? Today's Treasure explains it perfectly. Paraphrase Proverbs 25:28 in the space below:**

_____

_____

Without self-control, we are like a city with broken-down walls! To understand the significance of such a terrible dilemma we must remember a crucial characteristic of ancient architecture: a city was only as secure as the walls which surrounded it. A city's walls were its fortification. Archeologists estimate that three chariots could ride side by side on the wall of Nineveh. The walls of Babylon were so wide that six chariots could ride abreast on them![5] Their walls lent the reputation that they were practically impenetrable.

> **Read Deuteronomy 1:22-28. How did the "spies" describe the cities in the promised land? (Check one or more.)**
> ❑ **The armies are huge and the walls are impenetrable.**
> ❑ **The cities are large with walls that reach up to the sky.**
> ❑ **We can conquer the cities with the Lord's help.**

The Hebrew word for *walls* in Proverbs 25:28 says it all. The word *chowmah* simply means "a wall of protection."[6] Anything of value had to be protected.

> **What were the first structures Solomon built after He was crowned king? (1 Kings 3:1).**
>
> 1. _____
>
> 2. _____
>
> 3. _____

God demanded walls in every dwelling place He chose to grace. Even the tabernacle in the wilderness had a portable wall to provide security.

> **Where does the Holy Spirit dwell today? (1 Cor. 6:19-20).**
>
> _____

It is no accident that these verses reside in the very same chapter as our definitive phrase for self-control: "I will not be mastered by anything" (v. 12). We are the temple of God...and self-control is our wall of protection! It fortifies all that is within. The quality of self-control is that which secures our freedom to love, to experience joy, to know peace, to respond with patience, to have a kind disposition, to act out of goodness, to step out in faithfulness, and to agree with gentleness. How? Because self-control is the ability to make choices which invite and enhance the authority and filling of the Holy Spirit. Self-control is the decision to remain within the boundaries of victory!

> **According to the following Scriptures, what happens when the walls of fortification are broken down?**
>
> Ezekiel 26:7-14 _____
>
> _____

Ezekiel 38:11 _____

_____

◐ Can you think of a way in which the enemy has stolen victory from you through a broken-down wall in your life?

_____

_____

Any out-of-control area in our lives, no matter how big or how small, is an open invitation to the enemy. Believe me, he has memorized every strength and every weakness in our lives. He is always on the lookout for that one crumbling section of your protective wall—that one out-of-control area—where he will enter and play havoc in your life. His weapons are your greatest temptations. Your wounds are guilt, shame, frustration, and failure; his goal is to hold you captive for as long as possible. I know. I've been there. Are you a prisoner of war? Have you been in captivity? Do you deeply desire an end to your defeat? Do you want to know the protection and daily victory of self-control?

Read Nehemiah 2:1-20. God's Word will tell you how to begin. Check off the steps you have already taken. Pray about the steps you need to take.

❑ **"I set out...with a few men" (v. 12). Enlist a few accountability partners!**

❑ **"I went out...examining the walls of Jerusalem, which had been broken down" (v. 13). Perform an honest self-examination. In what areas do you lack self-control?**

❑ **"Come, let us rebuild the wall of Jerusalem, and we will no longer be in disgrace" (v. 17). Admit that you have experienced internal or external disgrace in your areas of self-indulgence.**

❑ **"They replied, 'Let us start rebuilding.' So they began this good work" (v. 18). Don't put it off any longer. Begin immediately to cooperate with God's diligent work with you in your areas of captivity. God may work through a structured process such as a support group or counselor.**

❑ **"The God of heaven will give us success" (v. 20). Give it to God, then keep giving it to God over and over until you have overcome.**

You can succeed! "After 20 years of battling this addiction?" Yes! "After 50 years of living out of control?" Yes! Read 2 Corinthians 2:14. If you follow Christ, you'll have to march to success. It's the only direction He's going! Does it seem like too huge a task? Have you tried too many times before? Have those old habits been around a lifetime? Then you need to read Isaiah 58:12.

Write Isaiah 58:12 on a note card and begin to memorize it. God always has the bases covered, doesn't He?

How does God want you to respond to what He showed you today?

_____

_____

_____

_____

_____

_____

_____

192

Day 2

Two Examples

On day 1, we considered the extreme importance of self-control in the life of believers. We learned that self-control is like a wall of protection surrounding us, dramatically reducing our vulnerability to the enemy. Today we are going to study biblical examples of two Greek words we learned on day 1: *akrasia,* which means excessive and indulgent, and *egkrateia,* which means temperate, restrained, self-controlled. Today's study involves a lot of reading. Please complete each assignment, and you will be scripturally equipped for the day ahead!

PART ONE: A LIFE OF *AKRASIA*

1. Read Judges 13:1-25.
Before his conception, God ordained Samson's dedication to Him as a lifelong Nazarite.

> **Read Numbers 6:1-20. Record below at least three of the special actions required of one who took the Nazarite vow.**

_____

_____

_____

Under ordinary conditions, the Nazarite vow was a voluntary pledge of devotion and consecration before the Lord. It was usually taken by those who, for a time, desired to be totally focused and sanctified before God.

> **Read Acts 18:18. Why did Paul have a haircut after leaving Corinth?**

_____

Paul had taken the Nazarite vow for the length of time he ministered in Corinth. A student of cultures, he knew about the open perversion and unabashed sensuality practiced in that city. He wanted very much to minister in the needy places of the world without being personally defiled by the sin of the world. The uncut hair was an outward expression of total devotion. It was a means by which he could let his "moderation be known unto all" (Phil. 4:5, KJV).

The Nazarite vow was a vow of self-control, of restraint, of extreme personal discipline. And it was a vow God ordained for Samson for the length of his life.

⸿Today's Treasure:

"So I tell you this, and insist on it in the Lord, that you must no longer live as the Gentiles do, in the futility of their thinking. Having lost all sensitivity, they have given themselves over to sensuality so as to indulge in every kind of impurity, with a continual lust for more" (Eph. 4:17,19).

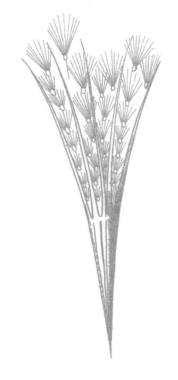

2. Read Judges 14:1-20.

From the first descriptions of Samson's life we observe two serious signs of *akrasia* or self-indulgence. First, Samson possessed a total disrespect for the sacred.

Where did he find the honey?

_____

What two things did he do with the honey? _____

_____

Samson not only disregarded his consecration by touching a dead animal, but he also disrespected his parents. He purposely caused them to unknowingly break Jewish law by eating from the carcass of an unclean animal. The prospect of his parents' disobedience obviously amused him. Beloved, it's dangerous to treat the character and commands of God with disrespect. Disrespect of God-given authority ultimately reaps dreadful results.

What do the following Scriptures teach us about the importance of respect?
Exodus 20:12 _____

_____

Galatians 6:7-8 _____

_____

The second sign of *akrasia* or self-indulgence we observe in Samson is his inappropriate sense of humor. He had an obvious affinity for practical jokes and riddles which were motivated by a lack of respect and were always at the expense of others. Often we can observe an unspoken rule of thumb among Christians: "Inappropriate subjects are admissible as long as they are humorous." We can tell an off-color joke as long as it's funny. We can show disrespect for a person as long as people laugh.

Ask yourself the following questions (which I also asked myself).
Do you have an appropriate sense of humor? ❏ Yes ❏ No

Are you more likely to laugh at an off-color joke than one that is "clean"? ❏ Yes ❏ No

Do you talk to others about inappropriate subjects? ❏ Yes ❏ No
Is it often for a laugh? ❏ Yes ❏ No

God loves laughter. His Word tells us in Proverbs 17:22 that "a cheerful heart is good medicine," but when it is at the expense of God's character, another's character, or our own character, the medicine becomes toxic. My friend, Wanda

Jean Hickey, once said, "We must never compromise holiness for the sake of humor." Excellent wisdom.

3. Read Judges 16:1-31.

Samson's weakness for women ultimately resulted in a fatal attraction. If love is blind, surely lust is twice as blind. His indulgence for the pleasures of the flesh was accompanied by his indulgence for practical jokes—and the mixture was lethal. Not surprisingly, Samson conquered a thousand men with the jawbone of a donkey (see 15:15), but he could not subdue one little woman. Delilah was the death of him. The eyes she caused to be gouged out had long since been blind to the things of God, family, and integrity. A man, whose entire existence was to be the epitome of devotion and restraint, lived practically his entire life out of control. Sadly, Samson was more effective in his death than in his life. Look at Today's Treasure. Samson was a living example of the warning extended in these two verses. By his example, we can draw the following conclusions:

- Self-indulgence robs sensitivity to the Holy Spirit. He had fallen so far away, he was completely unaware that the Holy Spirit's presence was missing.
- Self-indulgence saps us of much-needed strength. Samson's strength was never in his hair. His hair was simply the outward expression of a unique consecration. Samson's supernatural strength was created by the "Spirit of the Lord" who came upon him, and when he continued to ignore God and indulge the flesh, his strength left him.

Self-indulgence is absolutely insatiable. Lives given over to the passions of the flesh are never satisfied, and those who thirst for the perverse are never quenched. Self-indulgence is a never-ending cycle. Now let's look at a life in contrast to Samson's.

PART TWO: A LIFE OF *EGKRATEIA*

1. Read Daniel 1:1-21.

　　What type of food was offered to Daniel? _____

_____

　　What foods did he request? _____

_____

　　Why did he resist the king's foods? (v. 8). _____

_____

　　❧ **What was the difference between Daniel's attitude toward the king's food and Samson's attitude toward the honey?**

_____

_____

Mark the following results of Daniel's restraint true or false.

___ He and his companions were healthier than the young men.

___ They gained favor with the king's official.

___ The king ordered vegetables for all his servants.

___ God provided the four with knowledge and understanding.

2. Read Daniel 6:1-28.

What can you learn about Daniel from the concluding words of verse 10? (Check one.)

❑ He was faithful in prayer.

❑ He feared the government officials.

How did God intervene in Daniel's life? _____

_____

How did King Darius respond to Daniel's rescue? _____

_____

What testimony does verse 28 provide for Daniel? _____

_____

Notice that Daniel did not panic, nor did he ignore the edict. He simply got down on his knees and made his petition. Let's draw several basic conclusions from Daniel's *egkrateia* or self-control:

- Physical discipline and spiritual discipline often go hand in hand. Samson had neither; Daniel had both.
- Prior discipline prepares us for present dilemmas. The time to prepare for a crisis is in advance and through the practice of prayer. It requires discipline to form the habit of prayer and self-control to withstand the obstacles that compete for time.
- Self-control enhances effectiveness; self-indulgence limits effectiveness. Many of us will never fully affect this planet in the ways God planned because of our sheer lack of self-control and discipline. Any effectiveness may seem random and accidental.
- Self-control for God's sake invites God's blessing. Self-control prospers; self-indulgence perishes.

Consider this. Two healthy, red-blooded boys.

- One denied his call of consecration. One chose it.
- One took more than he was offered. One resisted what he was offered.
- One assumed the power of God and ultimately lost it. One asked for the power of God and ultimately found it.
- One was overcome by his enemy. One overcame his enemy.
- One was victorious in his death. One was victorious in his life.

Both young men had everything going for them—with only one major difference: one was protected by the wall of self-discipline; one was not. Ouch.

How does God want you to respond to what He showed you today?

_____

_____

_____

_____

_____

_____

_____

✎ What part most affected you today in 1) Samson's story; 2) Daniel's story?

_____

_____

_____

_____

D a y   3

Chasing the Wind

He had it all. He inherited the largest and most powerful kingdom in his region of the world. He commanded the strongest army on earth. He controlled the trade routes of many kingdoms. His income, excluding trade revenue and taxes, amounted annually to 25 tons of gold. The magnificence of his palace was incomparable. His reputation was larger than life. The wisest on the earth bowed before him. He had it all and then some. His name was Solomon, and he is the focus of our study today.

As we study self-control, we would be remiss to exclude the study of excess. We live in a culture motivated by one major goal—a little bit more. We work too hard and make too little. We have more than enough to live complicated lives, but less than enough to be contented. Let's allow the Word of God to address our obsession with money, position, and possessions by observing the state of one man's soul once he finally attained it all.

Read Ecclesiastes 1:1-11 and answer the following questions.

Paraphrase Solomon's words in verse 2._____

_____

What does he say about the eye? (Check one.)
❑ The eye is evil.
❑ The eye never gets enough.
❑ They eye is the window to the soul.

Fill in the blanks: "What has _____ will be _____,

what has been _____ will be _____ again; there

is _____" (v. 9).

🍂**Today's Treasure:**

"Remember your Creator in the days of your youth, before the days of trouble come and the years approach when you will say, 'I find no pleasure in them'" (Eccl. 12:1).

What is Solomon's point in verse 11? _____

_____

Read Ecclesiastes 1:12-18. How does Solomon describe the pursuit of wisdom?

_____

_____

Read Ecclesiastes 2:1-11 and answer the following questions.
What else proved to be "meaningless" in verses 1-3? (Check one.)
❑ work   ❑ love   ❑ pleasure   ❑ sex

What happened when Solomon undertook great projects? (Check one.)
❑ All his accomplishments were meaningless.
❑ His accomplishments achieved his goal of meaning and purpose.

What was Solomon's apparent philosophy according to verse 10?
❑ self-denial   ❑ hedonism   ❑ anarchy

What was gained by his philosophy? (v. 11).

_____

_____

Read Ecclesiastes 2:12-26 and answer the following questions.
What was Solomon's reaction to the "meaninglessness" of all he had pursued? (v. 17).

_____

Why did he hate all the things he had "toiled for under the sun"?
(vv. 18,21).

_____

What does Solomon say in verse 26 about climbing the ladder to

success? _____

Read Ecclesiastes 5:10-20.
Complete verse 10: "Whoever loves money _____

_____; whoever loves wealth _____

_____ with his income."

What does "wealth hoarded to the harm of its owner" (v. 13) mean to you?

_____

_____

What is "a gift of God"? (v. 19). _____

_____

Two very important points of emphasis appear in this verse:
- God gives wealth and possessions.
- Only God can enable us to enjoy them.

Are you finding it difficult to "accept" your lot? Only God can give you a heart of acceptance! Are you miserable in your job? Only God can make you happy in your work! Contentment with your present position and state of prosperity, no matter how vast or small, can come only from Him! But only you can allow God to work contentment in you.

> **Now read Ecclesiastes 12:9-14. What is Solomon's final "conclusion of the matter"?**

_____

_____

Many other Scriptures in God's Word instruct us about self-control related to material possessions. What insights do the following Scriptures offer about the shortcomings of money and wealth?

> **☙ Read Matthew 6:24. What happens when we attempt to serve both God and money?**

_____

_____

Now read Proverbs 23:5. How stable are riches? _____

_____

Proverbs 15:16 suggests that turmoil follows when the fear of the Lord is not present? Why?

_____

_____

Which of the following statements best summarizes the principle being taught in Haggai 1:5-6? (Check one.)
❑ **Little is much when the Lord is present.**
❑ **Without God we can never find true satisfaction.**
❑ **Your response:** _____

In his wonderful book, *Seasons of Life,* Chuck Swindoll tells the story of a man by the name of Yussif, or better known as "The Terrible Turk."

He was a 350-pound wrestler who won it all in Europe before coming to America to grab more glory. Yussif challenged Strangler Lewis, our 200-pound champion grappler. The Turk tossed the Strangler around like a teddy bear and won. The new world champ picked up what he loved the most—money—5,000 dollars of it, which he demanded in U.S. gold. He crammed it into the money belt he wore around his huge circumference before setting sail back to Europe on the S.S. Burgoyne.

Many miles at sea, the ship began to sink. Yussif went over the side with his bulging belt full of gold still strapped around his enormous frame. The added weight was too much for even the Terrible Turk to stay afloat. Before the lifeboats could reach him, he plunged straight to the bottom of the Atlantic like an oversize iron cannon...never to be seen again.[7]

What good will it be for a man if he gains the whole world, yet forfeits his soul? (Matt. 16:26).

Read 1 Timothy 6:3-10. What is great gain?

_____

We often reason that our pursuit of money and possessions is for the good of our children...for their "security." Read Proverbs 14:26 to determine how parents can build a secure fortress for their children.

_____

Conclude today's study by reading Proverbs 30:7-9. What wisdom do you find for relating to wealth?

_____

_____

_____

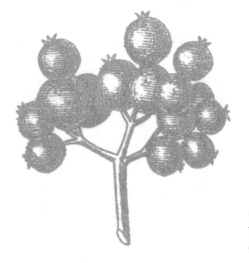

Lord, let me never have such riches that I forget you, nor such poverty that I steal and dishonor your name. Most of us are already there, Beloved, in that nice, safe place where we depend on God every single day just to make ends meet. If that stack of bills helps you never forget He is God, praise Him for it! If that paycheck keeps you from dishonoring His name, Hallelujah! You're right where you belong—within the secure walls of self-control, where excess is an unwelcome guest.

He knows our needs. He knows our vulnerabilities. He knows what we can endure...yet remain faithful. All things are His to give and His to take, but never ours to pursue. Ours is to gladly receive and gladly return. Solomon learned valuable lessons about material excesses in one way; God may instruct you in another.

 ☞ In the past, how has God helped you keep your priorities straight about money and possessions?

_____

_____

_____

Sometimes we discover we need to relearn some old lessons. Let's allow God to refresh the priorities He's taught us in the past, then recommit our futures to Him.

> **For the pagans run after all these things, and your heavenly Father knows that you need them. But seek first his kingdom and his righteousness, and all these things will be given to you as well. Therefore do not worry about tomorrow, for tomorrow will worry about itself. Each day has enough trouble of its own (Matt. 6:32-34).**

Day 4

An Exercise in Control

On day 1, we defined self-control and considered our desperate need for the wall of protection it provides. On day 2, we contrasted the lives of two men: one perishing and the other prospering over the basic issue of self-control. On day 3, we observed the futility of excess in the life of King Solomon. Today our study will be divided into two parts, the struggle to gain self-control over the mind and the mouth.

PART ONE: EXERCISING SELF-CONTROL OVER THE MIND

In several of our previous units we have observed the impact of properly feeding the mind; therefore, I will refrain from redundancy by focusing on one specific area in desperate need of our control: the television.

How does God want you to respond to what He showed you today?

_____

_____

_____

_____

_____

_____

☞ Today's Treasure:

"A man of knowledge uses words with restraint, and a man of understanding is even-tempered. Even a fool is thought wise if he keeps silent, and discerning if he holds his tongue" (Prov. 17:27-28).

Way back in 1979, *Good Housekeeping* printed an article written by Cathy Trost and Ellen Grzech called, "What Happened When 5 Families Stopped Watching TV?" A Detroit newspaper issued an offer of $500 each to 120 families who would cease watching television for one month. Of those 120 families, 93 turned down the offer. Of the remaining 27 families, 5 families who had been watching television from 40 to 70 hours a week became the study subjects. You can imagine what an adjustment these families faced after having watched an average of 6 to 10 hours of TV a day. The results, however, were closer family units; increased family activities such as games, piano playing, and singing; one-on-one time between parents and children; and patience! Families also reported an increase in creativity.

In an article he wrote for the *Christian Medical Science Journal* entitled "TV and Your Child," Urie Bronfenbrenn surmised, "The primary danger of the television screen lies not so much in the behavior it produces as the behavior it prevents." That was in 1978. Today's studies point to overwhelming evidence that the sex and violence depicted on TV appear to have a marked effect on behavior. An article in the *Houston Chronicle* by Joe Stinebaker (11-6-93) was entitled, "Gawkers' Growing Fascination with Violence Cited." It read like this:

> It's a still weekend night in southwest Houston. A young man's body lies face-down on a sidewalk outside an apartment complex, his life cut short by two bullets fired into his head at close range. A crowd has gathered outside the yellow tape-line set up by police only moments ago. Many in the crowd are carrying children—some perched on a parent's shoulders, to better take in the macabre scene. Such is the state of murder in Houston. No longer do parents feel the need to shield their children's eyes from the carnage of the streets. Murder has become urban theatre.

Is there any chance that a bird's-eye view of ongoing violence on an electric box in their living room has desensitized parents to what is acceptable and what is unacceptable? Two good reasons urge us to exercise self-control over what we watch and how much we watch—the behavior it prevents and the behavior it produces. Our children are not the only ones at risk. Recently I heard statistics which stated that more than 80 percent of all intimacy depicted on television is extramarital. And they make it look so exciting, so inviting.

It will take enormous self-control for some of us to reconsider and reduce what we watch on television. But, strangely, any self-control it costs us will be multiplied in more. It's time to trade in the remote control for a little self-control.

Examine each of the following Scriptures and consider how they relate to self-control in the area of television.

How can TV viewing contribute to our being in a "snare"? (Ps. 25:15).

When we "set before our eyes" the "deeds of faithless men" how can those deeds "cling to us"? (Ps. 101:3).

Fill in the blanks from Psalm 119:37: "Turn my eyes away from

_____ **things; preserve my** _____ **according**

to your word."

✎ Read Romans 12:2. In the past year, can you identify at least one specific way you have struggled to avoid being conformed to the pattern of this world? ❑ Yes ❑ No If so, explain.

_____

_____

What practical steps can you take to "take captive every thought" in

your life? (2 Cor. 10:5). _____

_____

_____

PART TWO: EXERCISING SELF-CONTROL OVER THE MOUTH

Two functions of the mouth need serious self-control: the ability to taste and the ability to talk. The remainder of today's study will, therefore, center on two issues—what we put in our mouths and what we send out of our mouths.

1. Controlling that which ENTERS the mouth.
Read 1 Corinthians 6:12. It should be familiar to you from day 1. Now look at the very next verse: "'Food for the stomach and the stomach for food'—but God will destroy them both." It is no accident that the subject of physical appetite is immediately followed by the exhortation to let nothing master us. Many Americans—bone thin to morbidly obese—are mastered by food.

Since overeating is neither immoral nor illegal, it is a common outlet for excess. Just last week on my favorite Christian radio station, the "call-in" topic was food addictions. One woman called in and stated proudly: "Mine is chocolate...any form, any time. I just have to have my chocolate." The radio personality inquired: "And what happens if you don't get it? I mean, do you get the shakes or anything?" She paused. A few silent moments passed before she finally said: "I don't know. That's never happened to me before!"

Craving food (not to be confused with requiring food) tends to be the acceptable Christian addiction. Its greater acceptability, however, does not produce greater benefits. Setting aside the physical effects, which I will leave to the experts, the loss of control and the addiction to overeating is deeply guilt-provoking and self-defeating. Equally devastating is the avoidance of food. Anorexia Nervosa is also considered a form of food addiction. It is not God's will for us to be mastered by anything other than Him. He wants us to be free from obsession: from the obsession of eating and from the obsession of not eating.

Write 1 Corinthians 10:31 in the space below.

_____

_____

Now reconsider the words of 1 Corinthians 6:12, also repeated in 1 Corinthians 10:23: "'Everything is permissible'—but not everything is beneficial." In the context of eating and drinking for the glory of God, what do you think this verse means?

_____

_____

I don't believe starvation forms of dieting are to the glory of God. I don't believe that crash dieting leads to much more than binging. The point is neither size nor shape. The point is freedom: a freedom that results from eating that which is beneficial to the body with not only the intent of losing weight, but also with the intent of glorifying God. This same resulting freedom leaves the results of our obedience up to Him. We'll be free. He'll be glorified, and we might just lose a pound or two in the process.

Your food-related addiction may be so overpowering that you have already surrendered to a life out of control. Please think about it, my Friend. The temporary comfort of food cannot begin to match the inevitable long-range guilt and self-defeat. If you have every other area under control but you are mastered by food, which is a portion of your broken-down wall, Satan will use it to trample you. If you often feel out of control and guilt-ridden after you eat, you need God's help to repair the broken wall. The process may be One-on-one, or God may lead you to "someone with a little skin on her" for encouragement. Christ-centered groups can help you feel less alone in your struggle.[8] Seek Him and find out. He already has a plan for your release.

Now, let's proceed from taste to talk.

2. Controlling that which EXITS the mouth.
Now we're getting down to the nitty-gritty of self-control. Check it out for yourself.

Read James 3:1-12 and answer the following questions.
✎ **What type of person is never at fault in what he says?**

_____

To what does James compare the tongue in verse 6?
❑ a raging fire   ❑ a devastating flood   ❑ a deadly plague

Think creatively for a moment. What comparisons could you draw between a fire and the tongue?

_____

What does James say can be tamed by humans? _____

_____

What does he say humans cannot tame? _____

_____

Why is it ironic that we bless God but curse men? (v. 9).
❑ **because we are sinners**
❑ **because humans are made in God's image**
❑ **because God blesses those we curse**

Ephesians 4:29 provides a standard for the words we say to others. Write that standard below in your own words.

_____

_____

Some of us may not to be talkers (fortunately for others), but we may be great listeners! Remember the catchy tune from the country variety show called "Hee Haw": "No, you'll never catch one of us repeating gossip. So you'd better be sure and listen close the first time!" Read 1 Thessalonians 4:11-12 and 2 Thessalonians 3:11. What are these verses saying? Mind your own business! Beloved, it takes great self-control to walk away from a great story. But you won't walk away alone, you'll walk away with your integrity.

When it comes to the mind and to the mouth, the goal is to take those four negative words of Felix used in Acts 24:25 and turn them into four positive words of self-control: "That's enough for now!"

Read 2 Peter 1:3-11. How can Peter's words help us in our battle to make choices in favor of self-control?

How does God want you to respond to what He showed you today?

_____

_____

_____

And add...to knowledge, self-control; and to self-control, perseverance; and to perseverance, godliness (2 Pet. 1:5-6).

We've been given the knowledge. It's our choice to add self-control. Look carefully. It's the only way to godliness.

You've worked hard this week, and the subject matter has been very difficult. By mustering enough self-control to get through this week's study, you have demonstrated great persistence and fortitude. You are walking in the right direction. Be encouraged!

Today's Treasure:

"Be imitators of God, therefore, as dearly loved children and live a life of love, just as Christ loved us and gave himself up for us as a fragrant offering and sacrifice to God" (Eph. 5:1-2).

Victorious Living

I write this final day's study with deep emotion. My heart is filled with gratitude to God for the privilege of sojourning alongside you these past weeks. The purpose of this study is practicality—the nuts and bolts of living the Spirit-filled life. A victorious life is the sum of many victorious days. Therefore, we will conclude on a practical note. Just how are we supposed to practice all that we've learned on a day-to-day basis? Let's take a look at…

A DAY IN THE LIFE OF A VICTOR

Read Psalm 63 aloud and with joy! This wonderful song of David is the perfect guide for living a day in victory from morning until night. Join me as we walk through a day of spiritual abundance…a day in the life of a victor.

GLORIOUS MORNING!

Look carefully at verse 1. The Hebrew word for *earnestly* is *shachar* and it means "dawn, early, to search for with painstaking, rise, seek diligently, in the morning."[9] We can conclude that the general idea of *shachar* is "rising in immediate pursuit." Psalm 63 opens in the earliest moment of the day, reminding us that a victorious day begins with a victorious morning! You may be saying, "But, I'm just not a morning person." I understand. But the problem is: God is a morning Person!

> Because of the Lord's great love we are not consumed, for his compassions never fail. They are new every morning; great is your faithfulness (Lam. 3:22-23).

What does Mark 1:35 tell us about Jesus' morning practice?

_____

_____

Psalm 5:3 tells us that David took two specific actions in the morning. What were they?

_____

_____

It may be that you have more time and opportunity to pray and study later in the day. However, please remember the words of Isaiah 50:4-5: we need to hear from God first thing in the morning! Whether or not you do the majority of your praying and studying in the morning, to experience abundant victory you must accomplish the following steps at this point in the day.

1. Acknowledge His authority!

Notice the repetition of the word *God* in Psalm 63:1. Did you know that those are actually two different Hebrew words? The first word translated *God* is the Hebrew word *elohiym* which is the plural form. I believe the plural to be a veiled reference pointing to the Holy Trinity. All three members of the Godhead were active in creation.

The second usage of the word *God* is *el*—the singular form of the word. It basically means "the one."[10] We can read the verse this way, "Oh, mighty Three in One, you are my only one!" The psalmist begins by acknowledging God as his God—the only focus of his worship. He rises up only to bow before the Lord.

Every victorious day should begin exactly this way. The moment you awake, settle the issue of authority. Awaken every morning to the challenge, "Choose… this day whom you will serve!" (Josh. 24:15). Remember, any day not surrendered to the Spirit is virtually surrendered to the flesh by simple default! We will slip back into what comes most naturally to us: our sin nature! Remember, the things of the Spirit come supernaturally to us by God's invitation.

As you acknowledge His lordship, confess to Him any thoughts, words, or deeds performed outside the realm of His authority. This is a perfect time for the repentance of all unconfessed sin and places Him in proper perspective and you in proper perspective. All sin boils down to an issue of authority. His will or my will?

2. Abound in His presence!

"My soul thirsts for you, my body longs for you" (Ps. 63:1). After you have acknowledged that He is Lord over you and you have asked Him to rid you of all self, you are standing before Him completely empty.

Read Matthew 12:43-45. What happened to the empty "house"?

_____

Although I believe Scripture teaches that we who are born again cannot be demon-possessed, our emptied vessel can be filled by a surpassing abundance of the flesh—and quickly. Never leave the vessel empty. Long for His presence. Ask Him to give you a spirit that desires to be full of Him. Right now, invite the filling of the Holy Spirit. Remember, cleansing + yielding = filling, and with the filling of the Spirit comes the fruit of the Spirit! As often as you are completely cleansed and yielded, you will possess a power that is completely beyond you…to love, to experience joy, to know peace, to express patience, to possess kindness and respond in goodness, to be faithful, gentle, and submissive to His will, restrained and under control.

3. Ask to see His glory and power!

Beloved, do you really want to experience God? Right here on this earth? Today? Seek Him.

What does Jeremiah 29:13 say? _____

_____

Only through the filling of the Holy Spirit can you truly see God in the daily grind of living because the things of the Spirit are spiritually discerned, and only those filled with the Spirit are spiritually discerning. Being filled with the Spirit means having our spiritual eyes opened. Like Elisha's servant, we will see God work in ways to which the carnal Christian is blinded!

What is it we want to see? His power and His glory! Look back at Psalm 63:2. Power appears in the works of God. Glory describes the ways of God. Power represents what He does. Glory represents who He is. Only the Spirit-filled Christian has the *chutzpah* to really ask to see God's power and glory. Only the Spirit-filled Christian can discern all the ways they've seen Him.

Be careful not to limit your eyes to the "big things." The ways God has most blessed me with His presence have undoubtedly been in the small, intimate details of my life. He proves repeatedly that He's really watching! If you ask to see Him and then agree to keep watching through the eyes of the Spirit, you will see His power and His glory everyday.

From glorious morning to marvelous day! Let's proceed to actions sparked in the morning and then spontaneous throughout the day.

4. Award Him with your mouth!

Take a look at Psalm 63:3: "Because your love is better than life, my lips will glorify you." Remember what we learned on day 4 of this week? The tongue is the hardest of all living things to tame. Pray for a mouth that glorifies Him all day long, and you will be filled with a sense of His love and approval.

> **Read each of the following Scriptures, and describe what they say about the mouth.**
>
> **Psalm 39:1** _____
>
> **Psalm 81:10** _____
>
> **Psalm 40:10** _____

Forget what your Mama said! When it comes to the things of the Spirit...never talk unless your mouth is full!

5. Approach Him with praise!

"I will praise you as long as I live" (Ps. 63:4). Praise Him off and on all day long. You don't have to have something specific to praise Him for...just praise Him for Who He is! He is worthy!

Here's something that works for me. Continuous praise in my ear is the catalyst for consistent praise coming out of my mouth. I listen to praise music continually. Even when I am totally unaware of it, praises are feeding my spirit and teaching me to praise. Every time I get in the car...every time I take a walk. Praise music. I have a strong carnal nature and I cannot afford to allow my mind to be idle. Music is one of the greatest praise catalysts as well as spiritual pleasures in my life. One of my most treasured moments is when I first awaken and my spirit is midway through a praise song. What a joy to realize that while we are sleeping, our spirits are often still praising. Hallelujah!

6. **Attribute all satisfaction to Him!**

       ✍ **Read Psalm 65:4. What does God do for the "blessed" person?**

_____

    The *King James Version* says it this way: "Blessed is the man whom thou choosest, and causest to approach unto thee, that he may dwell in thy courts: we shall be satisfied."

    The advertising industry of the United States of America is banking a billion dollars a year on a singular belief: they can convince you that you are not yet satisfied. You "need" a new car. You "need" a new house. You "need" some new furniture. You "need" a new VCR. Your children "need" the newest electronics. In a very literal sense, it is their business to perpetuate in you a spirit of dissatisfaction. If you ever realize that you are satisfied, they lose big bucks.

    Answering the invitation of access is the only thing that will ever truly satisfy. Then He will give you everything else (see Matt. 6:33), and when He does, enjoy it! Don't cling to it or idolize it, but enjoy it...and share it!

    Deuteronomy 26:11 says: "You and the Levites and the aliens among you shall rejoice in all the good things the LORD your God has given to you and your household." From glorious morning to marvelous day to blessed night! Now, we've come to the close of a day in the life of a victor. Did you notice that the end of the day is just as important as the beginning?

7. **Audit the manifold blessings!**
"On my bed I remember you" (Ps. 63:6). If you asked in the morning to see His power and His glory, and you allowed Him to adjust your spiritual vision and sought Him with all your heart, then you can be sure He worked in the course of the day. Recount His faithfulness to you. In your journal record the ways you have seen Him that day. Keep a diary of His activity in your life. A record of your history with God is an immeasurable asset to your Christian experience. How do you know He will care for you today? Because He cared for you yesterday! And the day before! And the day before! He never changes. He'll never forget you. When He discloses Himself to you, remember it, praise Him for it, and record it! Nighttime is prime time for remembering the day.

8. **Allow yourself to rest in His arms!**
"I sing in the shadow of your wings. My soul clings to you; your right hand upholds me" (Ps. 63:7-8). Turn your enemies over to Him (see vv. 9-11). Cast your cares at His feet, then crawl up under His everlasting arm and rest.

    Fill in the blanks from Psalm 4:8: "I will lie down and _____ in

    peace , for you alone, O LORD, make me dwell in _____."

    That, my precious Friend, is a day in the life of a victor. Praise His faithful name that we receive a new chance to begin again every single morning...complete with mercies enough to make it through another day...until He shouts. You may say, "But, Beth, I'll be thinking of Him off and on all day!" Yes, you will. Isaiah 26:3 says, "Thou wilt keep him in perfect peace, whose mind is stayed on thee" (KJV). He's worth it.

Living Beyond Yourself! It"s the only way to live. He's the only way to do it.

THE COMPANY I KEEP

Let me be known by the company I keep
By the One who determines each day that I greet
From the moment I wake til He rocks me to sleep
Let me be known by the company I keep!

Let me be known by the company I keep
When the valleys are low and the mountains are steep
By the One who holds fast when swift waters are deep
Let me be known by the company I keep!

Let me be known by the company I keep
By the One who implores me to sit at His feet
And quickens my soul to discern what is deep
Let me be known by the company I keep!

Let me be known by the company I keep
Eclipsed by your presence that I may decrease
Til all You have chosen this traveler to meet
No longer see me but the Company I keep.

—Beth

But the fruit of the Spirit is love, joy, peace, patience, kindness, goodness, faithfulness, gentleness, and self-control. Against such things there is no law (Gal. 5:22-23).

That's living proof.

✎ **How does God want you to respond to what He showed you in *Living Beyond Yourself?***

[1]Spiros Zodhiates et al., eds., *The Complete Word Study Dictionary: New Testament* (Chattanooga, TN: AMG Publishers, 1992), 499-500.
[2]John F. MacArthur, *The MacArthur New Testament Commentary Galatians* (Chicago: The Moody Bible Institute, 1987), 169.
[3]Ibid., 500.
[4]Ibid., 607.
[5]Trent C. Butler et al., eds., *Holman Bible Dictionary* (Nashville: Holman Bible Publishers, 1991), 1398.
[6]James Strong, from the *Hebrew and Chaldee Dictionary* of *The Exhaustive Concordance of the Bible* (Nashville: Holman Bible Publishers, n.d.), 37.
[7]Charles R. Swindoll, *Growing Strong in the Seasons of Life* (Portland, OR: Multnomah Press, 1983), 271.
[8]*Conquering Eating Disorders* is a Christ-Centered 12-Step process for persons dealing with eating disorders and is available from LifeWay Christian Resources. Another resource, *First Place: A Christ-Centered Health Program*, also available from LifeWay Christian Resources, helps individuals and groups follow a healthy lifestyle plan while utilizing biblical principles and Bible study. For more information about these resources, contact Customer Service at 1-800-458-2772.
[9]Strong, *Hebrew and Chaldee Dictionary*, 114.
[10]Ibid., 12.

Living Beyond Yourself

Leader's Guide

Introduction

Living Beyond Yourself is an in-depth, 10-week Bible study of the fruit of the Spirit.

LEADER QUALIFICATIONS

You do not need a long list of qualifications nor years of teaching experience to lead *Living Beyond Yourself.* You simply need a heart prepared by God with availability and teachability. Your role is that of a facilitator. You will not teach the material. You will help members learn for themselves.

Your success as a facilitator depends on:
- A heart committed to exploring crucial truths and the desire to lead others in the same pursuit;
- Your commitment to complete this study;
- Your faithfulness to each weekly meeting; and
- Your fulfilling the basic responsibilities described in this leader guide.

I have attempted to remove much of the guesswork you might have in preparing and guiding a group through *Living Beyond Yourself.* Follow the model that appears below for preparing before the session, conducting the session, and evaluating after the session.

BEFORE THE SESSION
1. Each week complete the activities in the member book.
2. Pray for each member of your group by name.
3. Pray for God's guidance in your preparation for this week's group session.
4. Carefully read through the session guide. Make sure you prepare for each suggested question and activity.
5. Arrange your room to meet the needs of your group. An intimate setting seems to be most beneficial.

DURING THE SESSION
1. Arrival Activity (10 mins.)
- Greet each member and distribute name tags. Learn every member's name and use it when you speak to her.
- Share prayer requests, graciously reminding members of the guidelines: please be brief and to the point!
- List requests as you receive them so that you can refer to them as you pray.

- Lead the group to pray for each request. Ask for God's presence and blessing throughout the session.

2. Review the Week's Principal Questions and Personal Discussion Questions (45 mins.)
You are looking for brief and basic answers to the Principal Questions. Seek to confirm that the study content was received and understood. Two to three minutes should be sufficient. Answers should be obvious as members complete the weekly reading and learning activities; however, ahead of time, compose basic answers to the questions and use to correct any misconceptions. Each day's Principal Question will be followed by a Personal Discussion Question.

Personal Discussion Questions can be answered by anyone who feels comfortable sharing. Do not pressure members to share personal answers, but allow them the opportunity to share. Ask them to be discreet and to never name another person who could be hurt by the discussion. Appropriate discussion of these questions is invaluable to the application of the unit. Be prepared to redirect if at any point the discussion becomes inappropriate. Pray for discretion and boldness to redirect at such times.

3. Conclude Session (5 mins.)
- Give a brief introduction to next week's study and encourage members to complete their home study.
- Close with prayer. Do not ask for prayer requests. (Remind members they were given that opportunity at the beginning of the session.)

If you followed the suggested time schedule, you will be able to dismiss your group five minutes early. However, you may need this five minutes to address any unexpected but brief needs or comments.

AFTER THE SESSION
1. While the session is still fresh on your mind, immediately record concerns or impressions to pray for any group member. Remember to pray for these concerns throughout the week.
2. Evaluate the session by asking yourself the following questions. Record your answers in your journal.
   - Was I adequately prepared for today's session?
   - Did I begin and end on time? If not, how can I use the time more wisely next session?

- Does anyone need extra encouragement this week? Note whether a card or a phone call is appropriate. Then remember to follow-up on each one.
- What was my overall impression of the session?

3. Read the next session guide in order to prepare for the next session.

HOW TO BEGIN A GROUP

1. Seek the approval of your pastor. Enlist his OK and, ideally, his blessing. Encourage him to announce this new opportunity for women. Since women fill many vital positions in the body of Christ, the deepening of their spiritual lives should be a high priority in any church.

2. Present the idea to the women of your church and ask how many would like to be involved. You need an approximate number, even before the registration session, to order books, enlist small-group leaders, and reserve room accommodations.

3. Choose 11 consecutive weeks on your church calendar that will allow maximum participation. Schedule one introductory session and 10 study sessions. Fall and spring sessions tend to have better attendance than summer sessions.

4. Determine from the level of interest whether to schedule sessions during the day, in the evening, or both. Try to offer a time slot that will meet the needs of women employed outside the home. I am deeply burdened for women who work outside the home.

5. Because this is a study designed for women, if at all possible offer childcare. This provision will increase your attendance and encourage mothers' weekly participation.

6. After approximating the number of participants, order materials direct from Customer Service Center by calling 1-800-458-2772. Or you may order from your local LifeWay Christian Store. Purchase one member book for each participant. Leader material is contained in this leader guide.

7. Enlist one facilitator or leader for each group of 12 women. If this is not possible, conduct the group Bible study anyway. Pray for God's guidance and blessings in spite of the leader/member ratio.

8. Once leaders have been enlisted and dates reserved on the church calendar, take advantage of whatever avenues your church offers for promoting *Living Beyond Yourself*. This study is a wonderful opportunity for church outreach. If possible, invite women from the community who are interested in a Bible-based study. Church bulletins, newsletters, handouts, posters, and word-of-mouth are excellent and inexpensive ways to advertise the study. Sometimes local radio stations announce impending events in the community (free of charge). Do a little research to discover available promotion ideas and then take advantage of them!

9. Pray, pray, and keep praying that God will bring both the members and the leaders that He desires and that He will validate this Bible-based study with His obvious presence and apparent activity!

After you have completed each of the preceding nine steps, you're on your way! Now it's time to prepare for registration and your introductory meeting!

Just Between Us...

Because of my love for in-depth Bible study, I've tried to make it my business to know what works and what doesn't in a ladies Bible-based study. Through the years I've asked many women what they liked or did not like about the way their Bible studies were conducted. I've also offered countless evaluations at the conclusion of those which I have taught. I believe women are looking for the following characteristics in the administration of their group Bible studies:

- Women want organization! Women have very little time in our busy culture. When they give the precious resource of their personal time, it is undoubtedly at the sacrifice of something else. They want to participate in a well-planned program and use their time wisely.
- Women who register for in-depth Bible study want the greater emphasis to remain on the Bible study. In other words, during discussion time, they are more interested in what God has to say and the response of the women to His Word than they are in haphazard opinions. The effective leader will keep discussions focused on the responses of the women to God's Word.
- Women desire well-respected guidelines rather than stringent restrictions about attendance and confidentiality. An effective leader makes the group aware that if guidelines are respected, there will be no need for restrictions.
- Women want to feel connected to their small group. They want to meet other members. They want to know they are missed when they are absent. And they want to know they are an addition to the group when they are present.

Introductory Session

GOALS FOR THIS SESSION

In this session you will—
- register all members for *Living Beyond Yourself;*
- develop a role or attendance sheet;
- distribute member books;
- welcome all members; and
- explain basics about the format.

BEFORE THE SESSION

1. If you are expecting 20 or more participants, arrange tables in the designated meeting room and place cards indicating a division of the alphabet at several check-in stations. For example, those with last names beginning with letters A–E will sign up at one station, F–J at the next, etc.
2. Enlist a volunteer or group leader to sit at each check-in station. Consider forming small groups by designating those each leader registers as members of her group. Adjust as necessary.
3. Instruct each "registrar," whether leader or volunteer, to be at her station 30 minutes before registration begins. Supply each with member books, registration cards or sign-up sheets (prepared by your church or study leader), pens, and name tags.
4. Each registrar assumes responsibility for each new member's first impression. Be sure registrars wear their name tags, greet new members with enthusiasm, anticipate questions and provide answers, make registering members feel welcome, and provide additional instructions. (After registration, members report to a joint session during the introductory session only. After the introductory meeting, members will begin each week in their discussion groups and each leader will take attendance.)

DURING THE SESSION

Introduction to *Living Beyond Yourself* (60 mins.)

1. Open with prayer.
2. Welcome members and introduce leadership. Consider asking each member to introduce herself or. create an icebreaker to introduce members.
3. After introductions, give instructions and information related to the course. Include the following and any additional information pertinent to your church facility:

a. Ask members to scan the first week's daily assignments. Emphasize that each week's study is to be completed prior to each weekly meeting. Say, For example, before the next meeting, complete the study and activities for week 1. Also explain that although the daily assignments are absolutely crucial to the study, members are urged to attend the weekly group sessions even if their work is incomplete. Each daily assignment will take approximately 30 to 45 minutes.

b. Encourage members to read the introduction in the member book before beginning their study.

c. Using the introduction to the member book, explain that the format and distinctive features were designed to enhance learning. Point out that the Principal Questions, listed in the introduction to each week, and the Personal Discussion Questions, appearing in green, will be discussed in the weekly group sessions.

d. Emphasize the following primary reasons for small-group discussion:
  - *To establish accountability.* In-depth Bible studies are most often completed successfully in a group.
  - *To underscore the basic biblical truths presented in the previous week's study.* This is accomplished through discussing answers to the Principal Questions, which ensure that the biblical information offered in the study has been received and understood.
  - *To identify ways to personally apply this Bible-based study.* This will be accomplished through discussing answers to the Personal Discussion Questions.

e. Express the need to be good stewards of the time scheduled for each session. Time consciousness can mean the success or failure of any group. Ask members to adopt the following time guidelines for the remaining sessions.
  - Leaders: Be early!
  - Members: Be on time!
  - Small-groups: Start on time! Leaders, make it a habit to start on time regardless of the number present.
  - Members: Personal comments are vital to the discussion time, but be brief and to the point.

4. After today's introductory meeting, instruct members to report first to discussion groups. Explain that they will receive a phone call within 24 hours iden-

tifying their leader and informing them where their group will meet for small-group discussion (sessions 1 through 10.) A total of 50 minutes is allotted for discussion divided according to the following.

- *Welcome and prayer (5 mins.).* If you ask for prayer requests, encourage members to state them in one brief sentence. Intervene graciously if a request becomes lengthy.
- *Discussion of the Principal Questions and Personal Discussion Questions (45 mins.).* Allow 8-9 minutes to discuss each day's assignments. Each day's Principal Question can be answered in 2-3 minutes leaving 5-6 minutes for Personal Discussion Questions. Write these time divisions on chart paper or a chalkboard and post as a reminder for all group members.

Closing Remarks and Prayer (5 mins.)
1. Present a brief introduction to week 1.
2. Answer any questions. If you do not know the answer, call the questioner as soon as you collect the information she desires. Gather name tags as the group departs.

AFTER THE SESSION
1. Compile all registration cards or lists and, if there are more than 12 members and more than 1 leader, divide the members into small groups. Ideally groups should include no more than 12 members.
2. Ask leader(s) to call members within the next 24 hours to introduce themselves and inform them of their group's meeting place the following week.
3. Ask a leader or volunteer to create attendance sheets (using the registration cards) for each leader. Distribute attendance sheets to small-group leaders prior to the next session.

You can do it! If you follow these guidelines you will be good stewards of the one-hour time period. Implement the suggestions in this introduction and you will ensure that women are receive the utmost from this Bible-based study.

Before we proceed to the session guides, I would like to share one final comment. As a leader of *Living Beyond Yourself*, you have the opportunity to witness lives being changed, not the least of which is your own! And so you ask me, "Beth, How can you say that having no idea how this Bible study will be received in my church?" Because God's Word changes lives! If a woman dedicates herself to this study in God's Word,

her life will undoubtedly be transformed. As a leader, be careful not to let your administration of this study eclipse your participation. Open God's Word and enjoy! Walk in faith toward the woman He designed you to become. His Word will not return void!

Just Between Us...
God has allowed me the most awesome privilege of getting to know women across the nation, who are involved in weekly Bible studies. I have come to the conclusion that women basically have the same expectations when they meet together each week. I pray that together we can meet and exceed their expectations!

–Beth

SESSION 1

Free at Last!

DURING THE SESSION
1. **Arrival Activity (10 mins.)**

2. **Review the Week's Principal Questions and Personal Discussion Questions (45 mins.)**
Day 1:
- *Principal Question:* How did Paul respond to persecution in the city of Lystra?
- *Personal Discussion Question:* Do you think you would have responded the way Paul and Barnabas did in Acts 14:2-3? Why or why not?
Day 2:
- *Principal Question:* What are four major reasons Christ died for us?
- *Personal Discussion Question:* For you, what would it mean to seek only God's approval?
Day 3:
- *Principal Question:* What reasons might Paul have cited to avoid confronting Peter?
- *Personal Discussion Question:* Read Matthew 27:32-44. Put yourself in Jesus' place. How difficult would it be to surrender your rights and not "come down from the cross and save yourself"?
Day 4:
- *Principal Question:* On what basis is righteousness credited to us?

• *Personal Discussion Question:* Can you describe an instance in which you were challenged to "believe" God and He showed Himself faithful?

Day 5:

• *Principal Question:* After careful deliberation, when did God decide to adopt you?

• *Personal Discussion Question:* In what way did the Father show His great love for you, and what does His demonstration suggest about His willingness to meet your needs?

If time allows, ask for ways God spoke directly to members as a result of week 1. Affirm your members' participation and grasp of the material. Give a brief introduction to week 2 and encourage members to complete their home study. Close with prayer.

If you followed the suggested time schedule, you can dismiss the group five minutes early. Chances are, however, you will need this five minutes for any unexpected, but brief questions, needs or comments.

> **Just Between Us…**
> *The first week always seems the worst! In spite of all the prayer, planning, and preparations I know you had a few surprises today. Rather than dwelling on the minor complications, think instead of the "major completions" God will do during this Bible study session. I pray you feel His lavish love in your life every single day.*
>
> –Beth

SESSION 2

To Live by the Spirit

DURING THE SESSION
1. **Arrival Activity (10 mins.)**

2. **Review the week's Principal Questions and Personal Discussion Questions (45 mins.)**
Remember you are looking for brief and basic answers to the Principal Questions that reveal comprehension of the content and learning activities. Be ready to answer if no member volunteers and to keep Personal Discussion Questions within appropriate bounds.

Day 1:
• *Principal Question:* What part did the Holy Spirit perform in creation?
• *Personal Discussion Question:* Can you recall a time or circumstance in your life that illustrates all three members of the Trinity at work? Describe that event.

Day 2:
• *Principal Question:* What is the mystery God has chosen to make known?
• *Personal Discussion Question:* Oh, Beloved, are you thankful you've had the opportunity to "begin again"? What is the clearest difference you remember experiencing as a person reborn in Christ?

Day 3:
• *Principal Question:* What does the Spirit do with the words of Jesus?
• *Personal Discussion Question:* Describe a time when you had to depend on the Spirit to intercede for you?

Day 4:
• *Principal Question:* What do you believe it means to "live by the Spirit"?
• *Personal Discussion Question:* In a society that, at its best, preaches "follow your heart," what does Jeremiah 17:9 have to say?

Day 5:
• *Principal Question:* Why is one without the Spirit incapable of understanding the things of the Spirit?
• *Personal Discussion Question:* How does the Holy Spirit "speak" (1 Cor. 2:13)?

Conclude discussion time by affirming your members' participation and their grasp of the material. Give a brief introduction to week 3 and encourage members to complete their home study. Close with prayer. Since prayer requests were taken at the beginning of discussion time, they are not necessary at this time.

> **Just Between Us…**
> *Are you already seeing the "fruit of your labor" in your group? Are you getting a fresh word from God? I am praying you will have a fresh, clean heart this week to hear what the Holy Spirit is teaching you and your group.*
>
> –Beth

SESSION 3

Greatest of These Is Love

DURING THE SESSION
1. **Arrival Activity (10 mins.)**

2. **Review the week's Principal Questions and Personal Discussion Questions (45 mins.)**
   Day 1:
   - *Principal Question:* How might an ongoing deprivation of your mate for inappropriate reasons be considered a unique form of adultery?
   - No *Personal Discussion Question* today.
   Day 2:
   - *Principal Question:* What caused Herod and Pilate to become friends?
   - *Personal Discussion Question:* In Christ, you and I are "blood relatives." How should our kinship affect our relationship?
   Day 3:
   - *Principal Question:* Why did God choose the foolish things of the world to shame the wise?
   - *Personal Discussion Question:* Proverbs 13:10 says "Pride only breeds quarrels." The last time you quarreled with someone, was any pride involved on your part?
   Day 4:
   - *Principal Question:* What does Psalm 145:8 tell us about God's anger?
   - *Personal Discussion Question:* Read Psalm 119:29-32. How would your life be different if you could wholeheartedly embrace the words and attitude of the psalm?
   Day 5:
   - *Principal Question:* What is the relationship between the Holy Spirit and *agape*?
   - *Personal Discussion Question:* Remember, God both told us He loved us and showed us He loved us. How do they know you love them? In other words, in what ways are you demonstrating *agape*?

Conclude discussion time by affirming your members' participation and their grasp of the material. Give a brief introduction to week 4 and encourage members to complete their home study. Close with prayer. Again, since prayer requests were taken at the beginning of discussion time, they are not necessary at this time.

> **Just Between Us...**
> *Week three marks a time when you are seeing some real commitment in your group. Recognize and encourage those who are staying the course. Ask God for specific ways to light a fire within your sisters who are falling behind and losing their vision. By the way...I am so proud of you for the course you have chosen. P.S. I love you, too!*
>
> –Beth

SESSION 4

The Joy of the Lord Is Our Strength

DURING THE SESSION
1. **Arrival Activity (10 mins.)**

2. **Review the week's Principal Questions and Personal Discussion Questions (45 mins.)**
   Day 1:
   - *Principal Question:* By what "record" or "reservation" will we enter the kingdom of heaven?
   - *Personal Discussion Question:* Notice all the things, persons, and places believers "have come to" in the New Jerusalem. From all the items identified, which two mean the most to you personally and why?
   Day 2:
   - *Principal Question:* How did Paul consider everything else to compare to the "surpassing greatness of knowing Christ Jesus"?
   - *Personal Discussion Question:* Have you ever found Him in the midst of your struggles? If so, when and what was your marvelous discovery?

Day 3:
- *Principal Question:* What two matters did Paul see as parts of "knowing Christ"?
- *Personal Discussion Question:* Can you remember a joy which accompanied the realization of restoration?

Day 4:
- *Principal Question:* Why has Christ told us to "remain" in Him?
- *Personal Discussion Question:* Review the list of joy cheaters on page 83. Which one have you most recently experienced?

Day 5:
- *Principal Question:* What did Paul consider to be his "joy" and "crown"?
- *Personal Discussion Question:* Which of the catalysts of joy has been most important to you in your present journey and why?

Conclude discussion time by affirming your members' participation and their grasp of the material. Give a brief introduction to week 5 and encourage members to complete their home study. Close with prayer.

Just Between Us...

Joy...one of my favorite attributes of the Christian life. I am so glad it is not about my strength, but His. I pray your group is a picture of His joy bubbling over! I pray also that you are getting to see personally the effect of joy on each of your precious women's lives.

–Beth

SESSION 5

Peace Be with You

DURING THE SESSION

1. **Arrival Activity (10 mins.)**

2. **Review the week's Principal Questions and Personal Discussion Questions (45 mins.)**

Day 1:
- *Principal Question:* How did Job's friends respond to his loss?

- *Personal Discussion Question:* Can you describe a circumstance of life that challenges your peace?

Day 2:
- *Principal Question:* Now that we have been reconciled to God, how does Christ present us in God's sight?
- *Personal Discussion Question:* Ephesians 2:18 shares the good news resulting from the outcome of our peace with God. What does access to the Father mean to you?

Day 3:
- *Principal Question:* Why did Christ withdraw into a mountain?
- *Personal Discussion Question:* How do you feel about God's promise to "graciously give us all things"? (Phil. 4:19 and Rom. 8:32).

Day 4:
- *Principal Question:* What is the guaranteed outcome of "believing" God?
- *Personal Discussion Question:* Are you waiting on the Lord right now? ❑ Yes ❑ No If so, how does this Scripture encourage you toward greater peace in the wait?

Day 5:
- *Principal Question:* What was Christ's only request of the soldiers?
- *Personal Discussion Question:* What is the most important thing God has taught you this week about "peace"?

Conclude discussion time by affirming your members' participation and their grasp of the material. Give a brief introduction to week 6 and encourage members toward the completion of their home study. Close with prayer.

Just Between Us...

Ephesians 2:14 tells us that Christ Himself is our peace and that He came to make two into one. I would have walked this journey all by myself if necessary. I am so thrilled that God willed that we would walk together with other believers. I am also grateful that we can walk in harmony. Are you seeing Him do a mighty work in your group? God is so faithful to mend fences, defuse anger and multiply instead of divide! Are you encouraged to see Him at work in hearts?

–Beth

SESSION 6

A Composite of Peculiar Patience

Just Between Us...
Can you believe you have six weeks behind you? What a wonderful time to study patience and perseverance. I have so prayed this will be a week of forgiveness and freedom for you and your wonderful group. I know that this week many of the ladies in your group will be walking happy and free for the first time in years. His yoke is so much easier than what the world would have us carry around. Isn't God good?

–Beth

DURING THE SESSION

1. **Arrival Activity (10 mins.)**

2. **Review the week's Principal Questions and Personal Discussion Questions (45 mins.)**
   Day 1:
   • *Principal Question:* Exactly what "inspired" the endurance of the Thessalonians?
   • *Personal Discussion Question:* Are you presently experiencing difficulty in regard to situations or circumstances? What hopes do you possess to help you persevere through this trial?
   Day 2:
   • *Principal Question:* What was God's promise to Noah, and what was the proof God gave to seal the covenant?
   • *Personal Discussion Question:* Considering Genesis 1:27,31, why must this observation that the earth was corrupt and full of violence have caused God such pain?
   Day 3:
   • *Principal Question:* What was David's attitude toward judgment after his sin of pride in 2 Samuel 24:14?
   • *Personal Discussion Question:* In light of the eleven reasons not to judge, read 2 Samuel 24:14. What does this verse say to you?
   Day 4:
   • *Principal Question:* How does God create ministry from misery?
   • *Personal Discussion Question:* In what ways do you think Satan takes advantage of you when you won't forgive? (2 Cor. 2:10-11).
   Day 5:
   • *Principal Question:* What percentage of our sin does God forgive?
   • *Personal Discussion Question:* What does unforgiveness do? (Eph 4:30-32).
   Conclude discussion time. Give a brief introduction to week 7.

SESSION 7

The Kindness and Goodness of God

DURING THE SESSION

1. **Arrival Activity (10 mins.)**

2. **Review the week's Principal Questions and Personal Discussion Questions (45 mins.)**
   Day 1:
   • *Principal Question:* What name did Hagar give God?
   • *Personal Discussion Question:* How do you suppose Abraham felt when he followed God's command and sent Hagar and Ishmael away?
   Day 2:
   • *Principal Question:* What assurance do we have that God will never forget His children?
   • *Personal Discussion Question:* Have you ever felt forgotten by God? ❑ Yes ❑ No If so, when?
   Day 3:
   • *Principal Question:* Is it possible to cause another person to sin?
   • *Personal Discussion Question:* Which example of Christ's heart reminded you most of a way He has dealt with you in the past and why?
   Day 4:
   • *Principal Question:* What are we to guard and how are we to guard it? (2 Tim. 1:14).
   • *Personal Discussion Question:* Are you doing too many things to do any ONE thing well for Christ? ❑ Yes ❑ No If so, what can you do about it?

Day 5:
- *Principal Question:* How did Paul's actions demonstrate *chrestotes*? (1 Thess. 2:6-8).
- *Personal Discussion Question:* Can you think of a time when you were either the object of kindness and goodness through a loving rebuke or the vessel of such kindness and goodness to another?

Conclude discussion time by affirming your members in their participation and their apparent grasp of the material. Give a brief introduction to week 8 and encourage members to complete their home study.

Just Between Us...

What a wonderful message and much needed reminder! God will never forget us. He is not likely to "loose our address" no matter how many times we move! Encourage everyone to "keep up" the good work and "guard the deposits" of faith God is making in each of their lives. I pray your "spiritual bank account" is growing beyond what you can think or even imagine.

—Beth

SESSION 8

Keep Believin'

DURING THE SESSION

1. **Arrival Activity (10 mins.)**

2. **Review the week's Principal Questions and Personal Discussion Questions (45 mins.)**

   Day 1:
   - *Principal Question:* In Moses' farewell address, what words did he use to describe God's faithfulness?
   - *Personal Discussion Question:* How has God shown compassion to you recently?

   Day 2:
   - *Principal Question:* What does Hebrews 11:6 specify that we are to believe?
   - *Personal Discussion Question:* Why does it take faith to walk with God?

   Day 3:
   - *Principal Question:* What did God tell Paul through an angel in Acts 27:23-24?

- *Personal Discussion Question:* Can you describe a time when God let you "run aground" into His will?

Day 4:
- *Principal Question:* Which piece of the whole armor of God does faith represent?
- *Personal Discussion Question:* Can you describe a time when God has been a shield about you, your glory, and the lifter of your head?

Day 5:
- *Principal Question:* What is Jesus Christ called in Revelation 1:5?
- *Personal Discussion Question:* What do Romans 3:3-4 and 2 Timothy 2:13 say to you in light of all we've learned about "faithfulness"?

Conclude discussion time by affirming your members in their participation today and their apparent grasp of the material. Give a brief introduction to week 9 and encourage members to complete their home study.

Just Between Us...

I pray God is teaching you mightily right now. Do not let Satan encourage you to lose your faith. Stay alert and turn to the One in whom you put your faith in the first place. He is worthy! He is the King of kings! He is FAITHFUL! There are just two more weeks to go. Ask God to encourage not only your own faithfulness, but also your group's.

—Beth

SESSION 9

Gentle Giants

DURING THE SESSION

1. **Arrival Activity (10 mins.)**

2. **Review the week's Principal Questions and Personal Discussion Questions (45 mins.)**

   Day 1:
   - *Principal Question:* What were some of the ways Paul had to suffer for Christ's sake?

- *Personal Discussion Question:* Can you recall a time when you submitted to God's will while He untangled your mess?

Day 2:
- *Principal Question:* What evidences do you see suggesting John the Baptist's humility?
- *Personal Discussion Question:* What are your ideas for esteeming others?

Day 3:
- *Principal Question:* What was Balaam's response to the words spoken by the angel of the Lord?
- *Personal Discussion Question:* Have you ever had a stubborn period like Balaam when you refused to listen to God?

Day 4:
- *Principal Question:* What was the proper way to carry the ark of God?
- *Personal Discussion Question:* How has God's Word strengthened you in the past, or how might you be strengthened in the future by His Word?

Day 5:
- *Principal Question:* What was the obvious text of Christ's teaching?
- *Personal Discussion Question:* How do you suppose knowledge and depth of insight results in love that abounds?

Conclude discussion time by affirming your members in their participation today and their apparent grasp of the material. Give a brief introduction to week 10 and encourage members to complete their home study.

Just Between Us...

Beloved, can you believe there is only one week to go? I pray that God has reminded you of some "precious memories" in your walk with Him. I am so proud of you and your commitment to God's Word and your commitment to your own little flock. I know you have made some new memories for all of eternity.

–Beth

SESSION 10

The Crucible of Self-Control

Dear Leader,
I am always sorry to see a wonderful vacation come to an end. It is not nearly as much fun to unpack as it was to prepare for the trip. How glorious that the journeys we take with God's people in His Word never end. Thank you for all your hard work and preparations. It was worth it! I rejoice in spirit with the fruit of your labors, and I long for the day we will celebrate together all of His blessings in glory.

–Beth

DURING THE SESSION
1. **Arrival Activity (10 mins.)**

2. **Unit Review of Principal Questions and Personal Discussion Questions (45 mins.)**
Day 1:
- *Principal Question:* Why do we need self-control?
- *Personal Discussion Question:* Can you think of a way in which the enemy has stolen victory from you through a broken-down wall in your life?

Day 2:
- *Principal Question:* What was the difference between Daniel's attitude toward the king's food and Samson's attitude toward the honey?
- *Personal Discussion Question:* What part most affected you today in 1) Samson's story; 2) Daniel's story?

Day 3:
- *Principal Question:* What happens when we attempt to serve both God and money?
- *Personal Discussion Question:* In the past, how has God helped you keep your priorities straight about money and possessions?

Day 4:
- *Principal Question:* What type of person is never at fault in what he says?
- *Personal Discussion Question:* In the past year, can you identify at least one specific way you have struggled to avoid being conformed to the pattern of this world?

Day 5:
- *Principal Question:* What does God do for the "blessed" person?
- *Personal Discussion Question:* How does God want you to respond to what He showed you in *Living Beyond Yourself*?

Conclude discussion time by affirming members participation throughout the last 10 weeks and their grasp of material that was often difficult. Dismiss with a closing prayer. Have a good laugh or a good cry depending on which seems appropriate!

Consider letting us hear from you. If God has spoken to you or done something significant in your life or the life of one of your members as a direct result of this Bible study, we would love for you to share a brief testimony with us. Write to us, and include your name, address, phone number, and church affiliation. Mail your testimony to the following address:

Adult Discipleship and Family Department
MSN 151
127 Ninth Avenue North
Nashville, Tennessee 37234-0151

Just Between Us...

You've turned the last page and said your good-byes to the members of your group. May the fullness of God's Spirit fill any empty places a finished work sometimes brings. May God compel you to take a quick breath and return soon to another study of His Word. Abundant life is a life which abides in God's Word. I pray you've discovered riches during these last 10 weeks and that your experience was vastly increased by your role as group facilitator. My friend, God has found you faithful. He has credited your every effort to a heavenly account of imperishable treasures. Thank you so, so much.

–Beth

CHRISTIAN GROWTH STUDY PLAN

Preparing Christians to Serve

In the **Christian Growth Study Plan (formerly Church Study Course)**, this book *Living Beyond Yourself: Exploring the Fruit of the Spirit* is a resource for course credit in the subject area **Personal Life** of the Christian Growth category of diploma plans. To receive credit, read the book, complete the learning activities, show your work to your pastor, a staff member or church leader, then complete the following information. This page may be duplicated. Send the completed page to:

Christian Growth Study Plan
127 Ninth Avenue, North, MSN 117
Nashville, TN 37234
FAX: (615)251-5067

For information about the Christian Growth Study Plan, refer to the current Christian Growth Study Plan Catalog. Your church office may have a copy. If not, request a free copy from the Christian Growth Study Plan office (615/251-2525).

Living Beyond Yourself: Exploring the Fruit of the Spirit
COURSE NUMBER: CG-0477

PARTICIPANT INFORMATION

Social Security Number (USA ONLY) | Personal CGSP Number* | Date of Birth (MONTH, DAY, YEAR)

Name (First, Middle, Last)
☐ Mr. ☐ Miss
☐ Mrs. ☐

Home Phone

Address (Street, Route, or P.O. Box) | City, State, or Province | Zip/Postal Code

CHURCH INFORMATION

Church Name

Address (Street, Route, or P.O. Box) | City, State, or Province | Zip/Postal Code

CHANGE REQUEST ONLY

☐ Former Name

☐ Former Address | City, State, or Province | Zip/Postal Code

☐ Former Church | City, State, or Province | Zip/Postal Code

Signature of Pastor, Conference Leader, or Other Church Leader | Date

*New participants are requested but not required to give SS# and date of birth. Existing participants, please give CGSP# when using SS# for the first time. Thereafter, only one ID# is required. **Mail to:** Christian Growth Study Plan, 127 Ninth Ave., North, Nashville, TN 37234-0117. Fax: (615)251-5067

223

Nurture Your Spiritual Growth

Congratulations, you've completed 10 weeks of intensive study in the Book of Galatians examining the fruit of the Spirit. Now catch your breath and get ready for Beth Moore's previous Bible studies: *A Heart Like His: Seeking the Heart of God Through a Study of David; A Woman's Heart: God's Dwelling Place; and To Live Is Christ: The Life and Ministry of Paul.*

Similar in design and format, these in-depth Bible studies will encourage and challenge you and your friends to apply practical Bible truths with life-changing results.

Each study features a 224-page personal study workbook; a leader kit that includes the member book, leader helps, and six videotapes with administrative help plus Beth Moore's presentations; and audiotapes that feature the audio portions of the videotapes and a listening guide.

Ask your church to schedule these studies soon—they're ideal in reaching and ministering to women of all ages.

To order these resources, write, call, or fax Customer Service Center, MSN 113; 127 Ninth Avenue North; Nashville, TN 37234; **1-800-458-2772.** Fax # (615) 251-5933. email to customerservice@lifeway.com.

Also available at your Baptist Book Store or Lifeway Christian Store.

To Live Is Christ: The Life and Ministry of Paul
Discover new insights about the apostle to the Gentiles, who said, "To live is Christ and to die is gain."
Member Book
ISBN 0767334124

To Live Is Christ Leader Kit
ISBN 0767334027

To Live Is Christ Audiotapes
ISBN 0767329953

A Heart Like His: Seeking the Heart of God Through a Study of David
Member Book
ISBN 0767325966

A Heart Like His Leader Kit
ISBN 0767326539

A Heart Like His audiotapes
ISBN 0767326520

A Woman's Heart: God's Dwelling Place
Member Book
ISBN 0805498362

A Woman's Heart Leader Kit
ISBN 0805498265

A Woman's Heart Leader Guide
Included in kit.
ISBN 0767334019

A Woman's Heart Audiotapes
ISBN 0805497978

Additional women's enrichment resources include:

Women Reaching Women: Beginning and Building a Growing Women's Enrichment Ministry
Compiled by Chris Adams, foreword by Anne Graham Lotz—A comprehensive leadership resource with the latest information on beginning and expanding women's ministry in your church.
ISBN 0767325931

Journey: A Woman's Guide to Intimacy with God
This monthly devotional magazine helps women grow closer to God by addressing needs and issues unique to women. Available in multiple copies.

Whispers of Hope
A unique prayer and devotional journal by Beth Moore designed to help women develop a consistent, daily habit of prayer.
ISBN 0767392787

For women's enrichment training, contact Chris Adams, (615) 251-2810, Fax# (615) 251-5058 or email to cadams@lifeway.com.

For women's events, contact Faith Whatley, (615) 251-2793, fax# (615) 251-5058 or email to fwhatle@lifeway.com.